D0407211

Always a
Bridesmaid
{ *for hire* }

Always a
Bridesmaid

{ *for hire* }

Stories on Growing Up, Looking
for Love, and Walking Down the Aisle for
Complete Strangers

JEN GLANTZ

ATRIA BOOKS

New York   London   Toronto   Sydney   New Delhi

ATRIA BOOKS

An Imprint of Simon & Schuster, Inc.
1230 Avenue of the Americas
New York, NY 10020

First Atria Books hardcover edition February 2017

ATRIA BOOKS and colophon are trademarks of Simon & Schuster, Inc.

For information about special discounts for bulk purchases, please contact Simon & Schuster Special Sales at 1-866-506-1949 or business@simonandschuster.com.

The Simon & Schuster Speakers Bureau can bring authors to your live event. For more information, or to book an event, contact the Simon & Schuster Speakers Bureau at 1-866-248-3049 or visit our website at www.simonspeakers.com.

Interior design by Joy O'Meara

Manufactured in the United States of America

10 9 8 7 6 5 4 3 2 1

Library of Congress Cataloging-in-Publication Data

Names: Glantz, Jen, author.
Title: Always a bridesmaid (for hire) : stories on growing up, looking for love, and walking down the aisle for complete strangers / Jen Glantz.
Description: New York : Atria Books, 2017.
Identifiers: LCCN 2016034746 (print) | LCCN 2016052247 (ebook) | ISBN 9781501139062 (hardback) | ISBN 9781501139079 (ebook)
Subjects: LCSH: Glantz, Jen. | Young women—United States—Biography. | Bridesmaids—Humor. | BISAC: BIOGRAPHY & AUTOBIOGRAPHY / Personal Memoirs.
Classification: LCC CT275.G465 A3 2017 (print) | LCC CT275.G465 (ebook) | DDC 305.242/2092 [B] —dc23
LC record available at https://lccn.loc.gov/2016034746

ISBN 978-1-5011-3906-2
ISBN 978-1-5011-3907-9 (ebook)

For those who told me to give up on being a writer, on being a professional bridesmaid, on being exactly who I am—which is equal parts stubborn and equal parts peculiar:

I'm really glad I never listened.

And for Laurie, Lloyd, and Jason Glantz, who always told me that I should, would, and without a doubt could:

You were right. My goodness, you were right all along.

I am going to do something, and I have a strange feeling it is going to be phantasmagorically different.

—Paul Zindel, author of *I Never Loved Your Mind*

You are terrifying and strange and beautiful.
Something not everyone knows how to love.

—Warsan Shire, poet

Jennifer, marry a dentist. They'll be able to replace your teeth, for free, when they start falling out.

—My eighty-three-year-old great-aunt Rita

Contents

Author's Note

I changed most names and some identifying details of people, places, and things throughout the book. Of course I did. The characters who gave a heartbeat to these stories are friends, and strangers who turned into friends. Oh, and guys who had the courage to take me on a date. I changed their names as a way of saying: Thank you, I'm sorry, I love you. Now go off and be well.

Always a
Bridesmaid
{ *for hire* }

Prologue

I "Uggghhh" Weddings

When you live in New York City, it's almost expected that people will see you at your very, very worst, very, very often. It's built into the price you pay to live here, because you will at some point fall into the trap of believing that every block, every subway car, every splinter-ridden park bench is your own personal territory for having a full-blown mental breakdown.

I pinky-promise you that eventually you'll stop thinking twice about walking down Third Avenue in the morning to buy a large cup of coffee, with your hair in a spider web of tangles and your bra everywhere but where it should be—which is on you. And you'll stop noticing that everyone is staring at you as you publicly break up with the person who has had an iron grip on your heart. After all, if there isn't a crowd of at least five total strangers watching, can you say it even really happened?

The comforting thing is that even when you're at your

worst, there's always someone else one-upping you one block over. That's why you don't need to bat an eye when tourists turn their chunky DSLRs away from the Empire State Building and zoom in on your face, mid-ugly-cry.

I, however, am the kind of person who tries to keep my humiliations private. Like the time I had to be rescued from the bottom of my own closet.

"Hello?" I whispered in a delicate panic to the kind soul at the other end of the line at 9:00 p.m. on a Sunday. I had been organizing my long-neglected closet, only to be rewarded with every shelf collapsing on top of me, along with an avalanche of forgotten clothes that should've been donated to Goodwill years ago. The only parts of my body that hadn't been temporarily paralyzed were my face and a single outstretched arm that had managed to reach my phone. I had dialed the only person I knew would pick up at that hour: my building's on-call maintenance man.

"What's the problem?" he asked, pushing a giant rock of phlegm up and down the bumpy lining of his esophagus.

"It's an emergency," I said, attempting to wiggle my toes beneath a pile of platform shoes that my friends and I had worn when we dressed up as the Spice Girls for Halloween. "My shelves collapsed, and now I'm trapped at the bottom of my closet."

"Can't you call someone else?" he asked, annoyed, clearly regretting giving me his personal cell phone number when I moved in.

"Well, I don't have a—"

"A what? A boyfriend? A best friend? The ability to dial 911?"

I took a deep breath and imagined what would happen if I called 911 and they transferred me to the NYPD's Seventeenth Precinct at 9:00 p.m. on a Sunday. I imagined what it would feel like to utter the words, "Help me! I'm trapped in my own mess of polyester and sequins," to the city's' finest; how I'd have to beg and plead for them to stop handcuffing the guy trying to break into a non-twenty-four-hour CVS, or quit patrolling Fifth Avenue to come to the twenty-sixth floor of my apartment in Murray Hill just to rescue me from a pile of T-shirts I had bought seven years ago.

"Please don't make me do that," I whispered. "If you come, I'll give you your Christmas bonus early."

Those turned out to be the magical words. He arrived just a few minutes later in his bathrobe, my knight in fuzzy armor. I smiled because I knew he'd seen worse. Much worse.

"How did this happen?" he asked, peeling back layer after layer of clothing.

"Well, I read that it's going to be fifty-five degrees tomorrow, so I was trying to grab a sweater from the top shelf when—"

"No," he cut me off. "Not that. *This!*"

I craned my neck to see that he was holding in his wide-palmed hands not one, not two, not four, but *nine* bridesmaid dresses.

"It's not what it looks like," I said, worried that his judgment would crush me faster than the contents of my closet. "Trust me, I don't even *like* weddings."

I wasn't totally lying to him either. When I was a little kid, the idea of my own wedding didn't take up much real estate in my mind. Whenever I found myself scoring an invitation to a sleepover or to a lunch table in middle school, the girls would giggle over the cuts of their future rings, the colors of their future flowers, and the flavors of their future cakes, while I'd be off in the corner of someone's bedroom or at the end of a table, crafting paper airplanes from expired love letters I was too afraid to send.

"You hate weddings?" my friend Samantha once asked me incredulously at her sleepover party, every syllable loaded with attitude. I watched as she brushed her Barbie doll's bleach-blonde hair, her fish-like lips pursed in sour disapproval.

"I don't hate them," I said. *Hate* was a very strong word that my mom put in the same bucket as curse words; I was never allowed to use it. Whenever I had a staring contest with a plate of broccoli or a pile of homework, I would say I "uggghhhed" them instead.

"But don't you want the flowers and the dress and the giant shiny ring?"

"Not really," I said, thinking for a second and realizing I had never thought about it before. I was seven years old, and the only thing that regularly crossed my mind was which toy I'd score in my McDonald's Happy Meal, or how I desperately wished I could sleep through the next lesson in long division.

All the other girls at Samantha's sleepover talked about how they wanted this flavor cake and that color rose. How their dress would be a cascading waterfall of lace and they'd spend all night twirling around in it. They never mentioned the ooey-gooey love part. They never mentioned the person who would be standing beside them in the photos, at the altar, for the rest of their lives. Maybe that's because back then, boys still had a major case of cooties.

"Look at her lopsided bangs," one of the girls said about

me as their tittering laughs ricocheted off the walls, hitting me right in the face.

"She'll never get married," another girl said as she slid into her Beauty and the Beast sleeping bag.

"You know what I think," I said, as my cheeks flushed magenta and my voice sounded as if someone was shaking me uncontrollably, though nobody was. "I think if you find your forever person, you two should just do whatever you want."

At that time, my forever person's name was Lucas, and we had never spoken more than ten words to each other. Amy was his forever person, and she was sitting across the room from me right now, painting her nails with a coat of glitter and plotting the coordinates of their wedding in some exotic place, like the Amalfi Coast.

I wouldn't say I was always averse to weddings—more like confused by them. I was three when I went to my first one. I was a junior flower girl, and my diaper matched my dress. My blanket, Mr. Blankenstein, was my plus-one. My mom had to bribe me with a caramel-flavored lollipop to stop sucking my thumb for a couple of minutes so I could use both hands to toss teardrop-shaped rose petals as I tiptoed in my Keds down the aisle.

I remember how the fragrance from the flowers tickled the edges of my nose, and when my uncle said, "I do," I sneezed so loud that the rabbi had to make my aunt and uncle repeat their promise that they would always stick by each other's side, no matter whose waistline expanded first.

I remember wondering why I was at a mini-circus, where everyone was drinking liquid that looked a little like pee and wearing fancy outfits that they could hardly move in, even though they had to spend the majority of the night moving around. I remember my dad cutting my food into tiny pieces and I remember sleeping a lot, passed out in my stroller beside someone's ninety-three-year-old grandpa and a cousin who was slurring his words, which I later learned meant that he was sloshed. Weddings then seemed like fancy schmancy birthday parties where everyone walked around looking like they had a wedgie. I wondered if I'd ever be able to understand the point.

Now I'm twenty-eight, and all of my assets are tied up in bridesmaid dresses. My passport has stamps only from bachelorette party destinations like Cancun and four of the seven Sandals resorts. Every scar on my body is from getting dragged into mosh pits while trying to wrap my arms around a tossed bouquet. I repeat marriage vows in my head the same way people sing lyrics from a catchy song they've heard on the radio. And I know never, and I mean *never*, to let a bride have a Diet Coke before she's about to walk down the aisle unless it's through a straw and there's a blanket splayed over her dress.

"So how did this happen?" the maintenance guy asked me once more, shaking a handful of chiffon.

"All of my friends got married," I said, miserably.

"Always a bridesmaid," he said, dropping the dress, grabbing both of my hands, and pulling me up from rock-bottom, sedentary state. "Never the bride."

He had no idea.

chapter one

A Familiar Kind of Love

My parents got married when they were twenty-six years old, so on my twenty-sixth birthday, while I was locked in a staring contest with a flotilla of skinny candles on my Carvel Fudgie the Whale cake, my mom asked if she could blow out the final flame that was stubbornly wiggling its fiery wick right in my face.

I agreed, and when it was over, I asked her what she had wished for. She just winked at me repeatedly, as if she had something stuck in her eyelid. She made sure the twinkle of her engagement ring, fused together with her white-gold wedding band, hit me right in the eye.

"I just want you to find a guy who makes you happy," she said, cutting the cake into three pieces: two miniature slivers for us and one extra-large slice with the most icing on top for my father. "But please, Jennifer," she went on, "try to do so while I'm still young enough to dance the electric slide with both of my original hips."

I mentally bristled. *There are a lot of guys who make me happy*, I thought to myself while running through an inventory of potential prospects.

There was my doorman, who always reminded me to go back upstairs to grab a heavier sweater and a knit hat when the chill in the air began to fog up the windows.

There was the guy who owned the rat-infested pizza shop across the street who always warmed up an extra slice for me, on the house, whenever I dragged my four-inch-stiletto-shod feet (courtesy of the Macy's clearance rack, of course) into the restaurant—which was usually after a cringe-worthy date. Those dates always ended with me knocking over a mostly full glass of Cabernet Sauvignon onto the guy's finely pressed Ralph Lauren button-down shirt, or him turning a friendly good-bye hug into an attempt to french my cochlea.

There was even the homeless guy who had built himself a tiny fort out of beat-up Home Depot cardboard boxes and marked his territory outside the Bank of America ATM machine on Third Avenue. He could often be found shaking his Starbucks cup full of change to the tune of a Ying Yang Twins song, and he always remembered to lift up his Yankees' cap to tell me that I was 57 percent more beautiful when I smiled.

I told my mom she had nothing to worry about as she whispered some ancient-sounding prayer in Hebrew before digging the tines of her silver fork into my birthday cake.

Even before I was in a training bra, and back when I was still on training wheels, I thought I would have absolutely no problem falling in love. I fell a little bit in love with every single person I met, and sometimes I even had trouble letting them go. Literally. The librarian at the after-school day care had to call my mom to pick me up early one evening because I latched onto her calf and wouldn't stop hugging it after she read us *Charlotte's Web*. The same exact thing happened with the mailman, a McDonald's employee monitoring the ball pit, and Mickey Mouse—all in the same week.

But I *truly* fell in love for the very first time when I was four years old. He had shaggy, tree-bark-colored hair, and a dresser full of well-fitting OshKosh B'gosh jean shorts. His name was Scott, and his eyes looked like the fabric buttons on Mr. Brown, my teddy bear.

Scott and I were the head of our preschool class's lines, and we took our job very seriously. We wondered if this was what it felt like to be the president and the first lady. If so, we were ready to take over the universe.

One afternoon, when Mrs. Kay shook us awake after nap time, Scott and I went behind a homemade rocket ship that was set up in the middle of our classroom. We pretended to be astronauts who had just successfully navigated their way to the farthermost spot on Pluto. We took our plastic cups of semifrozen, snack-time apple juice and clinked them together, a quick cheers to all we managed to accomplish before 2:00 p.m.

The next thing I knew, Scott's pillowy lips were planted smack on the middle of my right cheek. *Look at this,* I thought to myself. *Look how lucky I am to have found love at such a young age, and with such a handsome, motivated, future astronaut!*

But right as I went to kiss him back, to let Scott know that

I had the same heart-bursting feelings for him that he had for me, he turned to his left and planted his lips on the cheek of some floozy named Melissa. Talk about a mood killer.

That week, Mrs. Kay had taught us the importance of sharing. Rumor around our preschool class was that if we didn't understand how to do it, if we didn't give in and hand over our favorite Barbie to our best friend when she came over for a play date, or split our last Oreo when someone asked us nicely during lunchtime, we wouldn't be allowed to move on to kindergarten. We'd be held back for a year as punishment.

But I knew that love wasn't meant to be shared the way Scott had shared his precious lips with both me and that mini-bimbo Melissa. I was pretty sure of that.

When a guy finally gave me the undivided attention I longed for, it wasn't quite what I expected. I was in fourth grade and working overtime to make myself invisible so the other kids wouldn't make fun of me for being so painfully shy that I couldn't even utter my own name without breaking into hives and trembles. Jean was a transfer student from Nice, France, the new boy at my private school in the southwest corner of Boca Raton, Florida. He reminded me of someone out of a history book—Napoleon, perhaps. His shoulders always pointed back, his chin up, and his hands remained planted on his hips, as if he were about to make a profound declaration.

On his first day of school, Jean stopped me in the middle of the purple-speckled hallway carpet and asked me which way the bathroom was. I extended my arm to the left, hoping he wouldn't ask me anything else so I could go back to reading Harry Potter and developing my own invisibility cloak—a fleece sweater draped over my head, where I was determined to hide until it was time to graduate from elementary school.

My slanted bangs, crooked teeth, and dirty white Converse must have made quite the impression on Jean that afternoon, because the next day, during lunch, he planted his feet on top of a sailor-blue plastic chair and straightened to his full height of five-foot-one, ready to make an announcement.

"Listen up," he said as his prepubescent voice dipped low before hitting a high falsetto, the likes of which I'd never heard before. "I want all of you to know that I, Jean, am in love with Jennifer Glantz."

I coughed up my pizza bagel onto my orange lunch tray. I prayed that nobody in the lunchroom knew who Jennifer Glantz was. A perpetually shy girl can only dream.

Alas. Three hundred and forty-three pairs of eyes spun in circles until they found a pleasant resting spot on my forehead.

I wondered how well my invisibility cloak worked as I pulled the neckline of my sweater up over my noggin and tucked my legs up into the body of the sweater, hiding everything but my widow's peak. I closed my eyes tight. *Just get through this*, I chanted in my head, *and then maybe you'll finally be allowed to transfer to a middle school in some other galaxy.*

"I love her so much. I will do anything for her," he went on. "I'll even buy her tampons."

The room broke out into shrills of laughter. People began whooping and clapping their hands together as if they were welcoming Justin Timberlake onto our campus. A wave of "woos!" went through one of my ears and out the other. I hadn't even gotten my period yet, but now the entire student body thought I was a bleeding monster.

Was love supposed to be as uncomfortable as going to the dentist or, when I finally came of age to experience it, the gynecologist?

I'll never know why Jean fell in love with me after I pointed him to the bathroom, or why he proclaimed his love like he was conquering a brand-new territory, or why he felt the need to demonstrate the seriousness of his affection by volunteering to buy me tampons. Maybe it was because to Jean, I was a mystery. I was a girl of few words and only slightly more hand gestures, and maybe to him, and only him, that was enough.

By age fourteen, I thought that if I wanted the right guy to like me, I had to make him aware that I liked him by sticking my tongue down his throat. (I don't know when the girls I went to school with held a town hall meeting and decided that boys no longer had a flaming case of the cooties, but suddenly it was so, and now we had to kiss them. Which they did. All of them. Except for me.)

I would practice a lot in case my moment happened. I'd stand in front of the mirror and slather on some cherry Lip Smacker before placing my lips on the cold reflective glass, moving my tongue in rapid figure eight motions and tiny circles, making out with my own reflection.

When I finally found someone who told someone else he'd be okay with kissing me, I had a mouthful of braces and a deep psychological fear that if the boy also had braces, we'd lock together. Then we'd be rushed to the hospital and my parents would have to see me tangled up in a premarital situation with a guy who was just *okay* kissing me. They'd probably make him marry me, or at least attend our next Passover seder.

The day I got my braces off, I went to the movies with a group of guys and girls and told myself that before another car flipped over in *Fast and Furious* 3, my lips would be glued to a guy with the AOL screen name Bucs314. But I waited too long, and right as our chins touched and our lips pressed together, my right leg started to vibrate. My teal beeper was going off in my jeans, which meant one thing and one thing only: the movie was over, and my dad was waiting for me outside.

I wondered, then, if love was all about being in the right place at the right time. The never-been-kissed, fourteen-year-old version of myself deemed that I would probably have to wait forever for it. (Now I wonder if I need to fully dismantle my biological clock, or at least take the batteries out; these days, it's pulsing harder than a Kesha song right before the beat drops.)

After that ill-fated attempt at romance, with Vin Diesel watching over us, I managed to successfully touch tongues with five people before I met a guy named Ben in college and instantly fell in love. He was the head of Habitat for Humanity at my college and had a pretentious air about him that made him seem as if he was tightrope-walking thirteen stories above everybody else. I melted when he said my name, and I cooed when he repeated world news as if he were taking over Brian Williams's gig on Nightly News. We kissed for the first time in my dorm room, on the edge of my extra-long twin-sized bed, and by the time he left, I was planning our entire future together. We'd graduate and join the Peace Corps and be the kind of couple who didn't shower for weeks at a time as we traveled the world, adopting a handful of kids from Third World countries. But one week after our first smooch, he stopped calling. He stopped texting. He stopped responding to me when I sent him emails asking if he'd read the latest *National Geographic* article on genocide in Rwanda. I was getting ghosted before ghosting had become a thing.

I started to think that maybe love was just a game. A series of passionate, heart-racing hellos followed by radio-silent good-byes. A factory-defective puzzle in which, for me, the all-important middle piece was left out of the box. Other people seemed to have it all figured out, but I was always "losing a turn," Monopoly style, or shelling out my hard-earned (and decidedly real) money to fund some guy's steak dinner because he was on student loans and counting the pennies in his sock drawer.

Two years after sticking my diploma in a frame and thirty-six days after landing in New York City with a one-way ticket, I signed up for a JDate account and messaged sixty-five guys before finding one whose bio was made up of complete sentences and not just a series of abbreviations and winky faces. It was my first time on an online dating site, but beggars can't be choosers—the only guys knocking down my door were of the Seamless deliveryman variety.

When I walked into a Lower East Side wine bar to meet one particular date, I had no idea which guy he was. In front of me was a lineup of freshly shaven gentlemen in gingham button-down shirts, so I went up to each guy, one by one, and asked, "Are you David?" They all shrugged their shoulders and fumbled around with their phones, begging me to move aside so when their internet date walked in, they wouldn't be caught canoodling with a lost girl with messy blonde hair.

When David finally arrived, I commented that he didn't look a thing like his profile picture. He was five inches shorter and his hair color wasn't the same; in fact, he didn't have any hair at all. But we sat down and ordered two glasses of sauvignon blanc. I rattled off some of the headlines that Matt Lauer had delivered that morning in order to shatter the nervous silence that was beginning to suffocate us.

"Cheers," he said.

I raised my glass and dinged it against his.

"To what?" I replied.

"You're just way smarter than you look." He chuckled and placed his glass back down on the wobbly wooden table.

I told him I wasn't feeling well. It was winter, and as a Florida native, I wasn't used to getting frostbite on my exposed flesh every time I left my apartment. I gathered my things to get ready to leave, but when I put my coat on, my left arm got stuck in the sleeve and I knocked down his half-empty—and my half-full—glass of white wine. I watched in slow motion as the glasses shattered and little shards got stuck in the leather upper of his loafers. When the bill came, the restaurant charged us a 15 percent service fee for my performance, and he asked me to pay for the entire bill to cover the embarrassment I had caused him.

I wondered then, at twenty-three, if finding love meant having to share when I didn't want to, be uncomfortable, and play a game all at the same time. If so, I was already exhausted. I wondered if I had to earn it, like a child earns an extra gold star, like a teenager earns her driver's license, like a college kid earns her first win at beer pong. But how many times did I have to sit across from a guy while he swished around his half-empty glass of whiskey and yammered on about how he absolutely hated his job in investment banking and couldn't wait to retire to the sunny isles of Florida? Did I really have to use all of my 60 GB per month AT&T data plan to download sixteen different dating apps to find my Mr. Forever, all while politely smiling whenever someone asked me why I didn't already have a boyfriend? What did I need to do to find a guy who would eat Doritos Locos on the couch with me?

Now, at twenty-eight, I'm feeling a little more hopeful and a little less constipated about the whole thing. Maybe if I don't experience these bad dates, these email breakups, these Tinder messages full of bad grammar and lame come-ons, I won't know true love when it finally comes up to me and gently smacks me across the face.

After all, every person we meet is a plus or a minus to our heart. As I stuck my fingers into a glop of birthday cake icing and drew a faint little heart on my plate, I thought, *Maybe it all evens out.*

My parents have been married for forty years. I don't know many things that last that long. My shower curtain needs to be changed at least every seven years. My library card expires every ten years and requires proof of a pulse and a New York City address to get a new one. Even Carnation Instant Nonfat Dry Milk has a shelf life of only thirty-seven years.

My parents met on a blind date back when "I'll Google you" was something naughty you said after dessert, right before the bill came. My mom had just moved from Queens to Miami Beach. One night, her friend told her to paint her lips magenta and put on a pair of sleek bell-bottom jeans because they were going out on a double blind date.

My dad was visiting Miami Beach from Queens, and his friend told him to shower but not shave, because that night, they were going out with two groovy girls.

That's the night my dad and my mom met, but funnily enough, they weren't set up on the blind date with each other—they were matched with the other's friend. When the date was over, my dad called my mom and said, "I had fun with your friend, but you're the one I'd like to see again."

I fear that now, that would translate into a pathetically blasé text, like, "Yo, you wanna hang again without the other two?" I wonder how my mom would respond to that, or if she even would respond to that, if their meet-cute was adapted for modern times.

"How did you know Dad was the one?" I asked my mom after we had eaten our cake and I had peeled birthday candle wax from the dining room table. We both glanced over and watched him sitting on the couch, snoring, the TV buzzing on low volume like a lullaby.

"I didn't know," she said, tapping every button on the remote, trying to shut the TV off. "It just felt different yet familiar. A familiar kind of love."

Maybe, I thought to myself, *love doesn't need to be complicated; maybe it just needs to feel like everything else. Maybe it just needs to feel familiar.*

"Lloyd!" my mother yelled as my dad shook himself awake and tried to acclimate himself to his surroundings. There he was, on the soft cream leather couch, his eyes meeting the eyes of the same woman he'd been waking up to for forty years.

"Wake up!" she said. But her voice was filled with patience, and she smiled back at him, as she had so many times before.

chapter two

You Can Always Come Back Home

"Jennifer Sara Glantz."

She starts the conversation with my full name, which means only one thing: I'm about to be put in my place. And believe me, I need it.

You can usually figure out what someone wants to say to you by their tone and how they address you. If she had opened with, *my darling, sweetheart,* or simply *Jen,* I would know she was calling about something trivial, like the weather, or to ask for a play-by-play recap of my weekend. But today she's about to lay it all out there, to tell me like it is, holding nothing back.

"Mom," I say, mentally bargaining with my anxious body to calm down before the waterworks set in. "I'm sorry for being so upset. I just have no idea what to do or where to go."

"You stop this right now," she interrupts, powering through in full mom mode, "before you make yourself sick."

There are only three more days until graduation from the University of Central Florida, and while most of my friends are watching the minutes on the clock tick away like a New Year's Eve countdown, pressing their lips to glasses overflowing with champagne and toasting to a bright new future, I'm having a full-blown anxiety attack, curling my delicate limbs into the fetal position and hiding in the crevice between my sink and toilet.

The days of saying, "I'll figure out what I want to do with my life next year," are officially over. Now, I'm lying on a patch of frosted porcelain tile as my tears fall onto a piece of paper: a formal notice that I will need to vacate my college apartment by graduation.

"Jennifer," she begins again. "You can always come home. Do you hear me? I made your bed up with those sheets you like and bought you that deodorant that makes your armpits smell like fresh rain."

I never really understood what people meant when they said they were at rock bottom. Was it a spiritual place where their mental GPS left them? Or was it a physical location like, say, a bathroom floor? In this moment, it feels like both, because here I am, my mascara-streaked face smooshed against my sunflower-colored Urban Outfitters bath mat, with no job, no place to live, and no more than a couple of crumpled-up twenty-dollar bills that my Great Aunt Rita has been slipping to me every year since my bat mitzvah. I'm pretty sure this is *my* bottom.

No college freshman pushes open the lecture hall doors on day one and says, "I'm going to have a really good time here for a few years, and when it's all over, I'm going to move back home with my parents. I'm going to be unemployed and ultimately unsure of what kind of job I'm even qualified to do! But at least I'll get to hide in my childhood bed surrounded by Clay Aiken posters!"

When you're in college, you rarely think ahead past the next theme party, midterm, or even what you're going to microwave for dinner that night. No one's wasting precious extracurricular time wrestling with the possibility of ending up with a degree in poetry and not a clue what to do with it. You never realize that after you graduate, no one is going to dial your numbers and say to you, "I hear you just graduated with a degree in English! I would love to hire you as a paid assistant editor at *Marie Claire* in New York City."

My conversation with my mom ends with a summoning: "You'll move back home next week until you figure the rest out."

"Thank you, Mom," I say, before I respond with what I desperately would like to believe is the truth. "But I promise I won't be there for more than a month."

My family lives in Boca Raton, Florida, a place that's infamous for its early-bird specials and hearing aid discounts. There's not much of a social scene, and anything going on usually ends at 9:00 p.m. When I tell someone that I was born and raised there, they immediately say two things: "There are other people your age there?!" and "Do you know my grandparents?"

Its year-round paradise-like weather attracts people from all over the world to pack up their lives and settle down for retirement. But my life is supposed to be starting, not winding down toward eighteen holes of golf. I'm going to have to figure out my future and pick a career path among people who eat dinner at 5:00 p.m. and constantly smell like sunscreen and baby powder. How am I supposed to find inspiration or a mentor here? Someone who doesn't need to turn up a hearing aid to hear me ramble on, someone who would be up for being my wingman at the local bars, which—again—close before 9:00 p.m.!

But I pick myself up off the floor. Boca Raton, here I come.

My room is exactly how I left it when I began college four years ago. It's a shrine to myself, full of embarrassing photos of me with braces and baby fat and the kind of bad style that would alert Joan Rivers and the fashion police. If I were to bring a guy here, he'd think he was in some preschool playhouse, and the entire mood would be spoiled. Who would want to make out with me next to a giant stuffed animal giraffe in a magician's outfit eyeing him from a beanbag chair?

There's something about unpacking my collection of shot glasses, all purchased at exotic spring break locations, and lining them up next to my once-darling American Girl dolls that makes it clear that I've traded in the 4:00 a.m. dance floors for nights on the couch with my parents' DVR. I have officially said good-bye to flirting with fraternity boys and said hello to grocery shopping with my mom.

Which is exactly what I'm doing when I see Cheryl.

Cheryl was my first real friend. The one you'll find peeking over my left shoulder in all the Kodak prints from my childhood. The friend I'd eat my entire bowl of broccoli for so that my mom would let me have sleepovers at her house. The occupant of my top bunk at sleepaway camp. She stuck around for matching Halloween costumes, confessions of first kisses, and playing dress-up in clothes too mature for our lanky and undeveloped bodies.

But she didn't stick around—or talk to me ever again—after we hit puberty and she grew a pair of boobs that attracted the undivided attention of the male species. Meanwhile, I began sprouting pimples and decorating my overgrown chompers with a set of metal braces from Doctor Woolgoomooth.

My right eye gets tired from staring at tomatoes so it drifts across the produce aisle—and there she is: a grown-up version of my corduroy-overalls-wearing, monkey-bar-climbing, pinky-promising, used-to-be-best-friends-forever ex-friend.

"Oh my god!" Cheryl says, as she drops a bag of prewashed lettuce on the floor. "Jennifer Sara Glantz!"

Here we go with the full name, I think to myself.

I lean in as if we're going to hug, but we don't. I'm unsure how a person is supposed to greet another person who used to mean so much to her and now means the same amount as the guy with the hairnet behind the produce counter.

Her hand flails wildly, as if she's trying to get rid of a mosquito. So I do the same and wave back.

"When did you move home? What are you doing now?" she asks as her eyes wander from my stained Converse all the way up to my split ends.

"I just moved back," I say. "I, well, I'm trying to be a—"

"Well, I'm doing great," she cuts in before I even have the chance to ask. She tells me she does social media for a non-profit and got the job three months before she even strutted her full-priced Marc Jacobs wedges across the stage at graduation.

I'm glad she cuts me off because, to be honest, I don't have an inkling of what the heck I want to do with my life. I'm proficient in dissecting Shakespearean sonnets and writing headlines for breaking news about local house fires, which means I'm qualified for few real-world jobs and have to apply for a little bit of everything to find anything that'll stick.

"Jen," Cheryl continues, sensing that I stopped paying attention forty-five seconds ago. "I just got my nails done because Josh is asking me to marry him."

"You have a job, an apartment, and a guy?" I say, genuinely awed, but mostly jealous. "Good for you."

Cheryl places her hand on my back, as if she's about to tell me a secret filled with excitement and gossip, like we used to do when we were in the fifth grade. This time, though, she does it in a way that feels like a gesture of pity, as if she's about to whisper into my ear, *Honey, I'll pray for you.*

"Well, I'm moving to New York City next month," I say, delicately removing her hand and leaving it to land on an avocado. My mom, lingering in the background, hearing this breaking news for the very first time, nearly knocks over a display of on-sale cantaloupes. "I plan on doing something big and becoming something wonderful."

Competition shouldn't be a part of friendship or a part of any relationship we once valued. But can you blame me with this one? She went from peeing in her pants to becoming a social media director. I went from nap time crybaby to unemployed and living with my parents at twenty-two. I had to say something.

She giggles, flails her hand at me again, and says, "We should get together soon, or something."

"Yeah, or something," I reply.

Our shopping carts collide awkwardly before we untangle them and make our way toward different aisles—and different life paths. I know we'll never get together, never catch up over a cappuccino, or stuff our faces with kale salad and reminisce about our past. We'll just wait for the next time we bump into each other to compare how many ticks we've jumped in our grown-up time lines, never fulfilling the "forever" in our best-friend-forever promise.

Later that night, I find myself back in my childhood room, which looks like some strange museum of mismatched souvenirs from all the eras of my life so far.

It always boggles my mind how you can be inseparable from a person to the point where she knows all your disgustingly bad habits, intimate secrets, and darling dreams—and you, hers. And then one day, she walks by you like she would a stranger, as if you were never part of the blueprint of their life. As if you hadn't spent thirty-two consecutive Saturday nights wrapped up in Limited Too fleece pajamas, watching *All That* and making masterpieces out of lanyards and promises out of an unpredictable future. As if you were never more than just a comma in her life sentence, a brief pause before she continued on without you.

Places are like that too, I suppose. No matter how many Beanie Babies or board games or middle school love notes written in milky gel pen that we shove away in garbage bags, boxes, or the cavity beneath our mattress, what that place once meant to us will forever remain a major reason that we always find ourselves back at home again. A grounded memory that we can temporarily run away to until we're ready, again, to move on, to move forward, to move away.

I have to figure out a way to move to New York City or find

a new grocery store so that I never run into Cheryl again, because I know that in this town, I will.

My mom knocks on my door as I'm tossing a handful of Barbies into a box labeled, "Give Me Away Now, Please."

We hug tightly, and as my heart beats hard at the realization that this spur-of-the-moment promise to move to New York City could be the biggest disaster of my life yet, I whisper in her ear a simple, "What if?"

But before I can carry on, before I can let my words unravel around my boundless fears and the questions buzzing through my brain, she pulls me in a little bit tighter and whispers back, "Jennifer Sara Glantz."

That's how I know I'm about to be put in my place.

"You can always come back home."

That's how I know, once again, that everything will, eventually, somehow, be okay.

interlude

A Brief History of My Life after Graduation

- I lived in my childhood room in Boca Raton, surrounded by Beanie Babies and Clay Aiken posters. I watched a lot of HGTV shows and Hallmark movies with my mom.
- I worked as an assistant for six months at a local magazine for a woman who resembled Cruella de Vil. My unofficial job duties included picking up the poop of her two Chihuahuas, climbing ladders at her mansion to take down Halloween decorations, wrapping Christmas presents for her family, and doing her husband's taxes.
- I applied for nearly four hundred jobs during this time and did phone interviews in the bathroom or my car. My resume was pretty bare. At first glance, it looked like a haiku, a Shakespearean sonnet, or lyrics to a Jay Z song. The objective section contained a giant question mark.
- My first boyfriend (ever—I was a late bloomer in the

love department) broke up with me after four months, mid-job search, because he said I was too lost in my personal life to be found.

- I gained twenty pounds after graduation and realized that, if I wanted to be happier, I had to be healthier. I went to daily boot camp classes, where I learned that burpies aren't something you get after eating pasta with red sauce and having acid reflux. They're much worse than that.

- I finally got a job—in Manhattan!—at a two-person PR agency that represented nonprofits. I had zero PR experience, but I told them I'd be a fast learner if they'd be a fast payer.

- I booked a one-way ticket to New York City and moved into a three-month sublet with only two thousand dollars in my savings account. I met my new roommate, Kerri, who would end up becoming my best friend/therapist.

- My job turned out to be ruthless—and my new boss just as bad as my old one. I went on five job interviews a month, but since I still wasn't sure what I wanted to do, I didn't get a new job for another year and a half.

- After eight failed attempts to start a blog, I launched The Things I Learned From. I wrote once a week about applying for jobs, getting funny rejection letters, dealing with heartbreak, and my quest to move to NYC.

- I did a lot of karaoke.

- I often found myself in Queens or the Bronx because I got on the wrong subway train or didn't get off at the right stop.

- I read a poem at Bowery Poetry Club.

- I spent New Year's Eve in Times Square, because nothing says "Welcome to New York" like watching a glittery ball drop when it's seventeen degrees outside.
- I ate a ton of pizza since it was all I could afford. (Two slices and a cherry Coke for $2.25. Can't beat that.)
- I joined an ultimate Frisbee team as my last attempt to meet guys in person without having to download a dating app. It didn't work.
- I was very, very single, but my friends were very, very not. Which leads me to the rest of my story . . .

chapter three

Will You Be My Bras-Maid?

Ivanka eyes me from across the room and I reluctantly move toward her, doe-eyed and afraid.

She leads with her chest, or maybe it's her chest that leads her, but either way, she's marching toward me, her lips a thin slash of tomato-red lipstick, her eyebrows merging into a single, untweezed bush. She's dressed in all black, like a crypt keeper.

Some people have this twinkle of a superpower, where all they have to do to make you fall goo-goo eyes in love with them is just to say hello. My first boyfriend was blessed with that innate charm. I had been double-fisting pizza on the boardwalk in Santa Monica when he approached me, gawked at the mozzarella cheese hanging from my nose, said the magic word, and ta-da! Tiny little cartoon hearts were popping out of my ears for him that very instant.

Ivanka is the opposite. She skips the hello, the handshake, the "How are you doing today?" and looks me up and down as if her eyes are a TSA body scanner.

"What size are your babushkas?" She's draped in tape measures and staring pointedly at my chest.

My right eyebrow reaches the summit of my forehead as I try to think back to the Russian words my grandparents used to toss around whenever they pinched my cheeks or rewarded me with crisp ten-dollar bills for my birthday.

"Oh—you mean boobs! Well, this one is an A," I say pointing to the right side of my chest like a proud mom introducing my child for the first time at a casual neighborhood picnic. "And this one is a—"

Before I can finish my sentence, Ivanka is squeezing my avocados like she's checking to see if they're ripe enough to make a nice guacamole.

"It would have been nice if you bought me dinner first," I mumble into her eyebrow.

"You're a D," she shouts, as if she's announcing a special 10 percent off deal today at Victoria's Secret. "Maybe even a double-D."

"Excuse me?" I say in utter disbelief. Did my lady lumps explode overnight?

Maybe it was just a language barrier. Maybe she got her alphabet mixed up. When I was in first grade, I had trouble remembering the order of R, S, T, U, V, so I would mumble through that part when we had to sing the alphabet song out loud with the rest of the class. Maybe she temporarily got her Ds and Bs mixed up. Common mistake! I will forgive her.

"You mean B, as in bazooka, bumblebee, bee's knees?"

She hands me a 34D strapless nude bra with a chicken-cutlet-like padding double-stitched inside each cup. I gawk at it. If I were to fall out of an airplane and land on my stomach, I would be just fine.

The only thing worse than shopping for a new pair of hip-hugging jeans is shopping for a bra. Both garments require you to stuff your junk into tight, conforming contraptions that are cut to a specific body type that doesn't quite resemble the jingle-jangles of your own bodacious body. Except I really do not mind wearing pants—that is, if you consider leggings pants. But I am completely fed up with bras. If you ask me, they're a health hazard. Bras are an attention-grabbing, stage-five-clinging, suffocating relationship, and some days I really want out. And just like relationships, I always settle for the wrong bra—the ill-fitting one, the one that doesn't give me the kind of support that I desperately need, the one that sticks around for the sole reason that it has nowhere else to go. Everyone around me knows it too. That's the worst part. At work one day, someone anonymously left a business card on my desk for a place called Moshe's Bra Factory on the Lower East Side. Attached to it was a handwritten note that read, *Jen, it is time you let Moshe do a miracle for you.* But I didn't go, because just like with love, my coworker saw a harsh reality that I was too busy making excuses for, so I continued to wear sports bras underneath my business casual work attire.

The wake-up call happened when I was a bridesmaid for the first time and discovered, the morning of the wedding, that I didn't own a proper bra to hold up my baby girls in my strapless black chiffon dress.

Nine months earlier, during my family's Passover seder, I had just finished asking the four questions about why we have to spend seven days eating something that resembles a cardboard box when my cousin texted me to meet her in the pantry in five minutes because she had something very important to ask me. I thought to myself, *Yes! She's going to ask me if I want to sneak away and hit up Bob's Bagel Store or smuggle in some Papa John's pizza to slap this whole unleavened bread thing in the face.* But as she took my hand and led me deeper and deeper into her parents' walk-in pantry, past the Costco-sized boxes of Cheerios and Charmin, I knew this was much more than a plot to plan a late-evening carb fest.

"Jen," she said, her smile almost hitting her earlobes. "Will you be my bridesmaid?"

I remember feeling light-headed. Maybe that was from the lack of carbs, but I threw my arms around her and screamed out, "Yes, of course!" We exited the pantry right as the rest of our family was reading about the nine plagues and dipping their pinky fingers into cups of red wine.

I announced, on the spot, that I, Jennifer Sara Glantz, was going to be a bridesmaid. I felt as if I had just scored the supporting actress role in an Oscar-worthy movie. But just a few hours later, after I left my aunt and uncle's house, I remember sitting in the backseat of my parents' car, trying to wrap my head around what the heck I was supposed to do next.

How to be a bridesmaid is really something they should teach you in school. Right before you finish your final exam for your last class of your senior year, your professor should collect your blue book, break your number two pencil in half, and wrap up your twenty years of education with this statement:

"Just so you know, every single person you know is going to get engaged soon, and there's a good chance you'll be a bridesmaid. So learn how to make someone a bridal shower bow bouquet and be prepared to dance the hora beside someone's ninety-two-year-old Great Uncle Joe."

Being asked to be someone's bridesmaid for the first time felt to me like a rite of passage. Something that I could check off my bucket list of titles and honorifics I wanted to achieve in this lifetime, alongside CEO and pizza taste tester. Except I had no idea where to start, or if it was my job to start anything. I only knew what I had seen in movies like *My Best Friend's Wedding* and *The Wedding Singer,* or what I witnessed at the one wedding I went to when I was a flower girl, for which all the bridesmaids wore gigantic taffeta dresses like they were in some terrible fashion show in Milan.

"What do I need to do?" I asked my cousin, one week later.

"It's simple," she said. She was always experiencing everything four years before me, and because of that, I held on tightly to every piece of advice she gave. "Just get the dress, walk down the aisle, and maybe catch the bouquet."

She picked out a fitted black chiffon dress, and since I ordered it three months too late (rookie bridesmaid move), it arrived on the morning of the actual wedding. So when I tried it on for the very first time, I realized I didn't own the right bra. I owned bras with straps, racer backs, and even those suction cup things you place over your boobs to prevent you from taking on the world with a terrible case of nipple-itis. But no strapless bras.

I pulled out a bandeau bathing suit top and tried to zip the dress up over it. *This will work*, I began convincing myself. Except when I moved, even just a little bit, the printed flowers from the floral bathing suit popped out, bursting free from a dress that was fourteen times more expensive. I couldn't ruin my debut moment as a bridesmaid with a tropical paradise suddenly sprouting from my chest when I least expected it.

That's how I found myself doing the Argentine tango with Ivanka two hours before walking down the aisle.

I rush out of the store, robbed of forty-five dollars and every remaining ounce of my dignity. Everything I thought I knew about my knockers was suddenly in question. But if there ever was a reason to be an unquestioning, jumbo-bra-wearing fool, it was that I never wanted to tiptoe into another Victoria's Secret again and get pounded like a piece of veal by my brand-new gal pal, Ivanka.

I try on my bridesmaid dress one last time, a dress rehearsal before the main event. My cell phone buzzes against the wood of my dresser, echoing my own panic.

"How are the babushkas?" Ivanka asks, her voice three octaves deeper on the phone. I had forgotten that we exchanged phone numbers, became friends on Facebook, and made tentative plans to do this all again, next month, during the semiannual sale. I put her on speakerphone, ripped the tag off of my brand-new flotation device, and hooked it around my chest. But no matter how much I wiggle the thing around my anthills, it keeps falling down around my waist. "Victoria has a secret," I shout into the receiver. "She's a liar!"

I dump every single thing out of my purse and survey which items I can stuff my bra with. *Tissues? Yes, of course, those will do the trick. Spearmint Life Saver mints? I can work with that.*

By the time it's my turn to walk down the aisle, I've stuffed my strapless 34D bra with so many different household items that I'm a walking CVS, at risk of dropping Band-Aids and individual to-go packets of Advil with every step that I take. A bridesmaid behind me makes a casual remark that she wishes she had a hair tie. I reach into the sweetheart neckline of my dress and pull one out for her.

At the reception, things don't get any easier. "Will all the single ladies make their way onto the dance floor?" the DJ announces. I watch a cluster of single girls giggle their way to the center of the room. "It's time to see which lucky girl is going to catch the bouquet!"

I stay put at table number two, beside a crew of my married cousins, and think long and hard about my options. I've come to understand that this ritual is a spectator sport for the rest of the guests, and as a bridesmaid, I can hardly refuse to go. I could use my hands to make sure my bridesmaid dress doesn't slump down to my waist, taking my loose bra with it, or I can go hands-free and flash my ta-tas to a crowd of 300 people, 150 of whom are my blood-related family members.

I make my way to the dance floor. One girl digs the pointy edge of her heel into my pinky toe, while another hikes up the hem of her dress, getting down low in preparation for a jump-and-catch situation.

"Eyes on the prize!" someone screams from the crowd. I have an inkling that it's one of my family members who's hoping that my first time as a bridesmaid will also be the last time I attend a wedding single.

As my cousin tosses the bouquet, the bundle of fresh peonies comes zooming toward my forehead, and I have no choice but to reach up and grab it. To stick my hands up in the sky like Rafiki holding Simba aloft. But right as I reach for it, my treasure chest comes undone. The mints, the tissues, the Band-Aids, the Dr. Scholl's inserts: they all come tumbling out of my bra and land beneath the hemline of my brides-maid dress. The clunks and bangs of CVS inventory hitting the wooden dance floor frightens the other single gals, and their eyes turn from the bouquet to the floor almost instantly. I fall to the ground, slipping on a travel-size lint roller, and before I even get up, I notice the other girls have cleared the dance floor. But clutched in my left hand is the bouquet. Such is the price of victory.

My first experience as a bridesmaid will always be defined by two very important things: I caught the bouquet, and the entire wedding learned a secret that I already knew when I woke up that morning: I am not a D cup.

On the car ride home, I sit in the backseat, patching up the blisters on the bottom of my feet with extra-strength Neo-sporin and Power Rangers–themed Band-Aids. The strapless bra snuggles up beside me, like an innocent puppy who still manages to ruin everything, and the bundle of peonies rests in my lap.

"Catching the bouquet doesn't mean anything," I say to my mom as she slides into the passenger seat of the car.

I watch her buckle herself in, her smile as proud as any mother who watches her child win her second-grade spelling bee or say, "I do," to the man of her dreams.

"I'm telling you," she says, fidgeting with her diamond ring. "You have the flowers, the luck, and, now, the bra."

I start plucking off my fake eyelashes, one by one, desperate to peel off this bridesmaid costume and return back to the messy-haired, braless girl that I am, deep down to my sports-bra-wearing core.

"Now," she continues, adjusting the air-conditioning. "All you need is the guy."

chapter four

For the Love of JDate

Her voice is panicked, as if the world is coming to an end and she wants to make sure that I have enough canned food in the pantry and jugs of water hidden underneath my bed. As if Ann Taylor Loft is having a 50 percent off sale, which is a step above their usual 40 percent off sale, and she wants to make sure I snag another pair of business casual slacks to hang beside the five pairs I haven't worn yet.

"Jennifer, what are you doing right this second?" my mom asks, more curious than usual.

"I'm, umm," I look down at my shaggy cuticles, figuring I'll use them as an alibi since I can't tell her what I'm actually doing right now.

It's Sunday afternoon and I've fallen into my weekend routine of scrolling through my Facebook newsfeed and clicking on one friend's friend and stumbling all the way to a friend of her cousin to discover a wedding trailer of a bride and a groom I've never met and watching it on repeat until my keyboard is drenched with pathetic tears.

"I'm filing my nails," I reply, convincingly.

"Stop everything," she continues. "Check your email. There's something special in your inbox."

I will always view my life as two distinct periods: the time before my mom got a smartphone and a Facebook account, and the time after. The time before was, of course, simple. It was safe. If my mom wanted to know about my life, she had to pick up the house phone and pause from chopping onions to find out. Now, if she wants to know what I want for dinner or where I know my most recently added friend on Facebook from, all she has to do is post on my wall whenever she wants, still not understanding that all 2,032 Facebook friends of mine can read her frequent comments, like, "Remember to use your pimple cream tonight."

I press Pause on the muted wedding trailer that's playing for the sixth time in the background and switch over to my inbox.

There it is. An email from my mom with a subject line that reads: *Fwd: Living Social Deal of the Day: 70% off Match.com.*

I can hear my mom on the other end of the phone taking out a coffee cup from the top shelf of the cupboard and placing it underneath the coffee maker. I can hear her putting the phone closer to her ear to gauge my reaction. But I don't make a sound as I drag and drop the email into my spam folder, rolling my eyes and thinking, only briefly, about reporting it as illegal activity.

"You know," she starts up again, interrupting my silent treatment. "Susan's son met his wife on Match.com."

I break open my locked lips, eager to find out if Susan is real. "Who's Susan?"

"She is in our Thursday mah-jongg group."

The word *our* is casually thrown around here. Just because I'm perpetually single doesn't mean I'm thirty years too young to be part of any kind of mah-jongg, Tupperware, or Oprah's book club group.

I stick my claws out at the idea of online dating because none of my friends met their Mr. Forevers that way. They all met them in some amazing, movie-like, meet-cute way, so many years ago, when braces and midterms and money for fast food was all we really had going for us. But back then, I was just trying to get a first kiss, a second date, anything but a third-wheel kind of gig. I was what most would package up and label a serious late bloomer.

I have a (Facebook) friend who met her boyfriend seven years ago, in high school gym class, and now they're married with a minivan full of kids. I have a (real-life) friend who met her husband on her first day of work, when the elevator stopped thirteen floors short, and they were trapped inside for fifty-six minutes, staring at each other in sheer, desperate hope.

What's my online dating meet-cute going to be? We met after I liked the About Me section of his profile? We fell in love after he messaged me a winky face or a pickup line like, "Sup, cutie?" Will it be hopelessly romantic to admit that when we finally met in person, he looked absolutely nothing like his photos? Or that I accidently swiped right when I meant to swipe left and it was the best mistake I made in my twenties?

When I moved to New York City, I thought dating would be easy. I thought I would go to a bar and have a line of guys eager to shake my hand hello and ask me for my number so they could call the next day and ask me out. I thought I'd meet someone in line at the Chase Bank ATM or while waiting to speak with a Time Warner Cable representative about how I haven't been able to connect to Wi-Fi in my apartment in twenty-six days. But the only guys who seem to be knocking at my door are my landlords asking me to shell out enough cash for last month's rent, and delivery guys who never judge me for ordering the same meal three nights in a row or for wearing pajamas with teriyaki sauce stains on them.

"I'm sure this Susan lady's son was very successful with the online thing," I say, dragging and dropping the email from my spam folder and placing it in my permanently deleted folder instead. "But I'm not interested in giving it a try."

I hang up the phone and press Play on my video, crying once again, as if on cue.

If I'm going to give this whole online dating thing a whirl, I think to myself, I'm going to do it my way. I'm going to spend as much time as I want browsing profiles and running elaborate background checks, first through Google and then through the NYPD. If I find a guy I'd like to meet in person, I'll meet him—behind a glass window, prison visitation style.

I figure if we hit it off, we could then compose an elaborate story together, a blended version of each of our fantasy meet-cutes. Perhaps he'd want to say we met while running around the reservoir in Central Park, and since everyone who knows me knows I never run, I'll ask him to change our story to how we met while reaching for the same J. D. Salinger book at The Strand. Nobody will ever have to know we met online, ever.

I start typing Match.com into a new browser and quickly mash down on the backspace key. If I'm going to find someone to go on a date with, I should at least try to find a guy I can also bring home with me for Passover. I type in JDate.com and start drafting up my personal details:

Username: MyMomMadeMeDoThis1234

Location: Behind my Mac Book Pro, trying to scratch off the dried-up smear of peanut butter that's made itself at home between the G and the H keys.

Hair: Blonde. Okay fine; it's more of a Jack and Coke color, but every three months I give a chunk of my paycheck to a patient hairstylist who makes it look like champagne.

Body type: Fits nicely on an L-shaped couch.

I'm really good at: Knowing all the lyrics to Jay-Z's *Hard Knock Life* album, writing what I want to eat in haiku on napkins at fancy restaurants, fumbling around in my purse and trying to find my wallet when the bill comes.

Looking for: A mensch who likes me as much as I like pizza.

I upload three photos of myself from three years ago and go to press Send when, all of a sudden, a pop-up window enlarges and takes over my thirteen-inch monitor. "One more step until you can spin your dreidel around love," it reads. I contemplate shutting down this secret operation, tossing my laptop out the window, and erasing this whole premeditated attempt at finding a husband. "You just need to insert your credit card information."

I forgot that this thing cost money. I forgot how expensive finding love could actually be. I click the X at the corner of the window. I'm done.

Another pop-up ad zooms forward: "Did Hanukkah come

early this year? We think so. Sign up today for only $39/ month."

I can't afford that. I'm a bottom-level PR assistant at a three-person company, where my salary resembles that of a top-level intern. My paycheck is enough to cover my rent, a couple of slices of one-dollar pizza, and half of my Con Edison bill every month. Anything extra that I want has to be free. I've become really good at sneaking into fancy hotels and stealing soap, an hour on their gym's treadmill, and a muffin and some stale coffee from their continental breakfast.

As I go to delete my perhaps too-honest profile, a blue blinking box on the side of the website pulls my eyes toward it. It's for JDate's blog, and it says they're looking for new writers. *I've been writing about every detail of my life, publicly, on the Internet for years now*, I think to myself. A couple of thousand people read about how I really uggghhh wearing bras, or how I was rejected from 256 jobs before getting my first in-person interview, or how I have extreme sweating problems that allow me to wear only white or black. Why not introduce the world to my dating life, or painful lack thereof, in the name of getting a free JDate account? Count me in.

Two days later, I'm JDate's newest blogger, and ten days later, I'm on my very first online date with that guy named David who told me I was smarter than I looked. This was all totally paying off.

I manage to keep my newfound dating life and my blog tips a secret from everyone until one day, two months later, this happens.

My roommate, Kerri, screams at the top of her lungs, as if she just won the lottery. Kerri and I have been sharing a 500-square-foot apartment for a year and a half, and the only time her voice has climbed up an octave above normal was when she saw a mouse crawling around inside our refrigerator. Other than that moment, she's been as calm as a Buddhist monk.

"Your face, oh my god, your face!" she yells.

"What is wrong with my face? What's wrong with it?" I scream back, wondering if it's somehow on fire and I don't even know.

"It's—" She tries to continue but can't, pointing at the computer and allowing her face to turn red and then even redder until it looks like a pepper. "It's all over JDate!"

I grab her laptop out of her hand. My secret's out, but not because she found my profile or my blog posts, but because, on the very front page of JDate, at the very top, there's a giant banner ad with my photo. With my name. With a snippet from my profile reworked into copy: *Follow Jen Glantz as she searches for a mensch who loves pizza.*

"Jennifer," my mom screams when I pick up the phone, just minutes after Kerri discovered I was bartering prose for the chance to meet bros. "Barbara's cousin's sister, Michelle, said her son saw a Jen Glantz on the front page of JDate? Is that you?"

Now the secret was really out.

I can hear her breathing heavily into the phone, crossing her fingers, praying to Hashem.

"Mom," I say with every ounce of patience left inside of my newly exposed self. "How does Barbara's cousin's sister Michelle know that you know me?" I'm starting to think that there's some secret society for Jewish mothers with single children, an underground offline dating club.

"Not important," she goes on. "It is you! Isn't it? Have you met anyone on there yet? Oh, I am so proud. The guys must be, well, they must be messaging you by the second."

"Mom," I say, watching my roommate's eyes bulge as she zooms in on the banner ad, enlarging my face to take over her entire screen. "No, there's no one on there for me."

"I don't believe it," she says. "I bet if I went on for you, I'd find you a guy in twenty minutes."

I had been on JDate, secretly, for three months and had gone out with only three guys. After David, the second guy, told me he was still in a long-distance relationship, and the third guy rolled his eyes when I told him I was madly in love with pizza. I was sick of skimming through messages with spelling errors, addressed to another girl, laced with wink faces. I was sick of having to write five hundred words of dating tips a week just so I could have a free account. And now, here I was, sick of my face being advertised to over 2 million people as a single girl looking for a guy who loved pizza.

"Really, do you want to bet?"

"If I find you a guy," she says, her confidence climbing up a notch, "you have to go out on a date with him."

"And if you don't," I jump in, "you have to stop nagging me about dating for one whole year."

"Deal."

The deal did come with more terms. I said she could not be Skyped in for the date, and she said she had to choose the guy and send him the message. I said she couldn't be on our phone calls, and she said I could not preapprove the messages she sent. I said she could not plan our wedding, and she said I could not plan how this whole thing would come to a tragic end.

"Here's my log-in info," I say, typing my username and password into the body of an email. "Enjoy."

I grab the computer back from my roommate and type into Google, "Who do you call when you want to shut down the Internet forever?"

"Did you just give your mom permission to manage your online dating profile?" Kerri asked, concerned, wondering if I have some kind of stress-induced concussion.

"Is this even allowed?" I ask her, slowly coming back to awareness. I don't remember seeing anything in JDate's rules about your mom not being allowed to log on and take part in the most intimate details of your dating life for you.

None of my rabbis or Hebrew school teachers ever mentioned, when I turned thirteen and had to recite a Torah portion through my braces, that when I finally grew up to be twenty-five, my mom couldn't stick her nose into my dating life.

So here I am, over a thousand miles away from my mom, with the phone squished against my ear as I listen to her type my username and password into JDate's login box. I can tell she's overwhelmed the way a child would be as they paw through their collection of newly acquired Halloween candy.

"Look at this one!" she squeals, but I can't see. I refuse to be on the site at the same time.

Instead, I'm hiding under my covers, pretending to be invisible, pretending that what my dating life has succumbed to at that very moment—my mom hand-picking candidates off a website, as if we're shopping for vacuums on Amazon—is not actually happening.

But it is. My mother is scrolling through the profiles of

guys like "MazelTovMan0132" and "JacobTHEMensch2013," wondering why in the world I wasn't into them.

"Mom, come on," I plead. She begins to read their bios out loud. The "Jacob" guy used a ";)" on his profile, and MazelTov-Man mentioned that he was looking for a girl to cook him dinner and join his fantasy football league.

I glance down at my phone. We've been at this for one hour forty-seven minutes. That has to be some kind of online dating record, at least for me. Any second now, JDate's fraud team is going to call and report that someone has hacked into my account, because this is more activity than they've seen from my username than in three months combined.

"Oh! Here we go," she announces suddenly. "I've found the one."

Before I even hear who this "Jonathan" guy is, I imagine my mom texting our rabbi to see if he'll be free, in a year and a half, to marry us. Apparently Jonathan enjoys reading nonfiction, eating pizza, and has family in Florida too.

After Mom and I agree that he sounds like the most compatible person on the site so far, she asks the unthinkable: "Will you let me message him?"

I've come this far, I tell myself. And since Mom has expressed nothing but patience regarding my negative attitude over the past two hours, I figure this would be a proper prize. (Plus, if it does work out, what a funny story we'd have to tell our kids one day!)

She reads me the three short, formal sentences she wrote him: *Jonathan, we have a lot in common. I would like to chat further with you. Please respond if you are interested.*

Jonathan responds, almost immediately, with a simple answer. His tone, almost identical in its lack of enthusiasm and overseriousness, says, *Let's get a drink on Thursday, 7pm, at Wine 33.*

No witty banter about what we do for a living or how awful cubicles are. No pretending that I didn't spend my weekend on the couch, binge-watching thirteen episodes of *House of Cards.* He's direct—very direct—and to my mom, he is perfect.

At 6:45 p.m. on Thursday, my phone rings.

"Jennifer," she starts. "Are you wearing something clean? Without any stains and wrinkles?"

"I have to go, Mom," I reply.

"One more thing," she goes on, before I'm able to press the End Call button on my phone. "Give him a fair chance, please. And don't eat with your fingers!"

Fifteen minutes later, I see Jonathan walking toward me as I lean against the wall outside the restaurant, one foot on the pavement and one foot flat up against the wall in case I need to drop down into a sprinter's stance and run away.

Surprisingly, he looks exactly like his photos. He's attractive in an "I would bring him home to my mom kind of way," which is fitting, since my mom picked him out of a lineup. He doesn't have tattoos, wear a leather jacket, or have a beard or any visible piercings, like the last twelve guys I dated. But a bet is a bet, and I'm here, ready to give this whole thing a fair chance.

As we sit down, I break the awkward silence with my infamous game of Here is What Matt Lauer said on the *Today Show.* We find ourselves talking about Obamacare and a segment that we both watched about it on *60 Minutes* last week.

We're in a heated argument before the waitress even has a chance to come over and ask us what our drink of choice is. *Note to self: Find a new, less controversial topic to break the awkward first-date silence with in the future.*

I can hear my mom's voice inside my head. "Jennifer, be charming. Don't do this." So I politely smile and try to change the subject to something less provocative. Something I know very little about.

"So, those Mets," I go on.

"Who likes the Mets?" he says, showing me the background of his phone, which is a giant Yankees logo.

I can see this isn't going well. I can see he knows this isn't going well. So we don't even order a drink. I take a sip of my stale water and he reaches for his coat.

"It was nice meeting you," he starts. "But . . ."

"I know," I say. "I understand."

He walks toward the door and I linger at our table, fidgeting with the menu, with the rolled-up napkin, with the five-dollar bill he left as a tip for the waitress we never had the chance to meet.

It's 7:20 p.m. If I text my mom now, she's going to think something happened. Either he tried to kidnap me and I stuck him in his soft spot with my Payless clearance rack shoes, or it was love at first sight and I'm giving her a polite heads-up that she should jump on that sale she saw in the newspaper for hand-made wedding invitations.

He was awful. I type. *We argued over Obamacare and then he walked out on me.*

I press Send, collapsing my head into my hands and slamming the phone down on the wooden table. My mom is going to be so disappointed. She's going to think this is all my fault. She's going to remind me of a rule our gal pal Patti Stanger always says, which is to never talk about Obamacare on a first date. She's going to sign me up for Match.com and eHarmony.com and MothersWithPerpetuallySingleDaughters.com.

All of a sudden, as I go to grab my coat, as I go to leave behind the shortest first date in the history of first dates, I feel my phone buzz.

It's a text message from my mom.

Jonathan is old news, it reads, and I take an enormous deep breath. *I already found you someone else. His name is Mark.*

My mom, the online dating machine. The secret is out.

chapter five

All of My Friends Got Engaged

When my friends call me and say they have good news, I hang up, because now that news no longer involves me.

When we were in our early twenties, my friends used to call for three reasons. The first kind of call was the most common: "Hey, Jen! Wanna go out tonight and bar-hop across the Lower East Side and see how many guys with thick-rimmed glasses and a studied affinity for craft beer ask us out?"

Sometimes they would call to say, "Hey, Jen! Let's blow our savings accounts and book it to the Bahamas this spring. We can sprawl out on extra-large towels across super-hot sand, slather ourselves with globs of tanning oil, and bake under the sun with an overdue library book and a freshly blended piña colada while we pretend we don't have 563 unread messages in our Gmail inboxes."

I used to wait all week for this one: "Hey Jen! Let's spend

Friday night plopped on the couch and stuff our faces with handfuls of cheddar jalapeño–flavored Cheetos and Three Buck Chuck from Trader Joes. We can rewatch season one of *Gilmore Girls* on Netflix and laugh at all the other people posting Instagram photos of the unpronounceable food they're eating on their dates at fancy restaurants." *Escargots in their cargos*, we'd say, and take a swig of pinot gris directly from our bottle of wine that cost less than the round-trip subway ride to procure it. *Le Pew to you too!*

What I'm saying is that whenever my phone buzzed, I knew it meant that some kind of adventure would slap me across the face and drag me outside my apartment and bring me back home at around 4:00 a.m. with a phone full of photos that would lift my spirits through the next week of 9-to-5 days and meetings with stern-lipped people in boring three-piece suits.

But now that we're in our mid- to late twenties, I've been getting three very different kinds of phone calls from those same friends, in this order:

"Hey Jen. Guess what?" I should note that when I first started getting these "Guess what?" calls, I naively thought the big reveal would still involve me. I would assume that my friend had just won the lottery and was inviting me to travel around the world for ham and cheese sandwiches in Madrid and cliff-diving in Dubrovnik in Croatia. Or to tell me she had free tickets to the Maroon 5 concert and a plan to sneak backstage to take selfies with Adam Levine.

But that's not even close to the kind of heavy-hitting, world-spinning, exclusionary news that followed the new batch of "Guess what?" questions.

"We're engaged!"

"Who's 'we'?" I say, because it's always, somehow, a little bit shocking to me when friends get engaged, mostly because I still view us as sixteen-year-old versions of ourselves giggling over guys and cooties.

A year or two later, that same friend will call to say, "Hey, Jen. Guess what? We're gonna have a baby!"

"A what? How?" I say, a little pissed off because now there's yet another person pushing me out of the equation. "But you just got married. Also, didn't you just drink half a bottle of coffee-flavored Patrón and pee in your pants after laughing so hard at that YouTube video of a dog dancing to Backstreet Boys?"

But the third kind of call is the hardest, and no matter how hard I try to prepare myself, I'm never fully ready.

"Hey Jen, guess what?"

Do we have to do this again? I think. *It's beginning to sound like a knock-knock joke gone wrong—and I'm the punch line.*

"What now?"

"We're moving back home to Florida!"

This is the worst because I know what this means for them. It means they're going to take out a mortgage on a house with more square footage than the entire floor of my New York City apartment building. They'll probably have a pool with a marble surface and a lawn that needs constant grooming and flowers that need more attention than their darling hyperactive children. They'll have a dishwasher and a laundry machine and a two-car garage. They'll have space to grow into real-life adults, with investments beyond the savings bonds their grandparents gave to them at their bar and bat mitzvahs. They'll have family sit-down dinners prepared with gifts from their wedding registry, and they'll eat with utensils that aren't hoarded from the hole-in-the-wall Chinese restaurant across the street with a C grade in the window from the New York City Health Department.

Do you know what this means for me? Well, it could mean a booming career if I decided to start my own babysitting business. But what it really means is that while I was trying to land a job that paid me more money an hour than the price of a tomato mozzarella panini from Starbucks, and while I was learning how to use Tinder and wishing I could forget how to use JDate, all my friends were getting engaged. It was as if an alert popped up on their phones at around some point that said, *What are you waiting for, girl! Now's the time to start dropping hints to the person you've been dating for two years to let him know you're ready for that diamond ring and a monogamous life of expanding waistlines and synced iPhone calendars.*

While my friends were waking up on Sunday mornings with the guy of their dreams, sipping mocha cappuccinos in bed and binge-watching *The West Wing* on Netflix, I was inventing ways to remember all the guys I met online and documenting them in my phone with nicknames so I wouldn't confuse one Joshua with another, an Evan with a Steven, or a David with a Daniel.

While my friends were merging lives with guys who complemented their personalities, I was dating Chase the Cheapskate, who would never pick up the check when we went out for dinner and somehow, always, forgot his wallet when we went to happy hour on Friday nights. I went on exactly one date with Lucas the Lizard Tongue, who went in for a kiss on the first date and ended up making out with the side of my earlobe.

Forgive me, Father, but I will never, ever be able to forget Michael the Mensch who was a rabbi in training at the local synagogue and met me for brunch one weekend after finishing a circumcision on one of our neighbor's newborn babies and didn't wash his hands. There was even No Job, No Problem Rob, who thought the idea of sitting in a cubicle all day was a shameful waste of time and had vowed never to have a real job again, living purely off the land and paying whatever bills he had with money he made from teaching people how to hang-glide.

My friends, those lucky saints, never had to go on a date with Jeremiah the Jean Shorts Wearing guy from Williamsburg, who wouldn't drink coffee from mass production companies like Starbucks or Coffee Bean. They never had to sit through drinks with Ryan the Russian Riot, who would pick a fight with just about anyone who looked him in the eye, including in the middle of a JetBlue flight to California or while shopping for pillows at Macy's.

My friends were rounding up the rare Prince Charmings of the world, signing leases together for proper one-bedroom apartments, and going on dates to places that were reservation only. They had routines that involved yoga on Saturday mornings and sushi-making classes on Saturday afternoons.

I started to ask myself, *What the heck is wrong with me? Where did I go wrong?*

It was only appropriate that I started to wonder, to really wonder, if the batteries on my biological clock needed to be changed. For some reason, my clock wasn't ticking as fast as the rest of the women I knew. I felt so young and so completely and wholeheartedly unsure of myself. How could I even consider getting married at this age when the contents of my résumé were about as coherent as ancient Egyptian hieroglyphics to anyone but an Egyptologist?

I wanted a career before I wanted a husband. I wanted a closet filled with Ann Taylor Loft pencil skirts and cotton button-down shirts; I didn't want to make life-changing decisions with a closet full of Forever 21 lace crop tops. I wanted a 401(k) and a boss who would sit down with me once a year to give me a review and a 10 percent raise.

A part of me even wanted to keep dating. I wanted to make some more mistakes with Recovering Alcoholic Alex and Wannabe Stand-Up Comic Samuel. Sure, I wanted to find my Mr. Right, but I'm pretty sure that even at this very moment in my life, if he were standing right in front of me with a bouquet of freshly cut yellow roses and waving them frantically in my face, I would walk right by him.

College doesn't prepare you for the moment when all of your friends start getting engaged, though it really should. Your advisor should tell you that after you graduate, three things are likely to happen. First, you might not find a job right away. You'll probably have to take an internship at a company that will make you wake up in the middle of the night, soaking wet in your own stress sweat, trying to remember if you sent that email your boss asked you to send earlier that day. You'll work hard at that job, even though you could make more money working at McDonald's, forcing you to reevaluate why you just spent $25,000 (or lots more) a year on your education. Second, if you can't score that full-time job, you'll probably have to move back into your parents' house—if they'll have you. If you have too much pride to do that, you might start couch surfing until your friends who just got hired at their first jobs as accountants or preschool teachers or grad school teaching assistants have enough of you and your whininess about being unemployed. Third, all of your friends will suddenly get married.

I kind of thought we would suffer through the first two things together a little longer before I felt left behind, like one of those kids who fails the state standardized test in the fourth grade. I thought we would all meet at a dive bar every Thursday night for the rest of our lives, where the beer is four dollars a pint and the French fries are a little bit frozen, and talk about how writing cover letters feels like a giant waste of time, or how we just quit our third part-time job that year.

It all started to fall apart when I got a text message from my friend Gina, whom I'd known since my freshman year of college. My phone buzzed, and I unlocked the shattered screen of my iPhone 5. There it was: a picture of a gigantic diamond ring on Gina's itty-bitty ring finger.

"Oh, that is cute," I said out loud to myself. I thought she was just bored at a jewelry store and decided to try it on or that it was someone else's hand in the photo. Gina had been dating her boyfriend for only eight months, hardly enough time to truly know someone. They didn't even live in the same city. They hadn't even made it through one full circle of seasons together. But before I could write back or send a, "Is this an early April Fools *joke?*" my phone was buzzing again. Gina was calling me.

"Jen?" she said with hesitation, as if she were expecting someone else to answer my phone.

"What's with the photo, Gina?"

"Jen," she said again, this time certain she had the right girl on the phone. "Guess what? We're engaged!"

"Who's 'we'?"

"Jon and me. Duh!"

"Oh. Really? So soon and everything?"

"I know!" she said. I could hear the same note of excitement in her voice that used to be there when she'd invite me to hijack a dance floor in a gritty club with neon flashing lights. "I can't believe it!"

Neither could I. Maybe a part of me was jealous because I was being demoted from best friend status to third wheel. But I think a bigger chunk of me was jealous that my best friend found love, when all I could find were terrible Tinder dates. I was happy for her, but I was also starting to feel a tingle of desperation to experience that kind of happiness for myself.

As if things couldn't become any more traumatizing, exactly two months after the first ring picture, while I was trying to get home in the middle of a late-season New York City blizzard, my phone buzzed again. This time, the voice on the other end of the line sounded so jubilant that I knew something bad was about to happen.

It was Gina again. "Jen! So, I have a question for you."

"Sure," I said tentatively. "What's up?"

"Will you be my bridesmaid?"

I immediately pushed the End Call button with my chin and spent the next fifteen seconds considering my options. Should I call back, lie and say the call was dropped, and enthusiastically accept? Or should I throw my iPhone into a snowdrift and never look back? Before I could make a decision, before I could figure out a way to never receive these kinds of calls again, a text from Gina appeared on my screen.

I'll take that as a yes!

And so it began.

chapter six

Bridesmaid Is Just Another Name for a Warrior in a Taffeta Dress

Back when I was just a Nick-at-Nite-watching, fleece-pajama-wearing, brace-face preteen, I remember my baby-sitter Erica telling me a bedtime story about a wedding she went to where a bridesmaid passed out at the altar.

My knowledge of what a bridesmaid was and what a bridesmaid did was limited to what I'd seen at the first wedding I went to when I was three years old. I remember watching a girl in a bubblegum-colored gown saunter down the aisle as the rows of people to her left and right oohed and ahhed. I remember her holding the bride's bouquet and fluffing the edges of her lace dress. I remember them hugging and dancing and clinking glasses of pee-colored liquid together. I remember thinking being a bridesmaid was the most beautiful and exquisite thing you could grow up to be. I had no idea that being the bride's side chick could leave you temporarily comatose.

"How did she pass out?" I asked, relaxing in my twin bed, my face sticky from the Fruit Roll-Up I'd just eaten. "Did the priest pause the ceremony? Did the bride start to cry? Did the bridesmaid get off the floor?"

"No, Jen." Erica answered, in a hot flash, as if all of my comments would have sounded off the buzzer on the game show *Family Feud.* "They just went on with the ceremony."

"Did they get married over her passed-out body?" I asked as I snuggled under my polyester Power Ranger sheets.

"Someone in the front row dragged her out of the room, got her some water, and gave her a tissue."

I remember trying to picture the whole thing. A girl zonked out on the ground, pretty in pink, while the happy couple, front and center, kept things moving along, their gazes full of loaded promises to love one another through thick and thin, and the downfall of everyone around them.

"Weren't they worried about her?" I asked.

Erica just shrugged. "They slumped her next to the confessional booth for the rest of the ceremony."

At eleven years old, I was more horrified by this news than by an episode of *Are You Afraid of the Dark?*

That was the beginning of my realization that being a bridesmaid required way more than just zipping up a poufy confection of a dress and flirting with a half dozen handsome groomsmen in penguin-like tuxedos. It was a test of human survival. It was something you walked into belly-up and left, potentially, belly-down. It wasn't for the dainty, the manicured, or the high maintenance. It was for those who were strong as an ox, the resilient ones who could endure being screamed at by a bride one moment and hugged tightly by her the next. It was for the ones who approached a wedding like they would a Tough Mudder competition, power-crawling through the day on their elbows, dragging their bodies beneath barbed wire, covered in mud as thick as cheesecake. Because if you walked in there as if you were entering a safe zone, a home base, a massage day at the spa, there was a good chance you would leave with rug burns from being dragged across microfiber carpet and left alone, with a half-drunk water bottle from Aunt Matilda's purse and a handkerchief from a kind stranger in the first row.

When I was a wee bit older, a few years before becoming a serial bridesmaid for my soon-to-be-engaged posse of best friends, an older girl in my sorority took me out for coffee one morning and ended up telling me a story about her first time as a bridesmaid, topping it off by saying that she solemnly vowed to never do it again.

"Never ever again?" I asked, trying to get her to concede to the reality that she probably would have to do it again eventually. Our sorority had 167 sisters in it, and a good chunk of them would probably walk off the stage at graduation and sashay right down the aisle. "What if your best friend or your real sister gets married? You'd say no?"

"Yeah, no," she said firmly, as if this was a well-thought-out and inarguable decision. "I had the worst experience ever."

"Well, my old babysitter told me that one time she saw a bridesmaid pass out during the ceremony. Can you beat that?"

Bridesmaid horror stories were like random cards dealt at a poker table, each person trying to see who had the best hand, folding only when they heard a story more interesting, more unbelievable, and more absurdly laughable than their own.

"Easily," she went on, confident that her cards trumped the ones I was holding. "When I was a bridesmaid, the bride spilled Diet Coke all over her dress. Before the ceremony."

I figured in a situation like that, the bridesmaids would step in and grab a white napkin to twist and tie over the spot, or empty as many Tide to Go sticks as they could onto the offending stain. But at this wedding, nobody did anything.

"A couple of bridesmaids offered to go to CVS, but we were walking down the aisle in two minutes. There was nothing we could do."

Nothing they could do? Why wasn't there some kind of golden rule that bridesmaids shouldn't allow the bride to walk down the aisle in a freshly stained dress, even if the string quartet is well into Mendelssohn's Wedding March? Or that brides shouldn't leave their bridesmaids passed out beside an empty church confessional booth? Was it unreasonable for all of us to agree that the people involved in the wedding were more important than the wedding itself?

"The bride tried to blame this all on us, and she actually thought about calling the whole thing off just because of a little Diet Coke stain on her $3,000 dress."

I hoped that an accidental splash of soda on a sparkling organza wedding dress, like the unwanted presence of rain on one's wedding day, was good luck in some weird, superstitious way.

"What did she end up doing?"

"The only thing she could do: she held her waterfall bouquet of red roses over it and walked down the aisle in complete and utterly unhappy tears."

I felt a sudden episode of acid reflux kick in, knowing that when I was tapped to be a bridesmaid for my friends, I would have to be prepared. Being a bridesmaid meant that you were an ironclad warrior, equipped for sudden emotional turmoil that could strike at any time, at any moment, whether it be over a soggy salad, a no-show photographer, or a synthetic eyelash that was glued a little too far left on the bride's epicanthical fold. There was solid statistical evidence that when I finally became a bridesmaid, I would leave with bloody battle scars and emotional bruises after spending twelve hours in a war zone of temporarily chemically imbalanced family members, flaky vendors who showed up late, and the ultimate wedding crasher: Murphy's law.

I started prepping years before I ever zipped on my first polyester regalia. Most people collect minisoaps and hair conditioners for their next stay at an Airbnb, but I began hoarding tiny bottles of moisturizer, sample packets of Advil, spare bobby pins from hair salons, and tissues from the waiting room at doctors' offices for my debut as a bridesmaid, as if I was gathering supplies for an underground bomb shelter fit for a bridal party of ten.

After the first time I was asked to be a bridesmaid, I became a traveling toiletry section of CVS combined with the snack aisle of 7/11, my tote bags stuffed with individual packs of salted peanuts, fun-size Snickers bars, and Sara Lee muffins. I've learned, over the years, that the only way to handle being perpetually clumsy is to be painfully overprepared. At weddings, my survival kit became my plus-one, which wasn't all that different from a human plus-one, since I'd have to carry both out of the reception hall at the end of the night.

But my survival kit finally came in handy the third time I walked down the aisle, this time for my childhood friend Clarissa, when I found myself locked inside a hotel room closet with a hyperventilating, excessively sweaty bridesmaid who was speaking to me in gibberish.

"I—" she said, huffing and puffing, "can't—" she continued, her eyeballs darting around frantically, "find," she grabbed the lapels of my champagne satin bridesmaid robe, "my—" she shook me hard, "bridesmaid dress!"

I had figured out the problem long before she finished the sentence. I reached into my handy-dandy survival kit and pulled out a candy cane, asking her to nibble on it in hopes of calming her down just a smidge.

"Let's start from the beginning, Beverly," I said, switching from seasoned bridesmaid to CSI detective. This was my third time as a bridesmaid and the other girl's first. I was the other bridesmaids' go-to guru, solving problems and answering questions they feared would set the bride's Victoria Secret lace panties on fire. *Jen, can I wear this necklace to the wedding? Can I paint my nails Ballet Slippers pink with one surprise nail painted in gold glitter? Do you think it's okay if I ask my new hookup, Jonathan, to come at the end of the wedding once everyone is already drunk and loopy?*

I would answer text messages, respond to email chains, flag Facebook chats with the same answer: *No, no,* and *NO.*

But this situation was different. I was inside a hotel room

closet, eyeing an empty safe and sitting on top of a luggage rack, watching a bridesmaid bar the door with her derriere, asking me to pull her missing bridesmaid dress out of my suitcase, like only a well-trained and highly paid magician probably could.

"Where did you see it last?" I asked, pulling out a waiter's pad and a Holiday Inn pen to take notes for my search later on.

"The bellman took it and said he'd drop it off in the bridal suite. But it's not here and nobody at the front desk knows anything about it." She blew her nose hard, the tissue barely containing the force of her snot rockets. "Clarissa is going to flip out when she finds out I lost my dress, and now I have to walk down the aisle naked."

"You're not going to walk down the aisle naked," I reassured her, grabbing the pile of mucus-filled tissues that were now surrounding our feet and tossing them into the safe—a treasure locked up tight for the next group of panicked bridesmaids to find.

"You're right, Jen," she said, sniffling. "I'll have to walk out in just my Spanx."

I handed her a *People* magazine with Channing Tatum on the cover and told her not to move from this spot until I came back. The last thing I needed was for her to be on the loose, rallying up more bridesmaids to embark on her FIND MY DRESS mission. I didn't want a flustered bride discovering the problem and taking revenge on the hotel concierge staff with a can of hairspray to the eyes.

I was going to handle this. I was going to somehow find the dress or make one for her, in two hours or less.

I pinned back my freshly curled hair and fanned my heavily

made-up face, pulling off my nude Guess stilettos and lacing up my Asics. I might have looked like I was ready for a Black Friday shopping trip to Target, but I felt like I was ready for combat.

Right as I snuck out of the bridal suite and went to make a mad dash to the elevator so I could go down and question my first set of witnesses—the hotel lobby staff—I was intercepted by the mother of the bride, whose bum was parked on the carpet, her head against the door of room 413.

"Martha, are you okay?" I bent down, taking a closer look at the mascara-tinted tears sliding down her face. I thought about handing her a candy cane as well.

"The limo isn't coming. I booked it for the wrong day. Next Saturday, not this Saturday."

"Okay, okay. No problem. We can fix this." I didn't know how in that moment, but I was willing to try anything to get momma back on her feet before the bride was off of hers.

"It's not going to be okay." She slung her flip phone across the patterned hotel carpet, showing the first warning signs of an adult-sized temper tantrum. "We're going to have to walk to the wedding."

"No, we aren't," I said, shaking my head, unwrapping a candy cane for her. I had a plan B that might've been too ripe to say out loud at the moment, but it was a viable option: my dad could drive us. It wasn't the most romantic way to roll up to a wedding, but it was better than going on foot. I figured I'd tell her when the time was right, after I called the sixty-five local limo companies and got laughed off the phone.

"You're right," she said.

Look at us, making progress, I thought happily.

"My daughter's going to kick our butts there with her Manolo Blahniks."

I pulled out my notebook and pen and jotted down an official list of things I needed to do in the next two hours.

1. Find missing bridesmaid dress.
2. Hire a new limo.
3. Make sure bridesmaid stays locked in the closet and mother of the bride avoids the bride until #1 and #2 are taken care of.
4. Find coffee. Lots of coffee.

I put my sneakers to the test and jogged toward the elevator, but before I could press the Down button, I saw something no bridesmaid ever wants to see 120 minutes before a wedding ceremony: a hysterically crying groom.

"Jon? What are you doing on this floor? Why are you still in sweatpants?"

"I'm in trouble. Lots of trouble," he said, sliding backward away from me until he hit the wall—literally and figuratively.

It took two bridesmaid horror stories and three times as a bridesmaid myself to realize that weddings were a lot like Disney World. Weddings are supposed to be the happiest day of the couple's life, just like Disney is supposed to be the happiest place on earth. Yet neither truly is. Both are bursting with expectations, extreme emotional setbacks, and the occasional unidentified heat rash.

"Two of my groomsmen are hungover. Like, really hungover. They can't stand up straight."

"That's okay," I said, trying to rectify this problem so I

could start crossing things off my bridesmaid emergency to-do list. "I have Advil and animal crackers in my suitcase. I'll bring them up to your room, and we can nurse them back to health."

"I'm telling you, Jen, they're not going to be able to walk down the aisle."

"Don't say that." I checked the pockets of my robe for a third candy cane to give to the teary-eyed groom, but all I found was one of those gel silica packets that keep new clothing dry and are boldly labeled DO NOT EAT. I figured now was not the time to ignore a warning label. "I'll get them to walk a straight line in no time."

"That's not a bad idea," he said, drying his eyes and stepping away from the wall. "You could walk down the aisle with both of them, one on each arm."

I whipped out my trusty pen and paper and wrote down another point.

5. Bring two rum-drunk groomsmen back to life and get them down the aisle.

My hair had completely fallen flat, the curls packing up their bags and skipping town, uneager to be a part of this wedding anymore. My makeup wasn't getting along with my sweat glands and was slowly slipping off my face. I watched my airbrushed tan slide ever so gently down my arm. It was as if my super-bridesmaid costume was coming off, and with it my superpowers. But I had less than two hours now to find a dress, get a limo, and babysit two groomsmen.

So when I found myself eye-to-eye with the receptionist

at the front desk and asked her about a periwinkle bridesmaid dress on the loose, I had no time to process her squinty facial expressions that made her look like Bozo the Clown.

"Well, lookie here," she said, in a thick-as-gravy accent, as if I was at the front desk of a hotel in Charleston, South Carolina, and not within spitting distance of Miami Beach.

"I need to find this missing dress, book a limo, and pray for a miracle that will hydrate two hungover groomsmen," I said, cutting off whatever excuse she was about to give me. I detailed all of my problems for her, and surprisingly, she heard me out. I guess helping me was easier than addressing another guest's complaints about someone who was playing Justin Bieber songs too loudly, on repeat.

She offered to help, but after a few minutes, she emerged from a back room with nothing more than a small package clutched inside of her hand instead of the garment bag I was expecting. She wasn't the saint I thought she would be.

"Can't find the dress, but I do have a number for our in-house limo service. They can show up in an hour."

"I'll take it," I said, pulling out my notebook and crossing the task off my list, as if I were shopping for groceries and just found the cantaloupes.

I snuck back inside the bridal suite and knocked twice on the closet door, hoping the bucked-up bridesmaid would let me in so I could gather supplies from my suitcase and head to the groomsmen's suite.

She did, greeting me ever so sweetly.

"Dress or no dress?" I guess she only wanted to let me in if it was the former, not the latter.

"I'm working on it, Beverly," I said, pushing open the door

and biting my tongue so I wouldn't blurt out what I desperately wanted to say: *Why can't you pull your twenty-seven-year-old self together and help me look!*

I popped my head out, noticing the bride in a chair in the corner of the room, her back to me. She had no idea one of her bridesmaids, her mother, and her husband-to-be were all simultaneously, hysterically, having a meltdown and about to make this day memorable for all the wrong reasons.

I decided to write a new list, one that was more practical than a list of things I wouldn't have time to do:

How to Save a Wedding in under 30 Minutes

1. Missing dress:
   - *Cut pieces of fabric off the other bridesmaid dresses and use a needle and thread to sew something together.*
   - *Run to a fabric store. Find anything periwinkle. Wrap it around the bridesmaid like it's a toga. Tell the bride the alternative was her walking down the aisle in just Spanx. The kind that go all the way up to your neck.*
   - *Give the bridesmaid my dress and I'll wear my flower-patterned, champagne-colored robe and Asics down the aisle. So much for finding a guy to smooch me at this wedding.*

I left the bridal suite and went to the groomsmen suite, which smelled like ashy cigars and stale whiskey spilled out of a tumbler and left to soak into the carpet. Two of the groomsmen were alive and well, on the couch playing video games. The groom was behind them, pacing back and forth,

clinking together the wedding rings nervously, perhaps wondering if they would make it to their rightful destinations
that day.

But in the bathroom, next to the trash can and the toilet
seat, were my two helpless victims, in need of a quick pick-
me-up and a gallon of water. I dropped a bag of crackers, a
pack of Advil, and a candy cane beside each of them, instruct-
ing them to eat it all up and then take a warm shower and a
power nap.

As I went to leave and begin my duties as a seamstress,
making something out of nothing for the bridesmaid with no
dress, one of the groomsmen paused from playing Call of Duty,
looked me in the eyes, and spoke up.

"You kind of look like the Tasmanian devil right now."

The groom broke out of his pout session long enough to
smile, and the drunken groomsmen on the floor snorted in
laughter. Even I started to tingle with the urge to laugh or
cry; in my experience, both sensations originate from the same
area of your twisted gut anyway.

Maybe the older girl in my sorority was right when she told
me that being a bridesmaid was something you did only once
and never again. Maybe doing it over and over again caused
premature wrinkles, bouts of acid reflux, and the inability to
sleep at night without waking up in cold sweats, screaming,
We need a limo! We need a limo!

It was just then, in the middle of that thought, that I saw
something I never thought I would find in the hotel room of
a pack of groomsmen lounging around in their boxer shorts,
smelling like burps.

Scrunched up beneath the butts of the two innocent boys

jamming their thumbs against the buttons of their Xbox controllers was a twinkle of periwinkle. I rushed over to them like I was a linebacker ready to tackle a running back, pushed them off the couch, and grabbed the dress out from underneath them.

"I found it!!!" I screamed so loud I was sure the front desk would get a noise complaint. I was filled with extreme joy and anger all at the same time.

The groomsmen scratched their heads, unsure of how the dress ended up on the couch or why I was so out of breath, body shaking as if I had just crossed the finish line at an Ironman competition. But they gave up trying to figure it out and instead went back to their video game, and I went back to the bridal suite.

"Put this on and smile," I said to Beverly, handing off her loot. "And never tell anybody about this, at least not until tomorrow. Okay?"

She hugged me so tightly that the only curl I had left on my head unwound itself and tiptoed out of the closet before I had the chance to.

The bride caught us hugging, and jerked me aside by my pinky. I had just saved the day, and now I was in trouble.

"Jen, why do you look like a complete mess?" she said, sighing with disappointment. We had fifteen minutes until call time, until we'd all be gliding down the aisle as if we spent the morning lounging by the pool, sipping piña coladas, and getting our feet massaged by a strong-handed pool boy.

I broke away from her grip wordlessly and took a seat on the couch, unwrapped the plastic off a gas station muffin, and starting chugging semihot black coffee straight from the pot. As I watched Beverly suck in her tummy and zip up her dress, I realized, right then and there, that being a bridesmaid was truly no different from being a warrior. The only difference is that bridesmaids go to battle in a periwinkle taffeta dress.

chapter seven

The Curious Case of the Serial Bouquet Catcher

I was the center of attention in middle school, but not for reasons that made the other nine-year-olds want to snag a seat beside me during lunchtime, or eager to copy my every move, word, or Limited Too outfit. Quite the opposite, actually.

They enjoyed me as an easy target for spitballs, a great punch line for any impromptu joke, the poster child for what every other middle schooler never wanted to become: awkward, shy, clumsy, a little pudgy around the edges, and a tomboy, one who didn't actually play sports but wore the uniform. Back then, and even sometimes now, I think Nike mesh athletic shorts and a sports bra are more comfortable to toss on than skinny jeans and a crop top.

After a herd of girls with Sour Patch Kid faces and matching ponytails chased me around the gym, sling-shotting hair ties at me and giggling like hyenas high on sugar, just because

I decided to wear two different shoes to school that day—my style resembled someone who frequently got dressed in the dark—I decided to take action. I was going to do something about my social situation, which was definitely a "situation" since my two best friends were the school nurse and janitor. I would go out into the world and become part of a team. I would become a softball player.

Who am I trying to fool? That's not how that happened. I wish the nine-year-old version of me had that much confidence and a clear-headed, compass-like sense of direction. I wish I didn't care what other people thought of my prepubescent acneic T-zone and garage sale jewelry, as if I were an offbeat character in a John Hughes movie. But the truth is, my parents wanted to find an activity for me where I could socialize with other kids my age, since my idea of "spending an afternoon with the girls" was camping out at the library with tea sandwiches and Dunkaroos and spending some quality time with Hermione Granger and Nancy Drew.

My parents saw a sign for a brand-new softball league in the park right next to our house. Tryouts weren't required, which meant I had a guaranteed in. I hadn't made the cut for the cheerleading squad, the chorus, or the emerging calligraphers' club, but a spot on the softball team and, at minimum, a participant's trophy at the end of the season, was mine for the price of $186 and a signed waiver from an adult. *Softball*, I thought to myself, as my parents' car rolled up to the edge of the field on the first day of practice. *Here I come?*

I was not good at sports, though I dressed like I was. Whenever I made eye contact with a ball, whether it was a soccer ball, tennis ball, or basketball, I did what I thought any normal person with a healthy misunderstanding of "survival of the fittest" would do: I threw my hands in the air and ran away as quickly as I could.

Growing up in Florida, I was always taught that when an alligator is chasing you, you should never run away in a straight line. You should always zigzag. So that's exactly what I did on my first day at softball practice. When the coach batted balls into the outfield for us to catch, I zigged and zagged all over the park.

After much thought, I decided that the best position on the team for me was benchwarmer. So I took my spot, resting peacefully beside a Costco-sized box of Chewy Granola Bars and defrosted Capri Suns. But before I got settled in, before I could unlace my cleats and pop open *The Diary of Anne Frank*, my coach slung open the dugout door and sat beside me.

"Jennifer," he said, eyeing me as I shoved five empty granola bar wrappers into my shorts pocket. "What are you doing?"

"Oh, I just think it's best if I stay here for the season," I said, pointing to the splinter-ridden, gum-stained bench.

"Not happening," he said, motioning for me to get up. "All members of the team must play. We need you out there."

I said good-bye to Anne, tossed my empty Capri Sun onto the crimson dirt, and walked onto the field. I was a member of a team—a lousy member but, still, a member. I could not let my teammates down.

They found a quiet little home for me as the fourth outfielder and told me to stand behind the other three, as close to the chain-link fence as possible. I stuck a milky pen inside my glove and entertained the other players on the field with haikus, games of MASH (a fortune-telling game that ruled the lives of middle-schoolers in the '90s and early aughts), and stick figure drawings of our coach. That, right there, was my role on the team.

I didn't quit after the first season. How could I? I finally made friends and became a fundamental part of the team. I was the fourth outfielder and the seventeenth person at bat. The team needed me. Plus, I was able to hold my head high once my reputation as a tough softball player began drifting around the halls of my middle school. Kids started coming up to me, asking how I got these watercolor-like bruises all over my legs, and I'd say they were from sliding into home plate during the ninth inning, when all of the bases were loaded and there were two outs. But really, most of them were from when I was twirling around to "Wannabe" by the Spice Girls, using the bat as a prop, trying to land a series of pas de bour-rées.

I played year after year, and eventually, as we all started to grow up a little bit, and some of us went through puberty, and some of us started drinking protein shakes and lifting heavier objects than our Barbie dolls, the balls started making their way to my Area 51–like territory.

The game was officially on. I had to put my pen away and start using my glove for its one true purpose: to cover my entire face when a ball was hit in my immediate direction. One year, I watched Darcy Munchausen get hit in the face with a fly ball and have her front two incisors knocked out. How was I ever going to get a first kiss with no front teeth? It was hard enough finding someone to give me a smooch with my teeth behind a metal cage of braces. I couldn't let that happen to me, so I became extra focused, and whenever a ball was hit into the sky, I would find it, stand right underneath it, reach my glove up as high as I could, and catch it.

Within a matter of four years, I went from MUP (most use-less player) to MVP.

I wanted to take my softball talents to the big leagues and snag a spot on my high school's junior varsity team, but there were tryouts, and on day one, when I was up at bat, my eyes drifted to a senior football player with no shirt on and bulging washboard abs walking on the other side of the fence, and I forgot to swing. I just stood there, with my eyes on a very different prize, as the ball hit my hand at seventy-six miles per hour. A broken thumb and my name not appearing on the roster became the official end of my mighty softball career.

Or so I thought.

I have an 87 percent success rate when it comes to catching the bouquet at weddings. If I ever win a Guinness World Record for this, I will thank my parents for putting me in the position of learning that when something is flying at you, you stick your hands up and find a way to catch it. So when I was twenty-two and at a wedding almost every month, on the dance floor, beside a pack of hungry single women, all stretching their freshly gel-manicured hands up to the ceiling, I would get right underneath the flying bouquet, stick my left hand up, and watch as it fell right into my palm.

I quickly became a threat among the other single girls of Boca Raton, Florida. People started whispering about me as I walked down the aisle. They pointed right at my face during cocktail hour as they were biting into an avocado mousse barquette and washing it down with a beverage from the open bar, saying, "That's the Glantz girl. She's the one who *always* catches the bouquet."

At twenty-four, right before I went to take my seat at table number five for dinner, a bridesmaid I had just met that evening grabbed my hand and dragged me into the handicap stall of the bathroom.

"Jen," she began as a single tear followed a distinct path from the top of her cheekbone down to her chin. "I'm just really sick of being single, and I was hoping that tonight I could catch the bouquet."

"You know," I said, lowering my voice and placing my hand on her shoulder. "I've caught that thing about twenty times and I'm still single. Very single."

"I know," she said, rolling her eyes as if there had been some kind of *New York Times* feature story on my bouquet-catching achievements juxtaposed with my dating catastrophes. "I just really could use some luck over here, okay?"

"Okay, fine," I said. How could I argue with that? To me, it was just a clump of soon-to-be-dead flowers tied together with a ribbon. To her, it was a golden ticket to finding love.

She wrapped her arms around my neck and gave me a squeeze. But before she went to open the bathroom stall door, she did something that nobody had ever done to me before. She grabbed my hand, pulled open my fingers, and slipped me a twenty-dollar bill.

"If you don't mind," she said, switching from sad girl tears to evil-girl grin. "When the bouquet goes up, just step away."

I was being paid off.

When the big moment came, I took a spot on the rear edge

of the dance floor, fingering the crisp twenty and feeling accomplished because, even though I wasn't going to catch the bouquet that night, I now had enough money for an Uber ride home, and I wouldn't have to wait for my dad to come pick me up from another wedding.

I became a bouquet-catching old-timer, and as more of my friends got married, I watched my competition start to dwindle down until it was completely nonexistent. At twenty-three, it was a mosh pit out there, as if we were trying to grab a selfie with Justin Timberlake at an NSYNC reunion concert. But now, you can almost see the tumbleweeds blowing onto the dance floor as a couple of unmarried women tiptoe forward, competing for something that, they all know by now, means absolutely nothing.

At twenty-six, I went to a wedding and waited for my cue. The DJ cranked up Beyoncé's "All the Single Ladies," and I dropped my salad fork onto a silver charger and put down my third buttered roll of the evening and started doing the one-handed single ladies shimmy as I made my way onto the dance floor, proudly mouthing the words, "All the single ladies, all the single ladies, now put your hands up."

The crowd started roaring, clinking their glasses together, and at first, I thought it was because they all knew about my reputation and they were in awe that they were about to witness a living legend, live and in person. *I should start charging admission for the Jen Catches the Bouquet show,* I thought to myself as I gave onlookers a royal wave. But when the music suddenly cut out and all the guests became quiet, I noticed that the reason everyone was cheering was that no one else was on the dance floor.

"Where is everyone?" I whispered to the DJ, with a slight edge of panic in my voice.

He shrugged his shoulders and made one final, desperate plea on my pathetic behalf.

"All right, all right," he said. "Last call for all the single girls out there. Anyone without a diamond ring, please join Jen on the center of the dance floor."

Still, nobody got up from their linen-slipcovered chair. As I scanned the room, as I eyed people from table one all the way to table fifteen, I realized there wasn't another single woman at this wedding.

That was my real-life version of a nightmare.

I was used to going to weddings alone. When I was a bridesmaid and the other girls in the bridal party were married or engaged, or in a serious relationship with a guy they didn't just meet on Tinder a month ago, I was never given a plus-one.

Going solo to a wedding benefits no one. I am infamous for throwing off seating arrangements, since tables have an even number of chairs. The bride and groom are forced into playing a game of Battleship, trying to figure out where they can stick me since there's no room at the table filled with my coupled-up, procreating friends. They usually find me a spot at the leftover table of odd-numbered cousins, family members they invited but didn't think would show up, or those attending solo, of all ages, which is where I almost always find one or two other single girls without plus-ones.

Everyone likes the idea that the leftover mismatched singles table is where I'll find my Mr. Forever. They think the success rate of meeting my match at a wedding is 75 percent because their neighbor has a friend whose cousin met her husband at a wedding, once, in 1996. But in real life, meeting someone at the singles table is just as hard as meeting someone on Match.com. I know this to be true because I once saw a single guy at a wedding, on his phone using the Match.com dating app, spoon-feeding himself a plate of soggy salad.

Being one of the few single gals at a wedding means that the bride and the groom are plotting for months who they want to pair you off with for the night. It becomes part of their wedding planning time line. They pick out their flowers, they chose a DJ, and they figure out which eligible guy they can get you to canoodle with.

A groom once texted me, eight days before his wedding, and said, "Don't get too excited Jen. We've spent the last hour trying to figure out what single groomsman we can set you up with, and, well, there aren't any." I responded with a quick text message back that said, "Well then, rent one."

I was never able to wrap my head around, or forgive a bride for, not letting me bring a plus-one to their wedding. Other people were allowed to not go empty-handed just because they were in a successful relationship. But me, the person who was in charge of holding up the bride's dress while she tinkled or running around to fifteen different beauty supply stores so she could find the perfect shade of pink lipstick, had to show up and occupy the dance floor alone.

Okay, fine. I get that if I had a plus-one, I wouldn't have anyone to bring. Maybe I would have to find someone from JDate or eHarmony, but leave that up to me. I promise to run a background check on them through the Palm Beach County Sheriff's office and heavily vet their social media history. If they have a MySpace page but no LinkedIn page, I'm smart enough to know they don't belong in my life or at your wedding.

But worse than having to slow dance to a Miranda Lambert song all by myself, or find out that I'm sitting at a table beside a recently divorced uncle and a single groomsman who's eating mashed potatoes with his hands, is hearing the DJ call for "all the single ladies to make their way on the dance floor!" and finding out that there's nobody left to go out there but me.

Which is where I found myself on that fateful night, looking like the feature act of a circus show.

"Dance for us," a drunken groomsman with a wife and three kids under the age of five yelled out.

The bride hurried onto the dance floor.

"Marissa," I said, as if I was about to talk someone out of jumping from a ledge. "Please don't throw it. Please don't make me do this."

"Jen, I'm so sorry. This is so embarrassing for you."

"Can you just hand me the flowers and tell the DJ to put on 'Gangnam Style' so that we can divert the attention away from me?"

I had been standing out there for five minutes, and my face was watermelon red. I wanted this to end. People were putting down their forks, looking at me like I was the saddest girl ever to walk a dance floor.

I wasn't sad. I was okay with being single, with being the only single one left. A part of me enjoyed attending weddings alone so I could dance like I was being electrocuted and eat all the leftover cake on tables when people weren't looking. But here I was, on display to over 250 guests who all had the one thing I didn't. Who all had something I was starting to believe

I never would find. Someone who loved every single inch of them.

"Well it looks like we just have one single girl in the room," the DJ chimed in, stating the obvious.

Marissa finally handed me the bouquet of peonies and I scurried back to my table, in the very back, and resumed eating my dinner roll.

There was a roar of whispers, and people at my table tried not to make eye contact with me as they sipped champagne and thanked their lucky stars that this wasn't happening to them.

I put the bouquet of flowers in a glass of water, grabbed my purse and a slice of cake, and headed for the parking lot.

If I learned anything from my softball-playing days, it's that you have to know when to walk off the field and retire from the team before you break your thumb—or, in this case, your very own heart.

chapter eight

Women Seeking Women—
Professional Bridesmaid

"Will you be my bridesmaid?" Liz asks. The coffee spills right out of my mouth, like I'm a baby who's been prematurely burped. There should be a universal rule that you have to wait at least thirty seconds after liquid or food enters someone's mouth before asking them any sort of high-pressure questions.

"Excuse me?" I respond, wiping off the communal marble table at the restaurant where Liz and I are having coffee. "What did you just ask me?"

Liz's face turns a shade of burgundy as she pushes her fingers into the ridges of her cappuccino's cardboard coffee cup sleeve. "I just wanted to know if you would consider being my bridesmaid."

My eyes bulge as I pull apart every syllable of that question, taking inventory on the words she spit out of her mouth for the second time.

"I know, I know," she backtracks, realizing that something is very wrong here. "This must seem so random to you."

Liz and I haven't seen each other in over eleven months. The last time we hugged hello was when we found ourselves in side-by-side dressing rooms, trying on a mountain of clothing at Forever 21. It was unplanned, like the downward trend of our once-solid friendship. We chatted back and forth until the dressing room attendant threw us out, bought matching pairs of distressed skinny jeans, and pinky-promised that we wouldn't let another year pass before seeing each other again. We made good on that promise, by just one month, when she called and asked if I would meet her for a quick Friday mid-afternoon cup of coffee.

It wasn't that our friendship was pulled apart by a series of nasty comments or one final conversation that made one of us go AWOL. It was exactly the opposite. Ours was friendship at first sight when we dove into being instant *best* friends during my sophomore year of college. But after two years, we just drifted. The daily calls turned into weekly text messages that turned into occasional Instagram likes, and finally dissolved into questions from mutual friends, over a sticky bun at brunch, about how the heck Liz was doing.

This happens a lot when we're in our twenties. Our roster of friends suddenly goes from too long with an attached waiting list, to not quite having enough for a list at all. And as we get older, we understand that's just how friendship works. You go from practically joined together at the hip to waiting, patiently, for the next time you'll bump into her at the mall or get a butt-dialed voice mail from her at 3:00 a.m. on a Sunday morning so you can laugh about it for a few days and then go back to forgetting to remember that a deep-rooted, secret-swapping, matching-outfit kind of friendship ever flowed between the two of you.

Yet here we are, sitting across from each other, discussing the side effects of the NuvaRing when, out of the blue, she asks a question that would have made sense four years ago— not now, when our friendship is full of spider webs and dust.

"Well," I say, brushing away the crumbs from my low-fat, gluten-free blueberry muffin. "Why me?"

"I know that we haven't been close lately," she says, shuffling around in her purse and handing me a small box and an envelope. "But do me a favor? Open this and read that, and then let me know your answer."

She covers her face with heart-shaped sunglasses and heads for the door, leaving me here to clean up the mess she created on aisle What Just Happened?

Speaking of aisles, I had walked down four of them that year already. I was a living manual on how to be a bridesmaid without making a mess. I had gotten all my mistakes out of my system early on, and now I was a well-oiled machine. I knew not to bring lingerie to the bridal shower unless you want to give the bride's eighty-seven-year-old grandma heart palpitations, and I knew that if I ever waited until the month before the wedding to order my bridesmaid dress again, I would have to go to a Jo-Ann Fabrics store and make the dress myself. I started giving the other rookie bridesmaids unsolicited advice the way Greenpeace workers, with clipboards, on the sidewalks of New York City start giving you facts about the environment.

When girls in my sorority wanted to know how they could find a bridesmaid dress for under two hundred dollars, plan a bachelorette party that didn't involve strippers dancing around to "The Thong Song," or handle a bridezilla who asked them to grow their hair out four to six inches for her wedding day, the answer was always, "Call Jen."

But saying yes to being a bridesmaid for someone I hadn't seen in almost a year, even though she lived twelve blocks away from me, was something I felt weird about. It made me wonder, for the very first time, if Liz was asking me because she really, genuinely wanted me by her side or if she was asking me because she knew that I was good at it.

The pear-shaped box and envelope are staring up at me from where they are sitting patiently, next to the cream and sugar. I pick up the envelope first, tearing it open like a child eager to see what she's been given for her birthday. I pull out photographs of us and a handwritten letter.

Dear Jen, I read out loud to the fine folks at Starbucks, most of whom are too busy typing away on their MacBook Airs to care. *You know, our friendship started over flimsy things like Wednesday afternoon ice cream and trips to the dollar section at Target. But before we even understood how two strangers could turn into soul mates, there you were, having my back.*

I run my fingers over the words, written in magenta Sharpie, and think back to the day Liz and I met and how she lost her cell phone. We spent four hours on a scavenger hunt looking for her iPhone 3, pretending we were on safari searching for an *Addax nasomaculatus*, until finally, underneath a bush by the pond in the middle of the campus, there it was.

Jen, I can't do this without you. So, will you be my brides-maid?"

I pick up my phone to call Liz. I have an answer ready, even though I haven't opened the box patiently sitting right in front of me.

"That was fast," she says. "I'm only four blocks away."

"Liz, listen," I begin, touching the gloss of the CVS-printed photos, wishing I could bring those days back into my life now. "My answer is . . ."

But before I can finish my sentence, my phone begins to shake violently in my hand. It's my friend Maria calling on the other line. She hasn't called me since we graduated from high school, back when we were using our parents' hand-me-down flip phones. When someone calls you like this, out of the blue, you answer, assuming the reason she's reaching out is either really awful or really good. Either the person won a million dollars and decided to make good on the offer pinky-promised while you were braiding lanyard on the top bunk of your summer camp cabin when you were in middle school or someone died. There is rarely an in-between.

"Liz, can I put you on hold for a sec? I'm getting another call." I click over. "Tell me you struck gold."

"Jen," she whispers.

"Oh my god, Maria. Who died?"

"Jen," she begins again, this time sounding excited. "I'm calling because I have something to ask you."

Oh no, not again, I think. *Not again.* I saw on Facebook a few months ago that Maria had gotten engaged, the same day twenty-five other people on Facebook did, and so I decided to block her on my newsfeed. She's either calling me to ask if she can borrow my password for Pinterest to stalk the wedding boards I've curated over the years, or for something far worse.

"Will you be my bridesmaid?" she blurts out before taking a deep breath right into the receiver of the phone.

"Oh god," I say, my reaction completely unfiltered. There really should be some sort of drinking game where, whenever I get asked to be a bridesmaid, everyone in a one-mile vicinity has to drink a bottle of Patrón—including me.

In the last year, I began keeping tabs on which question I get asked more often: "Why are you still single?" or "Will you be my bridesmaid?" Both questions seemed to enter conversations when I least expected them to and left me foaming at the mouth.

My phone begins to buzz again. At this point, I'm standing on the corner of 34th Street and Fifth Avenue with an unopened box in my hand and heart palpitations in my chest.

I click over, leaving Maria and her question to simmer, like a stir-fry I don't want to eat.

"Is that a yes?" Liz asks.

I switch back to the other line.

"So, is that a yes?" Maria asks.

I hang up on both and turn my phone on airplane mode and shove it into the bottom of my purse, below the tissues, the empty gum wrappers, and the expired Bed Bath & Beyond coupons, before seamlessly entering a crowd of New Yorkers who are all trying to avoid something. I'm bobbing and weaving and dodging elbows, walking the fifteen city blocks home too emotionally dehydrated to handle the situation at hand.

When you're in that state of mind, you can't think clearly. You walk a block too far because you're not paying attention to the street signs. Or you decide it's a better idea to climb twenty-six flights of stairs to your apartment instead of taking the elevator. I do both, which is why I collapse onto the laminate floor of my apartment, exhausted and out of breath, as if I've just been kidnapped and escaped all in one day.

My roommate walks toward me, thermometer in mouth, tissues stuck all over her T-shirt, as if she's trying to make an avant-garde fashion statement. She's got a weekend bag in her hand, hoping to recover in a more stable and calm environment: her parents' house on Long Island.

"You are not okay," the girl with the flu says to me.

I tuck my body into the fetal position, hugging my knees and falling apart.

"I was asked to be a bridesmaid today," I say, huffing to try and catch my breath. "Twice. By two people I haven't spoken to in a combined average of four years."

Kerri makes an attempt at a laugh but coughs uncontrollably instead. She's as miserable as I am but with a fever. She tosses me a Gatorade from the fridge, insisting I need the electrolytes to snap me back to life and become a functioning member of society once again.

I've lived with Kerri for four years now, so she knows that when I'm going through a prima-donna episode of hot flashes, the only thing she can do is make me laugh and get me back on my feet, usually with food or a drink.

I grab my phone from my purse and download every single dating app the iPhone store offers—my ritual after being asked to be a bridesmaid. I post an old About Me section that I have saved in my Notes app into all of my new profile pages.

"You're like a professional bridesmaid or something," Kerri

says, smiling in a way that lets me know that, even though, at this very moment, we both aren't doing so well, we will ultimately, eventually, be okay again.

"Yeah, or something," I mutter, lifting myself up and slamming myself right back down on the microfiber couch and into a pile of used tissues and cough drop wrappers.

I didn't know I closed my eyes until I open them again at 9:00 p.m. My phone has eighteen missed calls from Liz and Maria, and I discover that I'm sitting on top of an open, empty pizza box, with nibbled pieces of crust left inside, a half-drunk bottle of Three Buck Chuck on the coffee table. It's dark and Kerri is gone.

I grab the box that Liz gave me and pull it toward my chest, ripping it open to find a ring pop inside with a tag attached to it that reads, *Say I Do to Being My Bridesmaid*.

"Yeah, always a bridesmaid," I say, picking up the wine bottle with my index finger and thumb and doing an imaginary cheers with the stuffed animal moose tucked into the crook of my arm. "Always a professional bridesmaid?"

Maybe Kerri was onto something. People always tell you when you do the same thing over and over again and expect a different result, you're insane. Well, maybe I could do the same thing over and over again and expect . . . a paycheck?

"Hold on, Moose," I say, turning to him for moral guidance. "Do you think I could make this into a business?"

Maybe there were people out there who needed someone reliable, someone who could be there for them when their friends lived a thousand miles away, or had a minivan full of kids and two full-time jobs, or hadn't been in their lives for a while, kind of like what was happening with me and Liz.

I sit up straight and look around my apartment. There are bridesmaid dresses stuffed underneath the couch, Save the Dates taking up prime real estate on the fridge, and thank-you notes functioning as coasters on my coffee table from brides responsible for big-ticket line items on my credit card bill.

Kerri was right. I was a professional. An amateur one, but still. Maybe it was worth a try, worth seeing if anyone would hire me to be their bridesmaid so I could pay my credit card bills and my rent on time for once.

I shove a slice of half-eaten crust into my mouth and grab my computer. I flip it open, double-click on the bouncing Google Chrome icon, and enter a website I've never visited before.

"www.Craigslist.com," I say to Moose, who's watching me with rapt attention.

I suddenly remember what my mom used to repeat to me on a daily basis when I was in high school: nothing good can come from staying out past 11:00 p.m. or going on Craigslist. But where else could I test this idea with real results? I could post a Facebook status about it, but all people would do is comment with an LOL or smiley face emojis. I could call up my closest friends, but I'd probably be interrupting them in the middle of clinking glasses of some fancy vintage of Merlot with their SigNif to celebrate the end of a long workweek.

But Kerri thought it sounded good, and she's my voice of reason, even if she does have a 102-degree fever.

"What section, Moose?" I say. Moose sits there, stuffed and still, not trying to stop me, so I proceed.

Women looking for women. That seemed like a good home for this sort of thing. I open up a new post and I begin typing.

Title: Professional Bridesmaid for Hire—w4w—26 (NYC)

Post: When all of my friends started getting engaged, I decided to make new friends. So I did—but then they got engaged also, and for what felt like the hundredth time, I was asked to be a bridesmaid.

This year alone, I've been a bridesmaid 4 times. That's 4 different chiffon dresses, 4 different bachelorette parties filled with tequila shots and guys in thong underwear twerking way too close to my face, 4 different prewedding pep talks to the bride about how this is the happiest day of her life, and how marriage, probably, is just like riding a bike: a little shaky at first, but then she'll get the hang of it.

Right, she'll ask as she wipes the mascara-stained tears from her perfectly airbrushed face. Right, I'll say, though I don't really know. I only know what I've seen and that's a beautiful-looking bride walking down, down, down the aisle, one two, three, four times so far this year.

So let me be there for you this time if:

— You don't have any other girlfriends except your third cousin, twice removed, who is often found sticking her tongue down an empty bottle of red wine.

— Your fiancé has an extra groomsman and you're looking to even things out so your pictures don't look funny and there's not one single guy walking down the aisle by himself.

— You need someone to take control and make sure bridesmaid #4 buys her dress on time and doesn't show up 3 hours late the day of the wedding or paint her nails lime green.

Bridesmaid skills I'm exceptionally good at:

— Holding up the 18 layers of your dress so that you can pee with ease on your wedding day.

— Catching the bouquet and then following that moment up with
  my best Miss America–like "OMG, I can't believe this" speech.
— Doing the electric and the cha-cha slide.
— Responding in a timely manner to prewedding email chains
  created by other bridesmaids and the maid of honor.

"What are you looking at?" I say to Moose, who hasn't
moved since I started writing the ad and hasn't alerted the
authorities to grab my MacBook Pro out of my hands. That's
the benefit of having a stuffed animal moose as a best friend.
They let you be reckless, they let you do what you want, and
they sit there with an upward stitched mouth, cheering you on
with pure unadulterated mute bliss.

I find a carton of strawberry coconut milk ice cream in the
freezer and start eating it with the only clean kitchen utensil
we have: a whisk. I read the ad over once more.

Nobody is ever going to find this, I think to myself. *So why
not post it?*

I press Send, slam my computer lid shut, and place it on
the coffee table beside the memorabilia of a single girl's Friday
night bender.

I grab my phone and see another sixteen messages from
Liz and Maria.

Earth to Jen
Are you alive?

I slide my finger over each text message and press Delete,
deciding to read other messages—the kind from potential lov-
ers—on my newly downloaded Tinder profile instead.

One from Matt, 27, NYC, pops up.

> Your name must be Beyoncé, because when I clicked your profile, the power went out.

"Gross!" I shout out, to the infinite abyss of my Murray Hill apartment and toss my phone across the room, where it lands, screen up, on a dirty pile of clothes.

chapter nine

Bridesmaid for Hire—Crazy or Genius?

"Tell us what happened."

"Us" isn't just the guy sitting across from me wearing a starched button-down shirt and a black blazer, or the one, two, three, four people operating the camera, audio, and light equipment. "Us," in this live TV situation, is—I'm going to take a ballpark guess— a couple million people.

Do deep breaths show up on camera? What about armpit sweat? Oh no, I'm wearing a 70 percent polyester red dress. It doesn't breathe! Are people in America going to think that this professional bridesmaid girl has extreme sweating issues when they see the puddles forming near all of my sweat glands? Celebrities get endorsement deals all of the time. If this whole bridesmaid thing takes off for me, maybe I'll score one for a hyperhidrosis medication.

Is it my turn to speak? I can't tell. One reporter asked me a question, but then he started talking to other reporters about how this is the weirdest thing they've reported all week. Weird? I wouldn't say that. Weird is a story about a Florida man dressing up as Darth Vader to rob a grocery store. This is more adorable, unusual even, perhaps the greatest accident to ever happen to a perpetually single girl.

They're laughing like untamed hyenas. How does this whole live TV thing work? Am I supposed to just jump in and speak when I'm ready? I'm ready now. My heart thinks we're at Disney on the Tower of Terror ride. Any longer and it might hit me. I might realize I'm someplace scarier. I'm on live TV.

The camera is slowly coming closer to my face, as if it's the head of a turtle. Is there something in my teeth? Of course there's something in my teeth.

Where's my friend Katie? I think I can see her from over here. She's tapping her toes. Why is she nervous? All she's been doing is taking selfies with the studio equipment.

I'll start slowly. Let me try and pull myself together and hide this internal discharge of chaos behind my Crest White Strip–induced pearly white smile.

"Well, I posted an ad on Craigslist last Friday to offer my professional bridesmaid services to strangers."

"And then what happened? Tell it all to us!"

Here he goes again with the "us." Why is he leaning in closer? I swear he just winked at me when the camera cut over to show a screenshot of the Craigslist ad. At least it took a break from zooming in and out on my airbrushed face.

My eyes won't stop blinking. Can everyone watching from their hi-def TV sets see that? I know my mom is tuning in right now, sitting up straight on the beige leather sectional, with one hand cranking the volume on the remote up, up, up and the other snapping photos of me with her iPad, probably thinking I'm sending her some kind of Morse code with my eyelashes.

This reporter guy with bow-tie ears wants to know what happened next. Well, after I posted the ad, I fell asleep. Should I mention that? Then I woke up. It was Saturday, so I ate a couple of slices of pizza, took a stroll through the Kips Bay Public Library, went on a terrible date with a guy who described in unwarranted details the way his pee smells after he eats asparagus, and then I went to sleep. Alone. Again. The next day was a Groundhog Day kind of repeat of Saturday, sans the smelly pee guy. Then, before I knew it, it was Monday. That's when things started to get interesting. That's when, all of sudden, I learned the Internet is a very dangerous place, where your entire life can flip upside down with just one thing you post. I'll start the story there, in the middle of work, at my three-walled cubicle.

"A friend sent me a GChat message when I was at work with a link to some article on BuzzFeed about a girl offering her bridesmaid services to strangers through a Craigslist ad."

The reporter is looking at me now like this whole thing is completely bonkers, like it's some kind of joke. It's not. I was serious when I posted that ad. I really wanted to help strangers . . . and I wanted to get paid for my bridesmaid knowledge.

What's funny about this situation right now is that the reporter has something in his teeth. I see it. Oh boy, do I see it. I think it's a poppy seed or a red pepper flake. If he has something in his teeth and I have something in my teeth, maybe everyone watching will just think there's a stain on the LED glass of their Black Friday–purchased TV and spare us both some eternal embarrassment.

What's he going to ask next? I should come up with some-thing to say before he asks me another question. Should I tell him how I clicked on the link my friend Terri sent me while biting into a chocolate chip muffin the size of my kneecap and gulping down a cup of iced chai tea the length of my forearm? How I screamed, "AGHHHH!" so loud from my cubicle that the entire office of forty-five people took their hands off their keyboards, pressed Mute on their conference calls, turned around from the copy machine, the watercooler, and the snack jar to make sure that I was all right? How my coworkers thought I was having a premature heart attack? How one guy rushed over, ready to per-form CPR? I think he always had a crush on me. Maybe this was his way of getting some mouth-to-mouth action.

I had to convince everyone that I was okay. I couldn't tell them what was going on! I didn't even know what was going on. I needed to sort this situation out without potentially getting the boot from my boss over some ad I posted that's clouding up all of my focus and my search history on my company-issued computer. I put my hand over my mouth, signaled that all was well in cu-bicle D15 with a single hand wave, and sunk down in my desk chair as I watched my body break out in puffy hives.

I read the article over again, once more, mouthing the head-line to myself: Craigslist Ad Written by a Professional Brides-maid Is Ripe for a Rom-Com.

A rom-com? Is that what people were going to think of my subpar dating life and twenty-seven dresses-*style bridesmaid ex-periences? It sounded exciting. It sounded like I needed to figure out what to do next. Whether to forever stay anonymous or let the world, and the 15,672 people who already shared this article on Facebook, know that the girl behind the ad is me.*

Should I tell the reporter the truth? I really had no idea how BuzzFeed found the ad. I didn't tell anyone about this, not even my roommate, Kerri, who called me a professional bridesmaid in the first place, or my friend Jess, who I regularly text real-time updates of my life to. I certainly didn't tell the guy I went on a Saturday night date with who told me his pee smelled like rotten asparagus.

Maybe I'll mention that I Googled the words "Professional Bridesmaid" and "Craigslist" and saw that there were already five other articles about this, published in the last hour. That my ad was spreading like chicken pox on a preschool playground.

I remember typing back to my friend, OH MY GOD. THIS IS ME. But she didn't understand what I was saying. She just wrote back, I KNOW, WHOEVER POSTED THIS IS YOUR SOUL MATE. YOU SHOULD HAVE THOUGHT OF THIS IDEA FIRST!

I did. I did. I did! But nobody knew that yet, and I didn't know if anybody should know that, ever.

Should I tell him that people at work were starting to get suspicious? Someone told me I looked like I had just won the lottery. Another person told me I looked like I had just found out I was getting arrested for seventeen years' worth of library fines. My face flushed fuchsia, my body broke out in unidentifiable rashes, and my blue long-sleeved shirt was soaked, of course, in sweat.

I wonder if he wants to know how I ran into the bathroom and locked the door behind me. Hugging my cell phone and my chai tea in the corner, setting up a tiny fort out of paper towel rolls and Windex bottles, letting out the occasional oh no, oh no, oh no sigh as if I was in some kind of trouble? Was I? I had no clue.

"So you told your friend that you're the girl in the ad, right? You claimed it immediately?"

"No. I didn't say anything, actually. I just kept reading through the articles that were popping up everywhere thinking, *Oh my God, my mom is going to be so mad at me.*"

I must have been in the bathroom for a while. My butt was getting chilly from the tile floor and people were starting to knock on the door. After a while, they were getting angry that I was hogging the only women's stall, but I wasn't finished with my business in there. I still needed to call my mom.

It was probably around 3:00 p.m. by then, so the phone rang, rang, and rang before she picked up, startled and heavily confused. There are certain hours of the day when you can call the people you love and they won't think anything of it. But there are also blocks of time—say, midafternoon or after midnight—when they can become overwhelmed with panic if they see your name pop up on their phone screen.

I don't think she said "Hi" or "How are you?" I think she just jumped right to the point.

"Jennifer, what's wrong. Are you okay?"

"Yes, Mom, I'm fine, I just . . ."

"Oh my god, what happened? Where are you?"

"I'm at work; I just need to tell you something, okay? It's not a big deal . . . yet."

"Not a big deal yet? What in the world is going on, Jennifer?"

"I did something—something you told me never to do."

"You bought that winter coat for full price at Macy's?"

"No? No!"

"You kept your dishwasher running when you left your house?"

"No, mom. A little worse. I went on Craigslist."

"What? Why were you on there? For furniture? You can get whatever you're looking for at HomeGoods."

"I actually put myself on Craigslist."

"You did what? I think I need an oxygen mask for this conversation."

"Let me explain, okay? Liz and Maria both asked me to be a bridesmaid last week and so Kerri said I was becoming a professional bridesmaid and I took her seriously. I thought I could advertise myself on Craigslist and offer my bridesmaid services to strangers getting married."

". . ."

"Mom, are you still there?"

"Yes."

"And now the ad is going viral."

"You got a virus?"

"No, no, viral. The ad I posted is now all over the Internet. The news sites are starting to report about it. Everybody is about to know that I did this."

"Well, at least you won't have to pay out of pocket for ugly bridesmaid dresses anymore."

"So after you told your mom, what did you do next?"

He's raising his eyebrow at me like I'm a small child who still needs approval from her parents. He clearly does not know the kind of Jewish guilt I'm walking around with after twenty-six years on this planet. By now, I know better than to not pick up the phone and call my mom when something unusual happens. Something that I know she's better off hearing sooner rather than later. Later might involve the possibility of seeing the story on CNN, or getting it emailed to her by one of her mah-jongg gals, or having our community rabbi stop by the house and ask her if *the daughter she bat-mitzvahed thirteen years ago has gone completely mad.*

"I emailed BuzzFeed and told them that I'm Jen Glantz and I wrote the bridesmaid Craigslist ad."

"Why did you decide to do that? Didn't you think it might be better to keep this crazy idea under the table? Stay anonymous?"

"No. I wasn't ashamed. I posted the ad for a reason, and I was proud."

Well, the truth is, I had to leave the bathroom at this point. It had been a good thirty-five minutes and people were starting to pound louder and louder on the door. Some were asking if everything was okay in there. Everything was certainly not okay. Some were asking if they should go get me a bottle of Pepto-Bismol. I think this is one bathroom issue that pink juice can't address, even if it is extra strength. That last thing I wanted to do was create more commotion around myself or this undercover situation that nobody except for me, my mom, and the ten to fifteen Boca Raton residents she most likely told by now knows about, though they probably think Craigslist is some online dating website started by a guy named Craig Shulman. I wasn't worried about them.

I mushed up the homemade paper towel tepee and tossed it in the trash, opened the door with a smile, and walked calmly back to my cubicle, like nothing had happened. Like I didn't just hold myself hostage inside the office bathroom during the three o'clock hour.

I sent BuzzFeed an email right after that and told them the truth: I was the girl behind the ad. Within two minutes, the article was updated with my name and a link to my blog. That was officially the last two minutes of silence I can remember in days.

"After they added my name to the article, every other news site did too. That's when everything blew up and this ad went from cute idea to the real deal."

Should I tell him that Gmail shut down my email account soon after the ad went viral? I created a fake email, doigetaplus-one@gmail.com, *to post on Craigslist and it got so many emails that they thought it was a spam account and temporarily shut it down.*

I had over five hundred new emails. Inside that inbox were all kinds of gems just waiting to be read. I had brides wanting to hire me, guys proposing marriage, and women wanting to work for me, doing what I was doing as a professional bridesmaid. Work for me? I didn't even have a company. I just had an idea. Maybe I could make this into an official business. I don't know. What would I even call it? Professional Bridesmaid for Hire? Could I run a business? I majored in poetry and minored in stuffing my face at the all-you-can-eat buffet-style dining halls. I did take one business class in college, and all I can remember is that one day the vice president of marketing for Chick-Fil-A came in to chat with our class and hand out free chicken patty vouchers, and I raised my hand and asked about animal cruelty. I quickly became grilled like a piece of meat by the 450 students who wanted me to stop asking questions so they could start ordering their waffle fries. I wasn't fit to run a business. Though maybe I could learn now.

"So when did you decide to make this into a business?"

"After I made just one more phone call."

By now it was 5:00 p.m. and I snuck out of the office into

*the service elevator. My work there was clearly done. Plus I had
to call one more person, someone who knew me the longest and
wouldn't call me crazy unless I was truly crazy. Someone who was
business savvy enough to either tell me this was a cute idea and
a terrific way to catch the media's eye but it was never going to
work, or that this was a revolutionary way to keep the wedding
industry, and the world, on their toes.*

I called my older brother, Jason.

"That's you? Oh my god, I saw the article on the Huffington
Post.*"*

*"Yes, it's me. But what do I do? Jay, my inbox is out of control.
There are hundreds of people with questions, asking me to come
to their wedding, reporters wanting to get an interview, these reality show producers wanting to call me. I don't know what to
say."*

*"Jen, this is a great idea. We have to make something out of
all of this."*

"But, Jay, I have no idea how to start or run a business."

*"Well, congratulations on learning the secret to growing up.
None of us ever knows what we're doing. We just do it and figure
it out."*

"It was my brother's idea to make a website, to turn this
whole thing into an actual business and not just a one-time
ad."

"So who came up with the name?"

*"Give me a few days. I'll build the website; you write the copy
for it. We'll work together on packages and prices."*

*"Thanks for having my back, Jay. For being my professional
. . . brother?"*

"Thanks for being my weird little sister."

"*One more thing. What should we call this thing?*"

"*I'll tell you tomorrow.*"

"He came up with the name Bridesmaid for Hire. It just made sense and I loved it."

I really did love the name, but I didn't love what came next. Jay and I spent hours on the phone together trying to figure this whole thing out. I was the one with the bridesmaid knowledge, and he was the one who knew how to start a business.

"*How much do I charge for this thing? How do I background-check the brides who want to hire me?*"

"*We need to start with the basics before we jump into all of that. Let's start with what you actually think a professional bridesmaid would do.*"

"*Okay, okay. Well, personal things like lift up their dress to pee and be their human Xanax, calming them down before the wedding and on the day of.*"

"*So you're like the gal pal they never knew they needed?*"

"*Yeah, but during the time they need one the most.*"

"You say you have had hundreds of requests from brides. What are some of the oddest?"

The oddest ones weren't even from the brides, but I don't think he wants to know about those. One groom emailed saying he wanted to hire me because his fiancé lived in the Philippines and he was flying her in just for the wedding and she didn't know anybody in North Carolina. Twenty-six were from reality show production companies who thought this would make a great series on TLC or Bravo. But the worst part were the requests that followed me in person. I went back to work the next day, on Tuesday, hoping nobody there knew about my day-old alter ego, and surprisingly they didn't. But that didn't last long.

The receptionist swung by my cubicle wanting to know what I did to have the local news show up and ask for me. But she didn't believe me when I said nothing, which was probably a mistake. "Maybe they were looking for a Len or a Ken Glantz?" I'd said. She Googled my name and there it was: thirty-four articles in forty-eight hours, the newest one with a big fat headline that read, Jen Glantz and Bridesmaid for Hire: Crazy or Genius?

I guess you could say that in that moment, I was feeling like a little bit of both. But in that moment, I had two big problems I had to fix, both of which were under six feet tall and eyeing me for answers. I told the receptionist I'd buy her coffee for the next thirty days if she didn't tell anyone, anything. I told the reporter to please leave my full-time place of business and call me at exactly 6:05 p.m.

"The weirdest request I got so far was from a bride in India who asked if I could work a four-day wedding for her."

"Wow. So what would you say something like this cost?"

Oh, now he's going to toss me the hard questions? Right at the end of the interview when my face is burning from holding a smile and my body is begging for a nap? Can I phone a friend? Would it be out of line to ask on live TV if I can call my brother and have him help me answer that? Should I say it's TBD? I know I shouldn't say it's free. I know that's a terrible idea. People can probably tell I have no idea how to answer this one. I have to look right in the camera and say something.

"Right now, we're open to working with every budget. Even those who don't have any money at all."

We. Did anyone hear that? I just invented my own team. I hope he asks who we is, because I won't be embarrassed to say that we, right now, is me and my brother.

"Thanks for chatting with us Jen, and good luck to you and this Bridesmaid for Hire . . . thing!"

Us . . . thing . . . I nod my head seventeen times. My first live TV gig is over. I want pizza. I want to go home. But I don't know if I can get up from this seat yet, because it's soaking wet from my overactive sweat glands. How does my phone have fifteen missed calls? I don't even want to check my email. I just want to call my brother.

When I get home, I strip off my makeup, order a pizza, and call Jay.

"You did great, but we have a lot of work to do. Especially when it comes to talking about how much your services cost."

"I know, I know. I was so scared, Jay. I think I might have peed my pants a little bit. At least I didn't say that on live TV. Hold on, there's someone calling on the other line." I click over.

"Is this Jen?"

"It depends. Is this the New York Public Library?"

"Huh? No, it's Linda from *Good Morning America*."

"Oh, yes, this is Jen. Jen, this is!"

"We saw what you did with the Craigslist ad. We'd love to have you on the show."

What I did? I spent Friday night in the way every single girl's worst nightmare starts off: alone, with pizza, a bottle of wine, and Craigslist. I have to play it cool. I don't want to sound too desperate. Maybe I should tell her I'll think about it?

"Yes, I would love to. I'm free always, whenever!"

I'm very bad at playing anything cool.

"But we'd like to have you on with the first bride you decide to work with. Do you know who that will be?"

I could tell her about the India bride or one of the other requests I scrolled through when trying to sort through my emails. But I want the first bride I work with to have a story. To be the kind of bride who really needs somebody by her side, and not just because she wants an even number of bridesmaids and groomsmen. That's not the reason I wanted to start this business. I wanted this thing to take off, to really go somewhere, to help strangers who felt like they needed something from another stranger that they couldn't find in anyone else.

"Yes, of course, I have someone for sure."

Note to self: become a better liar.

"Great, what's her name?"

Note to self: this is why you should never lie.

"I'll send you her info. When do you need this by?"

Please say there's no rush.

"Tonight would be great."

"Tonight it is!"

I click back over. "Jay, *Good Morning America* just called. They want to know the bride I've chosen to work with first."

"Okay, let's keep reading through these emails."

"Should I just tell *Good Morning America* I'm not ready for all of this yet?"

"Okay, now you're finally sounding crazy. Of course not. I'm forwarding you a new email from a bride named Amy."

I keep Jay on the line and check my email.

Dear Jen,

Let me preface this by saying that I have never been a bridesmaid. I am one of the first of my friends to be getting married and am 25 years old. I am getting married this September, weekend after Labor Day, and it has been quite a learning experience at that. I had to let my maid of honor go, due to her issues of not being able to be part of the big day and rearrange. That was a stressful part of planning. :/

I knock the pizza box off my bed and put my brother on speakerphone, tapping the reply button as my eyes begin to flutter shut. My body clearly isn't on the same page with my brain, which is screaming that professional bridesmaids don't get to nap.

Dear Amy,

Thanks so much for taking the time to write to me. Congratulations on your upcoming wedding! It's great to hear about your interest in having me as a professional bridesmaid at your wedding, especially since you've had some problems with your maid of honor. I'm very sorry about that, by the way. I'd be happy to see what I can do to help between now and September.

I would love to jump on a call with you to chat more about this. Please let me know when is best for you.

All my love,

Jen Glantz

"I really hope she says yes, Jay. I think I could really be there for her. I think I could really help."

"I do too. But now . . ."

". . . we wait?"

"No. Now we go back to figuring out this business."

"Oh yeah. This Bridesmaid for Hire . . . thing."

chapter ten

The Strange Thing about Strangers

He says my name like I'm an Egyptian goddess who's getting fanned with a giant palm leaf on a warm sunny day.

"Jen, Jen, Jen."

"Say it again," I purr.

The third time he says it, there's a tap on my shoulder, and the fourth time, a little shake.

"Yes, my darling lover?" I say, squishing my lips together for a kiss, right before my eyes start to unglue themselves. The sand, pyramids, and camels dunking their faces into waterholes begin to melt away as I surface from sleep and remember I'm on an airplane, in the middle seat, and the Stranger Danger hunk of a guy in the window seat is shaking me awake.

I look around and there's nobody else left on the plane, which leads me to believe that he's been doing this for a while.

"Welcome to Minnesota," a cheery flight attendant with a missing bottom tooth says as she pulls my seat forward and grabs my zebra-print carry-on bag from the overhead compartment. "Aren't you such a cute little thing?" She hands me a moist towelette to dry up the drool that's now dripping onto my pleated Ann Taylor Loft clearance rack shirt.

This is where I am. This is who I'm with.

"Sorry about that," I say, grabbing *The Great Gatsby* from the pocket of the seat in front of me, tucked next to an empty Doritos bag, an unused puke pouch, and a crumpled-up *Sky Mall* magazine. My face is an attractive blend of all the shades of red from the Pantone color chart.

"You were out for a while," he says, in awe of my deep-sleep abilities.

"Are you from here?" I ask, rubbing clumps of dried mascara out of the corners of my eyelids, trying to salvage any chance I have of making him my future boyfriend.

"Ohio," he says. "I'm here for a wedding."

"Me too."

"Family?"

"No."

"Friend?"

"Kind of?"

His eyebrows climb to the top of his forehead and I can tell he's interested in hearing more. But more, I fear, will scare him worse than my drooling and sleep muttering already have.

"I'm a professional . . ." I begin, trying to feel out his reaction, to get comfortable saying something that's still very new for me. "Bridesmaid."

"Jen," he responds, his voice drags in a familiar and protective way. "You're not asleep anymore. You know that, right?"

"I know, I know. This is my first time. I just started a business, and I'm here to see if it works."

"So let me get this straight," he says, wiggling out of his seat, trying to get comfortable with the oversized baggage sitting next to him in 13B. "You've never done this before?"

Everything happened so fast. I remember posting the ad, reporters calling, brides emailing, friends stopping by to see if now was an acceptable time to toss me into the loony bin. I remember staying up late one night with my brother on the phone, reading through emails. I remember one from Amy, and how, after my eyes scanned her email, I wanted to call her right away. How I wanted to get on a plane to Minnesota, and be there for her on the most intimate and memorable day of her entire life.

I fall in love, just a little bit, with almost every person I meet. It might be the most dangerous thing about me. So although Amy and I had never sat across from each other ever or even had a conversation, I knew I had the tender cojones to fill in for her ex–maid of honor and be her step-in bridesmaid, her wildcard gal pal.

The morning after her reply hit my inbox, I splashed a handful of cold water over my limpid eyes, drank a chai tea latte out of a mug the size of my face, and dialed Amy to say hello and ask her if she would be the very first bride to hire me as a professional bridesmaid.

"I'd love to be your bridesmaid," I said to her, as if it were that easy. In most other situations, the bride does the asking. But in this case, things were different—very different—and I felt perfectly okay with shaking up the status quo.

"Listen, I don't really know what you do, or who you are, for that matter," she began, admitting the obvious up front, "but I wrote you because I have a situation and you seem to have an answer."

Her email had highlighted the details, but over the phone, she shared more.

Amy's maid of honor, Dani, was her best friend from high school. They were there to giggle about each other's first kiss, dance side by side at senior prom, and rip open college acceptance letters with their fingers crossed and a bottle of champagne chilling in the fridge. But when Amy got engaged, Dani switched from loyal friend to silent ghost, ignoring phone calls and telling Amy she'd rather work a double at Panera Bread than go dress shopping or cake testing with her.

Amy found herself with an aching heart and an MIA best friend. So two days before she emailed me and less than two months before her wedding, she told Dani she'd rather not have her as maid of honor, or even a guest at her wedding.

I wish this was the first time I've heard of a bride and her best friend having their friendship torn apart once an engagement ring came into the picture and the wedding plans seemed to crowd out any other plans. But weddings have a way of making everyone go just a little bit cuckoo, and sometimes the end result is the end of a once-beautiful friendship.

I saw a bride *fire* her maid of honor just one day before she was going to walk down the aisle with a bundle of pink and white peonies. I saw a bridesmaid not show up to a wedding as a premeditated way of saying a giant "I *uggghh* you" to the bride.

"I'll be there for you before your wedding and on the day

of," I said, laying out my offer: twelve phone sessions before August to chat about any challenges and go over her to-do list and a trip to Minnesota to toss on the dress and stand by her side. Anything she needed, even if it was a midafternoon vent session or writing her vows, would be my priority as her professional bridesmaid.

"Can I sleep on it?" she asked, warming up to an idea that she didn't even know existed before she read about my new company in The Knot, the online wedding-planning site.

"Of course," I said, realizing right then that I had another plot twist for her. "Just one more thing."

"What is it?" Amy asked, as if she weren't already making a big decision.

"*Good Morning America* wants to know if they can come too," I blurted out, like a nervous child asking her mom if she can have a sleepover party—a gigantic one, with two cameramen, a sound guy, and a lighting pro. "They'd like to film us together at your wedding. Maybe I can get them to fly you out to New York City so we can meet before."

There was an almost unbreakable hush of silence. *I need to get better at my sales calls*, I thought to myself. *Note to self: when chatting with potential brides, I probably shouldn't toss a mammoth proposition at them willy-nilly.* But this was my first Bridesmaid for Hire call, ever. I was allowed to make a mistake—or fifteen.

"Oh boy," she jumped in, thirty slow seconds later. "Let me digest all of this. I'll call you with my final answer tomorrow."

"Of course. No problem!"

There was something about Amy, and the way she told me

the story of her breakup with her maid of honor, that made me want to help her more than any of the other brides who had emailed me. Maybe it was her honesty, or the way she answered the call like she had already saved my number in her iPhone favorites list, but I felt my heart beating and my gut screaming, *This is right. This is why you started this whole thing in the first place.*

I had no idea if this business was going to work. Everyone was saying it was crazy. I was saying it was anything but. I needed Amy to help me find out, just as much as she needed me to help her out.

"Amy," I said, as if I'd said her name many times before over a bottomless mimosa brunch, as if we'd been friends since Montessori preschool. "Thanks for considering taking a chance on a stranger."

"You're not a stranger," she said, gulping down a nervous laugh. "At least not anymore. You already feel like a friend."

"13B and 13C," the flight attendant says sharply, interrupting our goo-goo-eyed get-to-know-you love fest. "You have to take this somewhere else."

I'm glad she interrupts because I need a minute to gather my belongings and pull myself together so I can make a grand exit off this plane and into my first gig as a bridesmaid for hire.

"So let me ask you," he starts back up again as we're keeping pace with each other on the jet bridge. "Do you think any of this is . . ." He pauses, looking for the right word to finish the sentence.

"Strange?" I say, giving him a hand with diction.

"Yeah, I guess so. You're jumping into someone's life pretty abruptly."

He wasn't wrong. When Amy and I met for the first time, it was abrupt as much as it was awkward. But not because it had been only four weeks since Amy phoned me and said, "Yes," or because we had talked only about ten times so far. It was because, when we met, at 6:00 p.m. outside a Starbucks in midtown Manhattan, three weeks before her wedding day, we went in for our first hug in front of a *Good Morning America* camera crew.

Amy, in person, was nothing like I imagined her to be. She was inches shorter, her dark brown hair longer, and her Midwest charm almost suffocating to a jaded New York City transplant, but in the most necessary kind of way. She couldn't get through a whole story without making me laugh, referred to me as "my dear" within just seconds of meeting me, and pulled me underneath her umbrella, without hesitation, when the raindrops threatened to ruin my freshly ironed dress.

She had never been to New York City before, so to her, meeting the place she'd only seen in episodes of *Sex and the City* was more terrifying than it was to meet me.

After the cameras filmed us shopping for dresses, honeymoon lingerie, and centerpiece flowers, we ditched our third wheel and went back to my apartment. We ordered linguine with meatballs and cheesecake and cannolis from a spot in Little Italy and spent the night playing an accelerated game of Who Are You?

"Is this whole thing strange to you?" I asked, stuffing down a peppermint-flavored cannoli the size of my forearm. After spending just forty-eight hours with Amy in person, I felt that she was a friend I'd known since the days of Barbie and Osh-Kosh B'gosh overalls.

"Not at all," she says. "Everyone you become good friends with was once a stranger."

Maybe Amy was on to something here.

I thought about Kerri, my sole voice of reason in this city. One day I knocked on the door of her already-decorated Manhattan apartment with two gigantic suitcases covered in luggage tags that read: *If found, please return to Boca Raton, Florida.* I had been to New York City only twice before and I had decided on the spur of the moment to pack up my belongings and move. So there I was, knocking at a stranger's door after we had connected on Facebook, giving her a hug hello, and saying something awkward like, "Hi, I'm Jen, looks like we'll be spending the rest of our lives together."

My best friend, Jaya, and I were strangers at a school of 65,000 students until we both signed up for the same dance competition and were matched as partners for the routine. When the day finally came for us to perform, she kicked me in the head and I dropped her—onstage. Ever since, we've spent nine birthdays together and a month traveling around Europe, and we live a few blocks away from each other in New York City.

Amy was right. Everyone we cherish in life starts out as a complete stranger, batting his eyes across the table on a first date, asking to borrow a pen during geometry class, craning to catch a glimpse of us on our first day on the job. Even people we no longer hold on to were strangers to us before they moved into and then out of our lives, becoming a stranger once again.

Which is what I fear is going to happen if Stranger Danger the Hunk doesn't ask for my number.

"Maybe that's the only way to enter someone's life?" I say, my eyebrows waggling in my puny attempt to be flirty.

My mystery man, aka potential future husband, shuffles his muddy Converse around the carpeted floor of Gate A17, ruminating over what his next move should be. He pulls out his phone. *Yes, he's going to ask for my digits! I did something right!* But he scrolls through Google Maps, eyes his next location, and puts his phone back in his pocket.

"Well, it was nice to meet you, Jen," he says, grabbing his brown leather messenger bag and slinging it over his head and across his chest.

Thanks for the shortest love affair I've ever had, I want to say, but I don't. I feel my heart sink down to my pelvis instead.

"Hey," I call out, as he starts to walk away. "How did you know my name this whole time?"

I remember Amy telling me that people from the Midwest are above and beyond nice. But I don't remember him shaking my hand or asking for my name. The butterflies in my stomach are starting to laugh at me, and I fear that during my sleep escapades, I was talking out loud and said something potentially harmful like, "I'm Jen Glantz and I love the way you sit with your elbows on the airplane windowsill."

"Look down," he says, swirling his finger in the air until it points to my ticket stub that's sticking out of my stolen library book.

My face can't keep cool any longer, and it darkens to a fire-engine red.

"That's the strange thing about strangers," he says, waving good-bye and walking away without an ending to that sentence.

•   •   •

Being a professional bridesmaid for Amy feels almost identical to what it was like to be a bridesmaid for my friends. Amy and I had a fast friendship, the kind where you condense years' worth of gabbing phone calls and coffee dates into a sixty-day time frame. But none of that matters on her wedding day. I'm there for her when she needs me. I help her lace up the silk corset of her wedding gown, sit by her side, and talk out the family drama surrounding her cousin, who brings a date without an invite or an RSVP—and whose date brings her own kids as well.

Yet unlike my friends' weddings, where I knew at least some of the bridesmaids, things are a little different this time.

The second I walk into the church dressing room where the bridal party is getting ready and say hello to the other women, questions start flying fast and furious at Amy in not-so-hushed whispers.

"You just met Jen two months ago?"

"You're paying her to do our job?"

"Have you gone completely bridezilla mad?"

Amy has three other bridesmaids, and she's honest with them about who I am and why I'm here.

"Her job is not to replace you," she says, and I nod furiously in the background, trying to make peace with them by mixing homemade mimosas out of champagne and a bottle of Orangina. "She's here to do some of the bridesmaid dirty work so you all can have fun."

Note to self: hire Amy as a spokeswoman for Bridesmaid for Hire, because she is on fire with these answers.

After a glass of bubbly and lending them a box of unopened bobby pins, the bridesmaids warm up to the idea of having me around.

One bridesmaid grabs me by my pinky and pulls me into the corner of the room; something sharp with a pointy edge flashes in her left hand.

Oh no, I think to myself. *Is this how it's all going to end for me?*

"Amy's bracelet is broken," she says, her eyes beginning to cloud with tears. "I went to put it on her and the stone popped off. We have to fix it before she finds out."

I reach into my duffle bag and pull out a tiny tube of false-eyelash adhesive. I rub it on the back of the stone and press it down firmly onto the silver bracelet, but it's flimsy, as if it's saying, *Let me out of this party.*

I look at my surroundings. We're in a church, and churches, my Jewish self thinks, must have art supply closets. I casually stroll out of the dressing room and raid the place until I find the goods—and a hot glue gun.

"Here," I say, handing the bracelet back to the bridesmaid, rubbing the burn I gave myself from sitting on the hot glue gun in my shorts. "This should do for now."

The bridesmaid gives me a hug, grabs the bracelet, and hands it over to Amy as if nothing had ever happened, as if everything has always been okay.

When it comes time for the ceremony to begin, someone grabs me by the pinky once more and drags me away—this time into the bathroom stall.

It's Amy, and she's completely in tears.

"Jen," she says, sweating into her bouquet of red roses. "I'm nervous about this."

Her three other bridesmaids are still in the dressing room, putting a coat of gloss over their lips and rubbing deodorant stains off their dresses with a paper towel lightly coated in soap and water.

She's known one bridesmaid since kindergarten, another since college, and the last since she moved into the neighborhood four years ago. *Why me?* I thought. Why is she telling me this, someone she's known for only a couple of weeks? Maybe that's the strange thing about strangers. You feel more comfortable telling them the truth because they have no fear, no shame, in telling you the truth right back.

"It's just that so many people will be looking at me and taking notes on this whole wedding," she went on. "I just feel a lot of pressure to make it perfect."

"Amy," I remind her, "remember what you said to me over cannolis and cheesecake? About strangers and how they affect your life?"

She looks at me oddly, as if we've had many memories, conversations, and inspirational quote-swapping sessions over cannolis and cheesecake.

"No, not really," she says, dabbing her tears with a piece of single-ply toilet paper.

"The guy you're about to walk down the aisle toward was once a stranger to you," I say, hoping she thinks about the start of their adventure and how she got here with him today. "Now he's the love of your life, and that's all you should be thinking about as you take those steps."

Her fake eyelashes flutter like the wings of a butterfly.

"Everything else," I go on, "is just background noise."

"Thank you for everything, Jen." We hug for the fourth time in the history of our sixty-day-old "situation."

"I'd really like it if we could be friends, you know, after this whole wedding thing," I say, as we head out of the bathroom and into the church.

I was new to this whole business thing, and I hadn't yet figured out how to draw a line between a work relationship and a postwedding friendship with the brides I worked with. I was never any good with boundaries anyway, and something inside my gut was screaming at me not to let Amy walk out of my life after she said "I do."

"I'd like that," she says with a laugh. "Considering you'll be in my wedding album and all."

"Considering I'll probably always have this scar on my arm," I say, telling her all about my experience with the stolen hot glue gun.

When it's all over, I find myself back in seat 13B, returning home after the wedding, hoping that the Stranger Danger Hunk will also be on my plane. Maybe this time he'll finish his sentence—and, perhaps, ask me out on a date. But he's not, and just before the door of the plane closes, the last person to step on board takes the window seat beside me. He's the new 13C, a man with a scruffy beard who jams the armrest down, partitioning our space, and lowers the window shade before falling asleep. He snores in perfect harmony with the flight attendants giving us instructions on how to use the oxygen mask.

"That's the strange thing about strangers," I mumble out loud, mocking my ex-potential lover, thinking of possible endings to that sentence.

They mean a lot to you and then you never see them again?

They have the potential to become your soul mate, but they don't ask you for your number?

I look over at the guy next to me, in la la land. *They teach you how to deal with mouth breathers?*

I flip open *The Great Gatsby* to the page bookmarked with my plane ticket. Sticking onto page 15 is a note from *my* stranger. *Please be his number. Please be his number. Please be his number.* This could be the meet-cute to end all meet-cutes. My friends will ooh and ahh when I tell them that I fell in love with a guy on an airplane and he left me a romantic note inside a forty-five-day-old library book that I have no intention of ever giving back. I sweep the hair out of my eyes, shimmy up in my seat, nudge the guy in 13C to stop hogging the armrest, and prepare to read a love letter that will become the source material for the sequel to *The Notebook*, but with a more positive ending.

Dear Sleeping Girl, the note begins. *Read* Let the Great World Spin. *It's my 2nd favorite to Gatsby.*

His handwriting is a little hard to make out, like a doctor's or a fourth grader's, so I read it once more. And then again, staring at it, twisting it, holding it up to the airplane reading light, hoping to find some encrypted code, a set of numbers, anything else. But there's nothing but a book recommendation written on a Delta Airlines cocktail napkin.

Maybe that's the strange thing about strangers: they have just as much control as you do over how the story ends. They can make you feel so much in such a short amount of time. But either way, they sure know how make life gain an extra heartbeat of pulsing excitement over the what-ifs, the unexpected unknowns. So maybe the strange thing about strangers is that there's nothing strange about them at all.

chapter eleven

The Perfect Match

She makes choosing a life partner feel like ordering a coffee at Starbucks.

"Tall? Short? Light? Dark? Fat? Nonfat?"

Kind. Passionate. Selfless. Forgiving, I sing over and over again in my head, taking a sip of stale warm water and staring at my matchmaker with an exhausted look.

"Earth to Jen! What does he look like?" she presses me once more, as if I have the ability to look right into the sparkling eyes of my Mr. Forever and describe him to her in 140 characters—or less.

Who knows where he is right now, or what he's even doing. Perhaps he's canoodling with some other blonde girl whom he thinks is The One, until he discovers she's twisting her tongue in some other guy's mouth when he's not looking. Maybe he's on a scuba trip with his high school buddies and taking selfies with the most exotic fish south of the Galapagos Islands. Or maybe he's in a cubicle right here in New York City, mistakenly hitting Reply All and picking his nose.

I hear the sound of an ambulance speed by outside. I wonder if my Mr. Forever is inside. Or maybe he's on his way to come and rescue me. That last one is the most unlikely, but a girl on the fourth floor of a matchmaker's office at 6:00 p.m. on a summer Friday can dream.

"He looks like Jake Gyllenhaal," I say, after I glance down at my phone and notice that our precious time together will be ending in ten minutes and I've yet to give her an answer that isn't totally blasé.

"But," I continue, picturing the version of Mr. Forever in his cubicle touching a booger, "he also looks like Jack Black."

She jots down my answers, critiques my body language, and swishes the water around in her cup, as if the liquid inside is from a bottle of well-aged chardonnay.

"Tell me this," she says, leaning in closer so that nobody else in the vacant Fifth Avenue, fourth-floor, stuffy shoebox office can hear. "What are three qualities you must have in a partner?"

"He has to like pizza," I say, letting loose a laugh that hits the ceiling and echoes through the room and bounces right back down to the white shaggy rug.

Her eyes bulge.

"Okay," I start again, leaning forward in my chair. "He should be passionate about something, anything. He should be understanding. He should be patient and forgiving."

It's a Friday night, and while other single women are probably slipping on a pair of cork wedges, spritzing their pulse points with Flower Bomb, and giving themselves a pep talk before a first, second, or even third date, I'm making googly eyes at a matchmaker.

It's not because there's something wrong with me.

Okay, maybe there is.

There's a little something wrong with all of us. We all have our "things." Some people are terrible at making decisions, too stubborn to get along with others, or too picky when searching for their perfect match.

I'm just stuck in this wild affair—with my couch. I spend nearly every free evening nestled deep against the cushions, spooning with the remote control. I've also found myself in a dysfunctional relationship with dating apps, downloading them and then deleting them from my phone more times than the average girl changes before heading out on a Saturday night.

"Does he love cats or dogs? Is he a doer or a dreamer? A night owl or an early bird?"

"Both! In the middle! The first one! Or how about a combo?" I say, thinking of another bird I'd prefer him to be. "What about a flamingo?"

When I was thirteen, I started having this recurring daydream that my meet-cute would be inside a bookstore during its buy-one-get-one-free sale. My arms would be wrapped around a stack of books up to my chin, and he would accidently bump into me but somehow catch every book before it hit the floor. Maybe he'd be an off-duty magician, or just really good at balancing, but his smile would make my cheeks flush fire-engine red, and he would feel so bad about almost knocking over my leaning tower of paperbacks that he would offer to buy me an iced chai latte. He'd even pay for the almond milk upcharge.

Someone knocks twice on the outside of the wood-paneled door, distracting me from my reverie. It must be her next victim.

I wipe away the sweat beads making their way down my sideburns.

"Just so you know," she says before getting up to answer the door. "I have the perfect guy for you."

"Really?" I ask. "Are you flying him in from Mars?" I laugh so hard I snort clumps of air. It sounds like I am popping popcorn from my nose. She shakes her head, as if I'm hopeless.

"You'll meet him in two days," she says.

I get up from the distressed brown leather chair and check behind me for any puddles of stress sweat I might've left behind.

"And, Jen," she says, as if we're long-time pals, the kind of friends who often browse the clearance racks at Bloomingdale's together or go halfsies on a chopped salad at the Cheesecake Factory. "Give him a fighting chance."

Once I'm out the door, I call my mom. "It's Friday night," she says. "Do you have a hot date?"

"I just left a matchmaker's office," I say as I exit the lobby of the building. I can almost hear my mom sitting up and pulling the home phone receiver closer to her face.

"You did?" she says, eyes probably expanding her eyelashes so wide they wiggle on her T-zone, ice water glasses being shoved away, a guide for mothers with no grandchildren being tossed into the recycling bin beside empty Zephyrhills water bottles and yesterday's newspaper.

"What did you say? Who did they find? Did you mention that he needs to have a job?"

I can see my mom already Googling available wedding venues for April 2017.

I had just deleted all of my dating apps for the sixteenth time this year. When I mustered up the courage to use them, I found the acid in my stomach start to bubble over messages that said things like, *Sup, Fool?* or *Want to chill 2night?*

Earlier that night, *Glamour* magazine's web video team had called after they saw a news article cracking jokes over how I was a professional bridesmaid but so single that I would never be a bride. They asked if I would be interested in doing a web show with them called *The Perfect Match.*

"Think *Millionaire Matchmaker* meets *The Bachelor* meets real-life Tinder," they said.

I had been wearing pajamas with holes in them, finishing off a bucket of Trader Joe's strawberry licorice that served seventeen and watching year-old episodes of *The Real Housewives of Atlanta* on my DVR. Basically, I was doing the least sexy thing I could do on a Friday night in New York City.

So when they called, I had no choice but to say yes. If I said no, it would be one more tick mark toward watching my expanding waistline creep up and down all alone.

I like to call my biological clock "Cynthia." That name seems so down to business, cut the bullshit, serious. The opposite of who I am and how I date. So whenever I download a dating app or agree to go out with a guy whose profile says he spends his free time going to the gym, doing laundry, and tanning, I know Cynthia's behind the wheel, steering me toward the path of reproduction, and whatever else my bodily to-do list says I need to get out of the way before menopause—at which point I imagine Cynthia will retire to a farm in Georgia with the other expired biological clocks.

"Cynthia made me do it," I say at Sunday brunch when my friends ask me, over hot oatmeal and berries, how I ended up having a staring contest with a matchmaker.

"Who's Cynthia?" they ask, before taking sips of their green juices.

I always think I'm one comment, one manic laugh, one dating story away from them tossing me in the loony bin and telling the good-looking guy at the front desk to throw away my bedazzled key.

"You," I point to the friend who is breast-pumping in the middle of a SoHo restaurant so her nipples won't leak all over her brand-new Gap maxi dress, "have a baby!"

"And you," I point to my friend who keeps using her non-dominant left hand to reach across the table for the salt shaker to flash us her engagement ring, "are practically in Lamaze classes already."

"I," I say as I brush a chunk of dried oatmeal from my eyebrow, "am hopeless."

In some strange and twisted way, it seems as though everyone I know who has already found their endless love thinks of themselves as a certified matchmaker.

It took a year and four months for an ex-coworker of mine, who is under thirty with two kids, a wife, and a mortgage in Long Island, to get me to agree to have dinner with his friend, whom he promised was my perfect match. So one night after work, I met the friend at a restaurant with nine tables and eight items on the menu. He sat across from me, cross-legged and phlegmatic, and stared into my eyes, as if he was trying to figure out what planet I traveled in from. He never spoke to me again.

My cousin, who lives in Westchester with two kids, a husband, a dog, and a house with a driveway she has to shovel after snowstorms, tried to set me up too. Except she tried to set me up with another cousin—a third cousin, but still, *a cousin*. We share family members, DNA, and slices of apple pie during Thanksgiving dinner. Were there no other eligible single guys in the area code, or the planet, that she could find for me?

"You don't need professional help," my breast-pumping pal says. "You just need to put yourself out there more."

"Step away from the computer screen," my engaged friend says, waving her fingers in the air so the entire restaurant can see her sparkle. "And charm them, not harm them."

Here I was, at Sunday brunch with the girls who once accompanied me onto dance floors until 4:00 a.m., or spring break trips to the Bahamas, or late-night phone calls discussing the whos and whats of the single guys who lived in our college apartment complex, treating me as if I'm on an episode of *Hoarders*. As if they are knocking on my door of boxed-up attempts at love, trying to fix the damage, to hand-pick the Mr. Nos and Mr. Wrongs off my puny heart to get me swept up and ready for the world once again. Except for a task this large, it was almost like they needed to call the National Guard. The Big Guns. The mobsters of love to pitch in and help out. Which is why I agreed to go to a matchmaker.

I needed a professional who didn't lead with, "Put yourself out there more."

This wasn't my first time flirting with professional help. I am indeed a proud member of Patti Stanger's Millionaire Matchmaker's club. But not as a millionaire or even one of the girls invited onto the TV mixers, in a suffocating dress and six-inch heels that squish your toes together until they look like soggy fish sticks.

I've always had a theory that Patti and my mom are related. They have the same edge, unwarranted opinions, and last name. So when my hairdresser in Boca, Vicky, told me that she used to color Patti's hair blonde and that I should reach out to her for help, I busted out my iPhone and wrote her a letter.

> Dear Patti,
> You might be my aunt. But you also might be my one-way ticket toward finding a guy who doesn't burp on a first date. Please reply.

It took forty-eight hours, but I heard back. Not from her, of course—if she read that email, she might also be on team "toss Jen into the loony bin"—but from her team. They gave me an application to fill out and asked that I send over seven unfiltered photos of myself.

"We have the perfect match for you," a lady with a squeaky voice, and the capacity to chew gum and form sentences at the same time, said to me over the phone six months after applying.

"Do I get to meet Patti?" I said, thinking how happy my mom would be to know that I finally found her long-lost potential sister. "You know, there's like a 15 percent chance she's my aunt because my mom and she have the same last name, and they look alike, kind of."

"This isn't *The Maury Povich Show*," she went on, popping a bubble in my ear. "Do you want to meet this guy or not?"

I agreed to a phone chat first with my mystery guy. His name was Bouyoung, and after chatting with him for ninety-five seconds, I learned that he was forty years my senior. Which was a shame, because we had a lot in common: a desire to retire in Boca Raton, Florida, and a mutual love for a chilled glass of prune juice.

I wrote back to Patti after I hung up the phone. This had to be a giant mistake. There had to be plenty of guys with good jobs and even better manners she could set me up with, someone in my age range.

> Dear Patti,
> Me again. Was there a glitch in the system? How about setting me up with a guy who doesn't have an AARP card sticking out of his wallet?
> Ps. My mom says hi. She's happy we're chatting. Let me know when we can swab the inside of your cheek. You know, so we can tell if you and she are the "perfect sibling match."

It took another forty-eight hours, but I heard back again for the last time. It seems my membership had been revoked, and my email had been blocked.

So when another opportunity to tango with a matchmaker and her superhuman love powers presented itself to me, I had no choice but to wipe the crumbs off my face and answer.

This is how I found myself on a Tuesday, at 10:00 a.m., fresh off the A train at the Hudson Street subway station, about to walk two blocks to have brunch with another perfect match victim, all while having the whole thing filmed and edited down to six minutes so that a couple million people could watch it for entertainment.

Maybe I should just go home, I mumble to myself as I try to orient myself and figure out which way is south. *What if he sees me and runs across the river to New Jersey? What if I have lipstick on my teeth?* I feel my teeth with my index finger, and, sure enough, my finger proves me to be correct. *What if I forget to speak in complete sentences? What if I forget to speak? Okay, what if I spill something? Oh my god, I always spill something! Can I cancel? Is it too late to call this whole thing off? They'll understand, right? I'll ask for his address and I'll send him an Edible Arrangement.*

By the time I talk myself out of the whole thing, I'm standing in front of the Hugo Hotel, with a trail of confused homeless people squatting behind me and a handful of tourists filming my mental predate breakdown on their iPhones attached to selfie sticks.

"He's over there," one of the producers tells me as she grabs my hand and stuffs me into a waiting area behind the lobby. They want our first hello to be under the bright lights and clear filter of a handful of cameras. So until then, we have to stay sequestered in separate coat closets.

I dig into my purse. "Here's five dollars and a nearly full punch card to Birch coffee. Go over there, snap a photo or two of him, and tell me what you think."

The coat closet attendant stares at me for a minute, then takes the punch card and walks away, in the opposite direction.

Exhausted by my flower girl duties, which turned out to involve more than throwing petals on the ground and stuffing my mouth with handfuls of cake.

Trying on my mom's wedding veil. Still at an age when I imagined I'd marry a Disney prince.

Slow-dancing with my brother after said cake.

My first time as a wedding guest, at age thirteen in New York City. As my brother would say, these were the "brace face" years.

Above: My first day in NYC!
Seeing snow for the very first
time, and leaving my mark—
literally—on my new hometown.

West Boca Diamonds Softball's
Most Valuable Benchwarmer.

The first time I ever used Craigslist was to advertise my professional bridesmaid services. It was surprisingly more successful than trying to buy a bedbug-free couch.

new york > manhattan > all personals > strictly platonic

prohibited [?]   Posted: 18 days ago

Professional Bridesmaid - w4w - 26 (NYC)

Expanding my skill set as a bridesmaid by helping my friend Mel with her wedding shoes.

Matching tank tops is an essential part of being a bridesmaid. I have the collection to prove it.

I failed ballroom dance class in college, so I usually overcompensate by laughing loudly in my partner's face.

Right before I asked Steve Harvey if he was hitting on me.

Listening to the producer count down in my ear before my first live TV interview.

The banner ad JDate ran on their website featuring me, mensch-hunter and pizza-lover.

A news outlet films me in my apartment one week after my Craigslist post went viral.

Tucker Carlson laughs at the idea of me being a professional bridesmaid. I whip out some hand motions to prove him wrong.

On *The Rachael Ray Show* to recommend last-minute desserts for couples who don't want a wedding cake. Last time I'd baked, I set off the fire alarm, so I'm not exactly qualified for this segment.

Bridesmaid and sole witness for an Australian couple's wedding in Times Square.

Celebratory drinks with my favorite Australian couple.

Right after fixing the bustle of this bride's gown with hair ties at a wedding at Battery Gardens in Manhattan.

Taking a selfie with the first bride who ever hired me, and her husband, in Minnesota.

Below: Bryn sent an invitation to Taylor Swift and saved a seat for her. Taylor didn't show up, but Bryn got me, at least!

Posing at a water fountain in Michigan with two of my pals whom I talked into going to a wedding with me for a bride who wanted three bridesmaids.

Right: My first gig as a bridesmaid, for my friend Alli.

Far right: Half of the wedding party for my friend Jamie, in Boca Raton, Florida.

A Brooklyn bride takes off her shoes, lets her hair down, and jumps on the bed to shake off her wedding jitters.

Just moments before I scooped up animal poop with my bare hands so the brides could walk down the aisle without ruining their silk dresses.

At *Glamour* magazine's office, waiting to see their professional matchmaker.

Two minutes into a stand-up routine at the Broadway Comedy Club.

Wishing for dry shampoo and pizza as I wait for a delayed flight to a wedding.

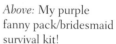

Above: My purple fanny pack/bridesmaid survival kit!

Left: Curling my hair five minutes before a wedding after a major flight delay. My eyes say everything.

My smile says, "I've got this," but this was the first time I'd ever used a steamer. My brain was screaming, "Don't destroy this $6,000 wedding gown!"

Wedding guest welcome bag in one hand, blue polyester bridesmaid gown in the other, aka, me pretty much every weekend.

Below: Proof that my wardrobe is made up entirely of T-shirts that say "Bridesmaid" on them.

My one true love who never lets me down: pizza.

With an adorable puppy named Katie Scarlet, who pooped on me right before we walked down the aisle together.

Reading a story about being a professional bridesmaid, in a bridesmaid dress, at a really prestigious literary event. Another writer brought a goat.

Speaking to middle school students with the founder of HerCampus.

Telling my life story at STORY in New York City.

Teaching a room full of entrepreneurs how to do their own PR—and warning them of the dangers of talking with your hands too much.

Trying on a bride's wedding veil. Still at an age when I imagined I'd marry a Disney prince.

When the red light flashes twice on the camera, the producer tells me to walk toward my perfect match of a date, who's already sitting down at a wooden table inside the hotel's restaurant. I approach him as my body trembles and my nose starts to run. As we're getting close enough to make out the defining characteristics of our human facial features, the lights go out. It's pitch black. The whole place—the entire hotel—is having a massive power outage.

How's that for love at first sight?

I go to hug him hello, but a producer grabs me with one hand and places the other one over my eyeballs.

"Cut," she yells. "Take Jen away. We need to film this whole thing again."

The second time is smoother. I walk toward him, camera all up in my grill, and hug him hello.

He sits down across from me, smiling, his blue eyes searching mine.

So this is my perfect match, I think to myself, feeling empty, like a gas tank that's been drained dry.

"Let's talk about the elephant in the room," I say, fogging up my water glass with my own petrified breath.

His eyes wander left and then right. "Huh?" He replies.

"The cameras everywhere?" I say, wondering if I've gone bonkers.

"Oh, yeah. This is pretty weird," he admits, before jumping into conversation that feels fluid and a little bit forced. Slowly, I begin to realize that he's everything I asked the matchmaker for.

Loves his family. Check.

Is passionate about a hobby. Check.

Seeks a good adventure. Check.

But even after an hour of conversation and checking items off my preconceived "perfect guy" shopping list, I realize my cart is painfully empty. Sure, I said I wanted the organic, home-grown, no-preservative stuff. But what do I know? Maybe I'm better off with Fruit Loops and Cheetos. Maybe I thought I would be okay with Splenda, but I want real cane sugar. I want someone whose voice tickles with excitement when he talks about the things he loves and who listens, with his eyes glued, when I talk about the things I love.

My match-made date was perfect on paper, but in person, he didn't have much of a personality and we didn't have much in common besides our dirty blonde shaggy hair and overactive sweat glands that poured through our shirts. When the date ends, I stick my arms out for a hug, but we end up, somehow, just high-fiving in the street.

"Maybe pizza next time?" I say hopefully, because if this is who an online certified matchmaker thinks I belong with, I'm willing to give him a second chance.

"Oh, I'm not a big pizza person," he says, reaching his arm up high to hail the nearest taxi.

Everyone has their thing, I thought to myself.

Even though I wasn't weak in the knees after our first date, I did hope there would be a second. Why not? Every-one deserves a second chance, even a guy who isn't on my pizza-loving level. But neither one of us had the courage or the desperate desire to exchange numbers. So we parted ways. He went back to Brooklyn, and I went back to Tinder.

•   •   •

A week after the date, I'm walking home with two sizzling slices of pizza on a paper plate and a stolen library book in the other, when I notice that I'm keeping pace with someone who looks familiar. Someone whose perfume makes my nose tingle and whose eyes I've spent quality time gazing into before.

I'm walking next to the matchmaker.

"Hey, there!" I say, stopping in my tracks as she keeps on walking farther and farther away.

She turns her head and catches my eye, and then she walks a step faster. It's as if matchmakers, like fairy godmothers or therapists or gynecologists, prefer not to be recognized in public, outside the confines of their offices.

"You're wrong about this matchmaking thing," I shout as she approaches the crosswalk and hurries across the street.

She turns around, fully amused, to look at my face. I'm certain there's mozzarella cheese in my hair and pizza sauce on my cheeks, and she giggles, looks at me, then laughs.

"Maybe you're right," she shouts back, winking at me as if she had a piece of fairy dust in her eye. As if she knew something I didn't. As if she had set me up on the most lethargic and boring date of my life for a reason.

Matchmakers, like weathermen, can only ever be 35.4 percent certain. They're not genies in a bottle. They don't know what will work for you and what won't. They simply force you to say what you think you want out loud and drill you with questions nobody else has the patience or courage to ask. And then they give you what you want. What you asked for. Maybe it's to show you that your list of qualities are pointless. That your perfect match on paper could be someone who makes you wish you could disappear into a fortress of napkins five minutes into the first date. Maybe the ideal guy, who dances around in your head, would have you rolling your eyes in real life.

Maybe this whole journey of love can't be plotted out along specific coordinates. Maybe it's completely random. Or maybe it's not. That's what cheap, sticky pizza is for: a rest stop for your brain and heart when nothing in New York City seems to make sense.

Maybe my Mr. Forever would bump into me but wouldn't catch a single book. Maybe his glasses would fall on the floor and I'd step on them while trying to pick up my purse. Maybe he'd ask to get coffee and I'd spill milk all over his backpack. Maybe he wouldn't be medium height, or a dog lover, or a fan of Salinger. But maybe he'd be interesting and interested, and maybe that's all that matters—at first and forever.

Maybe we need to take our list of demands and, instead of reading them to the world like a riot act, put them in the shredder and remind ourselves that, yes, we want certain things in theory, but in the end, what do we know? Maybe our perfect match is the most imperfect person, but he's got one hell of a heart.

Wherever my Mr. Forever is, right now, I hope he's reading this, knowing that I don't always have pizza on my face or lipstick on my teeth.

Who am I kidding. I do. I always do.

chapter twelve

A Time and a Square to Say I DO

To someone who has never been before, Times Square seems like a giant, well-lit playground in an underground nightclub. It's a plaza of brightly colored chaos, made up of converging avenues and neon signs. If you're a visitor, it's where you ask your taxi driver to take you after you drop your bags off in a hotel room that smells like Clorox bleach and meatloaf, ready to hunt for a slice of greasy street pizza.

People come to 42nd and Broadway from all over the world, passports popping out of their purses, phones clutched tightly in one hand, a well-worn paper map of the city in the other. But it doesn't take long for them to look away from their maps and up, up, and up without interruption, excused, for just a few minutes, of the view of bald spots and the butts of exaggerated coat jackets. They hope, or maybe they know for sure, that what they'll find here will be different than what they've seen before, printed on glossy cardstock postcards, triple-filtered on Instagram feeds, sitting up straight as the backdrop for a rom-com, where guy meets girl, and girl decides smack down in the middle of buzzing tourists and a burping homeless guy, that she wants to kiss him.

For people who are from New York City, Times Square is an Alexandrite gemstone that has completely lost its shine. It's the scent of roasted peanuts meeting the smell of unwashed armpits. It's the place where tourists fill up their camera rolls with pictures of a 5-foot-3 man dressed in a fur-stained Elmo suit, or a freshly painted Statue of Liberty human perched on a milk crate, collecting tips in her Lady Liberty torch while poking passersby. It's the place you go when you're craving a midday anxiety attack, if you want to get jostled in the ribs by careless elbows, giant shopping bags, and overstuffed purses. Most New Yorkers would rather walk fifteen minutes in the wrong direction instead of zig-zagging through the herd of saucer-eyed tourists.

The longer you live in Manhattan, the lower your tolerance gets for this suffocating and gimmicky circus. Yet Times Square, even for those with a permanent mailing address within the five boroughs, can possess the same allure for those who won't be staying long. It's a center stage for people to be and do and say whatever they want. Guys shilling twenty-five-dollar comedy show tickets, hip-hop performers barking about their next street show, passionate lovebirds kissing beside the TKTS sign—this is their proscenium.

I forget all of that when I find myself standing beneath the protruding awning of the New Amsterdam Theatre on 42nd Street, body-slamming tourists as I stare down at my phone, waiting for a text message that should have arrived twenty minutes ago. Everyone here is a stranger, but tonight I'm tapping my toes, waiting for two Australian guys who have hired me to stand beside them as they say, "I do."

> Meet on the corner, underneath the Broadway show's sign. We'll be in black tuxedos, purple pocket squares, holding hands; brown hair; over 6 feet.

I get the shakes, pacing back and forth underneath the meeting spot as the lights illuminating the *Aladdin* sign flicker on and off, like someone forgot to pay the electric bill.

What am I doing? Why am I here? A family of three, all blonde and buttoned up and waiting to see the show, begin to stare at me. The teenager with the same constellation-like pattern of acne that I used to have is probably tweeting, *New York is strange but the strangers who live here are stranger. #MeccaOfMadness #Pizza*

I check my phone again, but still, there's nothing. I pull up the last email from the couple and skim the details once more, worried that my gut is unable to intuit imminent danger.

> October 15, 2015—11:24am
> From: Rb40@aol.com
> To: Jen@bridesmaidforhire.com
> Darling! We'll see you tonight 6pm underneath the Aladdin sign. We are excited to get married in a place we've seen only in our dreams ;). It's going to be a night for all of us to remember, love. See you soon!
>> Kisses,
>> Rob + Chuck

I open up a blank text message and decide to confess to Kerri:

Have a weird feeling about this. Underneath the Aladdin sign. If I
don't text you in 45 minutes, send help?

I write her again, this time with more specific directions:

There's money for rent rolled up in a ball, zipped into my bedbug
mattress protector, if anything happens to me

July 2, 2014—5:15am
From: Rb40@aol.com
To: Jen@bridesmaidforhire.com

Jen Jen,
I'm Rob, next to me in a very tacky hospital bed right now, is Chuck!!!
He's recovering from having his tonsils out and what else do you do
while visiting a loved one in the hospital (especially one who can't talk)
but watch television? We heard them talk about you and Bridesmaid for
Hire and thought "This is interesting, we're getting married, just the two
of us, in Times Square in a few months."
Then we realized this chicky is in New York ;)!!! Chuck couldn't talk
but he looked at me and after 17 years, I knew I had to at least send
an email. We want you in October when we come to America for the
first time and proclaim our love in the Crossroads of the World, Times
Square!!!
How much and how can we get you to say yes?
                                        Kisses,
                                        Rob + Chuck

I'm rubbing morning crud out of my eyes when I read

this email, my covers wrapped around me tightly like I'm a well-made Chipotle burrito. A sharp tingle of uncertainty demands my half-awake attention, and something inside me thinks this email is a prank. I have a feeling it's from a friend who just got home from another late-night bender on the Lower East Side, writing this email as one last hurrah before her noggin hits the pillow. Something about the way it's written makes me paranoid that it's from someone trying to reel me in, someone concocting a lie to lure me away from my keyboard just so he can scope me out on the corner of 42nd Street.

You should see the kind of gobbledygook emails that I've bookmarked in a folder called *Say What?* ever since I posted the Craigslist ad for Bridesmaid for Hire.

There was a seventy-five-year-old man asking how much it would cost him for a cuddle, a guy from Slovakia asking to purchase the Bridesmaid By Your Side package because he wanted to use it as a way to take me on a first date. I had a couple dozen people read the ad and mistake it for my dating profile, responding with their age, sex, location, and a scanned photo that looked like it was from 1997. I had six marriage proposals in the first week.

But this email stood out. It had nine exclamation marks, a winky face, and the word *chicky.* I wasn't ready to place this one in the Say What? folder yet. I wanted to learn more. I wanted to give these guys a chance to prove me wrong.

July 2, 2014—7:15am
From: Jen@bridesmaidforhire.com
To: Rb40@aol.com

Rob & Chuck,

    Greetings from New York City. Thank you for writing. Sorry to hear about the tonsil operation, Chuck. I hope they are at least letting you clean out their freezers of ice cream.

    I'd love to learn more about the two of you. How about we Skype next week?

Love,

Jen Glantz

I'm pacing back and forth, feeling the blended juices in my stomach churning from my upper rib down to my intestines. My eyes shut tight, and I try to formulate a game plan: Do I stay, or do I go? My feet suddenly step on something soft and bony. I open my eyes to see that I'm standing on top of a New York City police officer's foot.

"Ma'am?" he says, trying to figure out if I'm lost or just waiting to be found. I wiggle my head as if I'm trying to get rid of lice, finding a way to say sorry and explain myself in the same breath.

"I'm so sorry," I start with the obvious one first. "I'm just a bridesmaid for hire, waiting to meet two strangers."

In the distance, police sirens wail, throwing off flashes of red and blue light that compete with the LED lights all around us. I realize what I just said must sound wacky. If this were a small town in Arkansas, where neighborhood police officers know last names, birthdays, the first kisses of all the residents, this news would have been enough to take me into the station for questioning. But this is Times Square. I have a lot to compete with.

"Have you met them before? Seen what they look like?"

the officer asks, as if this therapeutic kind of questioning is standard protocol.

Their email tells me they will be in tuxedos, that they are over six feet. It's a rare combination anywhere else but in Times Square, where men walking by in tuxedos are just as common as people in fluffy Disney character costumes. They could be anyone. I edge closer to the police officer, hoping, if they see me now, that they'll know I called in backup. They'll know the kind of guys I bring with me as my plus-one.

"No," I admit. Guiltily. "I haven't."

July 18, 2014—4:15pm
From: Rb40@aol.com
To: Jen@bridesmaidforhire.com

Jen Jen,

Oh snoot! We don't have Skype, or a webcam for that matter. But we would like to meet you on the 15 of October. Will you meet us then? Will you be our one and only bridesmaid and wedding guest?

Kisses,

Your Boys

I have watched enough of MTV's *Catfish* to know that when someone says they don't have a webcam, they 100 percent are not who they say they are. But still, for some odd reason, I decide to press on.

July 18, 2014—7:33pm
From: Jen@bridesmaidforhire.com
To: Rb40@aol.com

Rob,

    Are there any public libraries you can go to? Friends that have Wi-Fi or an iPhone? Would love to chat face-to-face.

                    Best,

                    Jen Glantz

I heard nothing back from them.

The crowds have started to thin, and the theaters on Broadway have begun sweeping the popcorn and ticket stubs off the rugs from their final show of the evening. I'm left feeling defeated. Feeling wrong about this whole thing. The police officer is mostly confused. It's been another thirty-five minutes and I haven't said a word to him, occasionally rolling my eyes or nodding my head, letting him know that while he doubts the outcome of this adventure, I still do not.

I throw my hands up in the air. "You're right," I say, backing away slowly, as if the officer and I have made a bet, which now has me surrendering and leaving the premises upon his silent request.

I head down into the subway, wondering how I fell for this. I've only been working as a Bridesmaid for Hire for a couple of months now. Maybe this whole thing was a premature decision—something that sounded really great on paper, but in real life, was a risky, unpredictable, and even potentially dangerous idea.

As I go to swipe my subway card and find a spot on the F train heading south, the text I've been waiting for all night flashes on my screen. It's from Rob.

Sorry love, traffic. We're here now. Tell me, are you?

The F train pulls up to the platform, and exhausted strap-hangers with doggy bags of overpriced restaurant food step inside.

I turn my back to the train and run away. I've waited this long to find out who my mystery men are, and I'm not going to lollygag the night away on my couch, stuffing my face with Doritos and Arizona Iced Tea, trying to figure it all out.

I run past the police officer, who can't help but look at me like I went down into the subway and came out a different woman, one who has now completely gone bonkers.

Underneath the flickering *Aladdin* sign are two guys and an officiant holding a book of handmade notes. The guys are in tuxes. They're brown-haired and over six feet. They're everything they said they would be, happily in love and miserably lost in Times Square.

I take a deep breath, whispering, "They're real, they're real."

October 14, 2014—1:15pm
From: Rb40@aol.com
To: Jen@bridesmaidforhire.com

Jen Jen,

Your boys here! Sorry we haven't been in touch sooner, love. We apologize. We haven't told you much. We're pretty private people but we want to tell you this. We've been together for 17 years and we work together every day. That seems like a lot for most people, but for us, it just works. We can't get married in our country, so we figured we'd go to a country and a place where you can feel and be anyone you please.

New York City tomorrow!! See you then? You know where!!

Hugs and kisses from the Grand Canyon.

> Your boys,
>
> R & C

I start typing a response but pause for a moment, realizing that whatever I send next, I will stick to: either I'll meet them or I'll tell them that this isn't going to work.

October 14, 2014— 8:47pm

From: Jen@bridesmaidforhire.com

To: Rb40@aol.com

Saved in draft folder

The next morning, I wake up and rub the crud out of my eyes. It's time to let them know if it's a yes or a no. Some things feel wrong, but even more feel right.

October 15, 2014—5:15am

From: Jen@bridesmaidforhire.com

To: Rb40@aol.com

> See you then.

> Love,
>
> Jen Glantz

The officiant performs the ceremony in less time than it takes for the light to turn red, then green, and red again. Rob and Chuck kiss, and then for the second time tonight, they give me a wide-eyed, wide-armed, hug.

They're complete opposites; one is clean shaven and the other has deep-rooted stubble. One laughs when he's nervous, and the other fidgets with a blue-beaded bracelet on his wrist. Both of them, stopping in the middle of a median, spend the first couple of minutes married to each other, breathing in taxicab exhaust and cigarette smoke, the scent of a late-night stroll in Times Square.

"I have to ask," I say, interrupting their stargazing, "what's the secret? What's the true way to make it seventeen years with someone?"

By now, Rob and Chuck have gone from being strangers to me, anonymous and questionable over the Internet waves, to being my love gurus.

Seventeen years, I think to myself, recalling my last relationship with a guy named Andy that lasted only seventeen days. That's seventeen New Year's Eve smooches, seventeen Fourth of July fireworks shows, seventeen Christmas presents (17 x 8 if you're Jewish).

"It just works," Rob says, feasting his eyes on a billboard for a phone company that reads #NeverSettle. "We're opposites but we communicate well to each other, though not so well online to others."

The three of us let out a laugh. My police officer, close by, does too.

Some love, I've noticed, much like Times Square itself, is resilient.

Some love, I've also seen, can be totally flimsy. It can't even survive a trip to IKEA, let alone a Thanksgiving where Aunt Beth is asking your significant other about his views on the government's tax system while piling up mashed potatoes on Grandma's 1914 hibiscus-patterned porcelain plates.

"Everything changes constantly," Chuck says, pointing out the differences between what he's seeing in front of him and what he imagined Times Square would look like from his years of seeing it in magazines. "You need someone who will latch onto you and love you no matter what season it is or what version of yourself you are that day."

I nod my head furiously, hoping one day I can stand in the middle of the busiest intersection in the world, with someone who loves me no matter what, even when the T-Mobile billboard turns into a Verizon one, or the shivers turn into sunburns.

chapter thirteen

Famous Last Words

The first time I was sent to the principal's office, I was only four years old.

I was in prekindergarten, sitting next to my two dearest friends in the world on a knotty, sunshine-colored area rug in my fire-engine red overalls, my hair a tangled, chlorine-tinted mess. Mrs. Kay gave us the task of counting silently to ourselves—which is exactly what I was doing, until suddenly, out of the blue, my friends presented me with a challenge: count to twenty-five, out loud, in front of the whole class.

I didn't question this random dare for a second. I was trying to rid myself of my reputation as a thumb-sucking baby who pees in her pants, and I figured that by accepting this dare, I would earn some street cred among my baby friends. (I should note that my preschool wasn't some rough-and-tumble jungle gym; it was in a synagogue in Boca Raton. Everything there was kosher, including our Play-Doh.)

I accepted the challenge and started screaming "Twenty-three! Twenty-four! Twenty-five!," so loudly that I felt my tonsils vibrate.

The next thing I knew, I was on my way to the principal's office, my little fingers locked in the hands of my teacher, Mrs. Kay, who was leading me down a long, red-carpeted hallway, straight to the place all of us tiny tots feared the most.

Back then, I wasn't shaking in my OshKosh B'gosh overalls because I thought this incident would be etched into my permanent record, which I always imagined as some kind of stone tablet, like the ones the Ten Commandments were carved on. And I wasn't worried that I'd be rejected from college one day because of this mishap. I was mostly concerned about what my immediate punishment was going to be. No graham crackers during snack time? No naps during nap time? No monkey-bar-swinging, jump-roping fun during recess?

I started to cry. I cried so long and loud that they had to call in backup: my mommy.

When she arrived, she held me tightly on her lap as the principal taught me a lesson that I would eventually file away under Things They Teach You in Diapers That Apply to Life in Big Girl Underpants. A lesson that would be taught to us next year, after we learned the importance of not shoving six Oreos into our mouths and sharing them with our pals instead, or why it's not very nice to eat with our fingers when a fork and knife are resting beside our plates.

"Jennifer," the principal said, looking at me as if I had personally pushed her buttons—or doused her desk in finger paint or stolen her peanut butter and jelly sandwich from her lunch box. "You need to think before you speak."

I remember asking my mom what that meant. It was a pretty heavy lesson to teach someone who had just traded in flailing hand motions for actual words less than a year ago and was still confined to training wheels and training pants.

My mom gave me a big kiss on the cheek, leaving a big, smeary lipstick mark on my face, and handed me a semimelted KitKat bar from her purse. "It just means to wait a couple of seconds before you speak so your brain and your mouth can hold hands."

I think what the principal really wanted me to learn that day was the difference between right and wrong when it came to using our words. That even if we feel something, like the desperate urge to go potty, we shouldn't announce it at the top of our lungs, in the middle of learning about what fruits are the color red or what animal makes a moo sound. We should wait until the teacher has a free moment, tug on the hemline of her Gap skirt, and let her know that we have some business to take care of.

But every so often—say, once a week for some of us, and once a year for us more disciplined and manners-focused humans—we let ourselves go. We revert back to our four-year-old, rule-breaking selves again. We stuff those six Oreos in our mouths instead of offering to share with our loved ones. We find ourselves yelling the wrong things at the wrong times, living in utter misery as they stick around to haunt us.

What I know now is that this principal of mine was actually trying to teach me something about having a filter: an imaginary device we rely on more and more as we grow up to prevent us from announcing every single thing we think and feel out loud to the world.

If my filter decided to stop working at this very moment, I would probably blurt out to a room full of macchiato-drinking strangers that I just felt a bead of sweat drip down my rib cage, or tap the guy sitting next to me with the Beats by Dre head-phones to tell him that his Adam's apple is almost as big as a baby turtle's shell.

My filter is working just fine these days. I think it finally learned its lesson after it was caught taking the afternoon off, lounging at the pool, slathering on sunscreen, and thumbing through the pages of a Nicholas Sparks novel, too busy to stop me from saying something I would later regret. At least, that's what I assume happened when I found myself in front of 350 people; twelve idle cameras; eight producers with walkie-talkies; and comedian, Emmy-winning television host, and bestselling author Mr. Steve Harvey.

"Now, Jen," he whispered to me at the end of our filmed segment together so nobody else in the studio could hear. "Are you single?"

"Steve!" I pulled away from our warm embrace, turned to the studio audience, the cameras, and the producers, and blurted out, in the same way I had belted out those numbers in pre-school, "Are you hitting on me?"

The words shot right out before my brain had a chance to catch them.

Oh no, oh no. Oh no, oh no. Did I just ask Steve Harvey, in front of all these people and these cameras, if he was hitting on me?

I was pinching my arm, squeezing my eyes shut tight,

asking my overworked/nonexistent fairy godmother for my eighteenth wish this year. I'm not very religious, but in that moment, I thought about getting down on both knees and praying to Hashem. But I didn't want to alarm the studio audience and Steve more than I already had. So I lightly clasped my hands together, looked up toward the crackling white ceiling, and prayed just a little bit.

Hello, up there. It's me. Jennifer Glantz. Yaffa is my Hebrew name, I think? I guess I should start by saying I'm sorry for eating pizza, pasta, and a veggie delight sandwich on wheat bread during Passover this year. Oh yeah, I'm also sorry for missing out on temple during Yom Kippur last month. I'm still feeling guilty about both of those things, okay? My great aunt won't let it go. She's constantly asking how my pants and my heart feel about myself after I stuffed my face with unleavened bread. I even ran into Rabbi Solomon last week outside the Second Avenue Deli. He asked me whose couch I was watching Netflix on when I was supposed to be at shul for the High Holidays this year.

Anyway, here I am, once again, asking for a favor. If you help me, I promise I'll give JDate another chance, and I promise to start fraternizing with more members of the tribe.

Just please, please tell me that was a dream. Please tell me I thought about asking Steve Harvey if he was hitting on me but my filter kicked in and I swallowed that thought before it had the chance to escape my mouth. If it wasn't a dream, if I did indeed say that to him, to a packed room of people, please tell me that he thought I said "kidding" or "knitting," not "hitting" on me. I don't care that those words wouldn't make sense; I'd rather him think I was Cuckoo for Coco Puffs than become known as the girl who accused him, a happily married TV host, of wanting to jump her bones.

"Did you all hear that?" he said, looking out at the audience, while his finger pointed directly at me. "She thinks I'm hitting on her."

In that moment, my filter decided to put down the Nicholas Sparks novel and kick into overdrive, erecting an iron wall between my vocal cords and the rest of the world. My brain followed suit. I couldn't even think of a way to defend myself.

"I'm a married man," he said, gesturing toward the stunned guests, showing off his wedding band in the act, as if he were a magician who had just pulled a rabbit out of his hat. He was waiting for the audience's applause. "I am *not* hitting on you."

I caught a reflection of my face on the screen behind me. The cameras were recording my word-vomit defense to Steve's accidental offense. My face was glowing the same fire engine red as my dress, and my eyes were desperately searching for the exit sign.

My ears were buzzing with the echoes of laughter. I felt as if I was back in the fourth grade, sitting in a plastic chair in the center of the lunchroom, listening to Jean tell me that he wanted to buy me tampons.

I wanted this moment to be over. I wanted someone to grab my wrist and drag me to the principal's office or, in this case, the executive producer's office, read me the Joan Rivers riot act, and ban me from network television so I wouldn't have the opportunity to embarrass myself again. I wondered whether, I cried hard enough, for long enough, my mommy would show up with a semimelted KitKat bar in her purse, ready to save me.

"I asked you if you're single," he went on, "because I'm a

matchmaker, and I may know someone who would want to take you out on a date."

At those words, I saw the image of my mother yanking the KitKat out of my hand. *You missed out on an opportunity to be set up on a date? On daytime TV? Oh, Jennifer.*

"I'm just really, really . . ." My mind struggled to match the right thought with the right words, but at that exact moment, my stomach let out a giant rumble, as if to say, *Get me out of here! I've had enough embarrassment for one pathetic lifetime. I just want to eat.*

Our stomachs don't have a filter. They always sound off when we wish they wouldn't, like in the middle of a buttoned-up business meeting or halfway through a lecture in algebra class. Whenever your stomach decides it's time to make itself known, it will whine like a puppy that's been left alone at home all day. At first, you convince yourself that nobody can hear it. It's your stomach, and it's buried somewhere deep down, between layers of flesh and blood and tummy flab. *Maybe it's just extra loud because it's bouncing off my muffin top*, you think. But you would be fooling yourself.

"Hungry?" Steve asked, laughing so hard he curled over and grabbed his own stomach. "Someone get her a pie from Giordano's and let's get on with this show."

The audience roared and a producer rushed forward to direct me offstage, like a crossing guard ushering people across a busy street.

"Wait, please, wait," I called out as she was shepherding me to a staircase that led back up to my dressing room. I felt as if I had just walked out of a courthouse with a guilty sentence for a crime I didn't mean to commit.

"Great job, Jen," the producer said, handing me a bottle of water and a washcloth so I could wipe my sweaty brow.

Had she missed the second half of my performance? The one where I went totally off script and out of my mind?

"I need to get back out there." I eyed her, letting her know that I had important business to take care of. "I need to say I'm sorry."

"I'm sorry," she said. "He's got to keep taping the show, and you have a plane to catch."

People always make such a big hoopla over first impressions. They always tell you that you need to have your hair combed, your shirt tucked, and your hand ready to deliver a strong and confident shake. They say the first words out of your mouth will decide if someone wants to hire you, befriend you, fall madly in love with you. But I don't think that's true. The truth is, I think it's the way we say good-bye that leaves more of an impression on a person than how we say hello.

I needed to fix my good-bye with Steve. But I didn't have the chance to. He would forever remember me as the girl who asked him if he was hitting on her.

Sometimes I wake up in the middle of the night, drenched in cold sweat, wondering, *Why, why, why, did you say that in front of 350 people?*

I blame this whole verbal snafu on the disturbing amount of hairspray fumes I ingested before I went on set. It fogged up my common sense. I kind of wish it had sprayed my mouth shut.

Maybe I was extra nervous this time because it was my first TV interview in front of a live audience. I had done a handful before, just in front of a camera or two and a news anchor. I wasn't used to having an auditorium of people watching. I felt like I was onstage at an off-Broadway musical, tap dancing along to my story of how I became a professional bridesmaid.

Or maybe it was because this time, they told me the questions they were going to ask beforehand, and I was practically on airplane mode, reading off a carefully constructed, premeditated, and memorized script. I spent a week role-playing with my brother, who helped shape my incomplete sentences into polished statements with his punch-in-the-gut rebuttals. I had become a rehearsed robot who was trying very hard not to improvise—until I finally let go and did.

Eleven months and six days later (I began keeping track in my head, recalling that moment at dinner tables and using it as my answer to the icebreaker question on a first date: "What was your most embarrassing moment ever?"), I found myself behind the scenes of another live-audience show, *The Rachael Ray Show*. As they were misting my hair with a tank-sized can of hair spray and flicking my lashes with a final touch of mascara, the producer ran through the topics Rachael wanted to cover, paused for a second, and asked if I had any questions.

"Yeah, actually, I'm curious. Who are the other guests on the show today?"

I was hoping for Justin Bieber. Maybe even Jake Gyllenhaal. I even would have settled for some shared airtime with Blake Lively. But her answer was someone I never imagined I would ever see again, let alone share a green room with.

"Well, we have you," she said, reading off her call sheet. "But right before you go on, we have Steve Harvey."

I dropped my phone, shattering the glass screen against the makeup room floor. I stood up from the chair abruptly, knocked the curling iron off the counter with my pointy elbows, and shouted over the lyrics Adele was belting through the computer speakers in the background: "I need to meet him!"

The producers and beautifiers chuckled.

"Wow, didn't know you were such a superfan of his, Jen," the producer said.

"No, no. It's not like that. I just need to tell him something."

I could see her looking down at her walkie-talkie, probably debating whether to signal to the crew backstage that this Bridesmaid for Hire girl was a little bit off her rocker.

"Don't think you'll be able to meet him. He's in and out."

I paced back and forth, dodging the curling iron and red lipstick the hair and makeup artists held out toward me. I had to meet him. What were the odds we'd be on the same show, at the same time? This was my chance to make a second, first, and last impression on him.

I waited backstage for him to finish his segment as I was getting mic'd up and debriefed for mine. Right as he stepped offstage and started walking in my direction, I ran toward him, but a group of security guards barred me from him with their strong arms, as if we were playing a game of Red Rover.

"Steve, Steve!" I squealed one last time, for good measure.

His head swung to the side, like a bird that heard a familiar chirp in the distance. He looked at me. His eyebrows turned downward, and I could tell that he wondered, for just a second, how he knew me and where he'd seen me before.

"Steve!" I called out from under the security guard's armpit, as if I were a fan girl trying to catch Harry Styles's attention outside a One Direction concert. "I'm sorry!" I shouted, completely oblivious to the fact that my voice could carry to the stage and that I might be embarrassing myself in front of a whole new studio audience.

By now, he was already through the double exit doors, which swung back and forth until, at last, they slammed shut.

But right before they closed, he turned, and his eyes met mine. And he smiled. I swear, I saw him smile.

chapter fourteen

What Ray Says, Goes

I announce myself like I'm a contestant in the Miss America pageant.

"I'm Jen Glantz!" I give a toothy grin, extend a beauty queen wave, adjust my arms into a Wonder Woman pose, and go on. "And I'm the founder of a company called Bridesmaid for Hire."

I'm not in front of a live studio audience at Planet Hollywood in Vegas or surrounded by panning cameras zooming in and out on my face. And—as much as I always wished this to be true—I am also not competing to win the title of Miss Florida Orange Grove.

I'm two feet deep into a closet-sized office, in the back of the Mid-Manhattan Library, on a Saturday morning, making goo-goo eyes at a business tutor named Ray, who isn't wasting any time trying to figure out how I found him. Instead, he's signaling for security.

I'm trying my hardest to look professional. This is a business meeting, and I'm a business owner. But when I went through my closet, all I could find were pleated leather skirts and long-sleeved tops with peekaboo cutouts from Forever 21. I settled on a button-down blouse from my "give to Goodwill" pile and ironed it (or thought about ironing it. In reality, I dunked it in water and fanned my blow dryer over it.)

I'm a walking, dry-clean-only mess.

Ray keeps silent after my introduction and slicks his gray hair back with one hand, sliding his chair closer to the cherry wood desk. He pierces me with his green eyes, and I hope he's about to say that he wants to learn more, that he's excited to tutor me in the wonderful world of business. But instead he says two words.

"Get out."

I'm used to getting thrown out of places. The library across the street from my apartment kicks me out all the time for chatting on my phone while browsing for books. The coffee shop around the block, with free Wi-Fi and samples of yesterday's breads, asks me to either buy another beverage or start paying rent whenever I try to discreetly camp out for eight hours with my computer. I've been on a date before in which, after fifteen minutes, he gently rolled on his coat, shook my hand, and ran.

It takes only a minute and forty-five seconds before Ray tries to show me the exit, a new record for me. While I'm completely taken back and a little shaken up, I'm also impressed.

"Get," he says slowly, pausing to take a deep breath before the next word, "out." He motions to the door like an angry-old-man version of Vanna White.

I wonder what I did to get him all riled up. I'm wearing the most professional shirt I own, after all. Maybe I sound too much like a cartoon character and not enough like a CEO?

But I came here to learn, and I came here for a one-hour session. I want my remaining fifty-seven minutes.

"No," I say, taking a seat and acting tougher than I am. I hide my hands underneath the desk so he can't see them shake. My once-retired button-down shirt is suddenly soaked with stress sweat.

The man across from me is probably in his eighties, has never lived anywhere outside Brooklyn (judging from his thick accent), and has probably bullied his fair share of rookie business owners. But these are all assumptions. What I know is that he is thin, his hands are wrinkled, and his shoes are the most modern thing about him. He has the exterior of a huggable grandpa and the mouth of a pit bull.

I grab the arms of my wooden chair, lean back, arch my eyebrows, and raise my chin in defiance, as if to tell him that I'm not going anywhere, not until somebody makes me.

He lets out a dry laugh, the way people do when they want to let you know that what you said, or what you did, isn't funny. At all.

"Ever seen an ugly baby before?" he asks, taking a sip of his coffee.

What an odd question. But I'm not here to judge his techniques, I'm here to learn, so I go with it and pull out my pen stolen from Bank of America and my notepad from TD Bank and jot down "Lesson One: Ugly Baby."

"Put that away!" he yells. I drop my pen and shove my paper to the side. "Have you ever seen an ugly baby before?"

"Well, I don't know. Maybe?"

His eye contact is stern, unbreakable. "Have you?"

"Yes," I finally confess, feeling exhausted, like I just admitted to something I was brainwashed to believe true.

"If you saw an ugly baby, would you tell the mother?"

Okay, now I'm really not sure what kind of business tutoring this is, but I have a feeling I'm not learning anything that will help me with Bridesmaid for Hire. At the most, I'm about to learn what to say to my friends every time they send me Snapchats of their newborn babies and ask me if he or she is the cutest thing I've ever seen.

"Well, I don't know. Probably not."

He pauses, looking me up and down, his eyes glued to the spot on my shirt where a button should be, hinting that I am indeed the ugly baby in the room.

"Your business . . ." He tries to go on, but I stop him.

"I get it. I get it."

He flicks his hand toward the door again, as if his work here is done. But it's only just beginning.

"You don't know a thing about my business."

"I know the name of it."

"Yeah, but there's more."

I don't know where to start or even how much to tell Ray at first. But I need him more than he realizes, more than my cherry-on-top personality makes it seem. The week before, I found myself crawling under my mattress pad, pushing my head into a firm pillow, and having a silent breakdown in my bed.

When you live in New York City, you don't have a lot of privacy to lose your mind without other people noticing. If you do it on the street, you have an audience of tourists swarming around you, with their street maps and selfie sticks, convinced that if they stay in Manhattan for too long, they'll also suffer from periodic emotional breakdowns outside Starbucks. If you do it in your apartment, you have neighbors who just want you to shut up so they can finish watching *The Voice* while your roommate keeps a silent running tally of how many of these you've had this month alone.

I was on my fifth. My business was eight months old, and all of a sudden I realized that I hadn't taken a deep breath, a day off, a moment to let it all sink in, since the day I posted the Craigslist ad. I was officially willing to admit I needed help. My website was broken, my business model and sales pitch had me losing money by the second, and my inbox was filling up with too many requests from too many people who all wanted something from me. I was trying to be my own lawyer, my own accountant, and my own investor.

If I was appearing on the TV show *The Shark Tank*, Mark Cuban would probably say, "Cute idea, but for that reason, I'm out." Mr. Wonderful would then say, "You're a complete mess and, for that reason, you're dead to me." My best shot would probably be with Barbara Corcoran, who, I imagine, would say, "Girl, you are in over your head. I'd have to spend way too much time holding your hand," and then, I would hope, follow up on that comment with a generous offer that I'd be too confused to know the meaning of and decide to decline before even considering it.

But none of that mattered, because here I was, in front of my very own Great White Shark, wondering if honesty would get me a deal or send me straight back out the door with nothing.

I found Ray while I was inside of my mattress pad, face down, telling myself that I couldn't do this anymore. I couldn't pretend I knew how to run a business, and I couldn't do the jobs of five people.

So I pulled out my computer, Googled "free business tutoring in New York City," and booked an appointment with the only tutor who was available on weekends—which is how I found myself at the Mid-Manhattan Library before lunchtime on a Saturday, sitting in what felt like a confessional booth at the local church.

I've never been good at keeping my mouth shut and not rambling on about what's on my mind, and my face is horrible at hiding my emotions. I'm prone to letting it all out, often accidentally and prematurely, and this moment was no exception; I told Ray the truth that, for the past 240 days, I have been too scared to tell anybody else.

"I'm running this business," I start to say as the tears slip from my eyes, "and sometimes I realize that I have no idea what I'm doing."

I tilt my face in the other direction. I stare up at the light. I cover my mouth with my hands. I'm trying every trick in the book to make him think the tears stubbornly falling down my face are just an illusion.

"Stop being so brave," he shouts. I flinch and turn my face toward him, revealing that I am indeed crying, that I am a Miss America wannabe with a missing button on my shirt who is secretly just a crybaby.

"Tell me this right now," he says. "What is your greatest failure?"

A hug would've been nice, or even an offer to split the

pumpernickel bagel and smear waiting patiently for him on his desk. But instead, he pretends that none of this is happening, that I'm not falling apart, piece by piece, in front of him. He's simply forcing me to go on.

"Well, my business isn't a failure." I decide to start with a positive first—and pull myself together. "I just need a little help."

"Tell me a failure!" He slams his fist down on the desk like an unhappy football coach who keeps watching his team turn over the ball.

I've failed. I've failed a lot. But I like to take my failures and crumple them up in a ball and shove them in the back of my mind like a pile of clothes that no longer zip all the way up, unacknowledged but there all the same. You know, just in case I want to pull them out and do a dance of self-loathing around the living room.

"Most recently," I mutter, "I failed because I gave up on writing a book that nobody said they would publish."

"Okay, what else?" He hit back, as if we're in a boxing ring and he's pushing me to keep throwing punches in his direction—except the person I'm really punching is myself.

"I guess you could say my savings account, or lack thereof, is quite the epic failure." I tap my fingers on my TD Bank notepad. "I'm two years away from thirty, and the money in my 401(k) has never reached four digits."

I fall silent again, hoping he'll pardon me from this exercise, hoping that he'll ring a bell and end this conversation. I'm ready to bow out.

He doesn't, so I go on. I have to fill the silence somehow.

"There's my love life. It's quite the cataclysmic mess."

I lock eyes with the fluorescent lights above me on the

speckled ceiling, as if to fool Ray into thinking, once more, that I'm thinking really hard about how to keep on answering this question. But I'm starting to cry again.

Finally, he breaks the silence. "Your problem," he says, "is that you're too scared to fail, so you don't even move."

He compares me to a piece on a chessboard that just stays put because it's too afraid of being tossed out of the game. He compares me to a small child who has just been caught stealing chocolate chip cookies from the pantry, and instead of running in the other direction, closes her eyes and hopes she won't get into too much trouble. He compares me to a toddler who's playing a game of freeze tag. And finally, he compares me to exactly what I am: a girl paralyzed in her own footsteps because she's constantly obsessed with the what-ifs.

"You want to be successful?" He leans in closer, muzzle fully removed. "You have to fail, fail, fail, and fail until you can sit here, in front of me, and recite every one of them so fluently and quickly that I'll get bored and ask you to stop. That is when I'll know you're ready to learn about success."

No one has ever told me this before. Most people say the exact opposite—that you shouldn't fail. That failing won't get you out of the third grade, it won't get you a spot on the baseball team, and it won't get you a fourth date with a guy whose presence makes you forget your constant urge to check your iPhone.

Failing isn't something I strive for or put at the very top of my to-do list. I cling tightly to the idea that I need to keep myself together, at least outwardly, avoiding risks and tiptoeing around my mistakes. That's what I had always believed would lead to success.

I wasn't ready to give in to this cuckoo crazy advice just yet, so I decided to change topics, to bring up something else.

"My ultimate dream is . . ." I clear my throat, sit up straight in my chair, and try to regain control of the conversation and myself. But before I can even tell him what that dream is, he cuts me off.

"Enough with the ultimate dream language," he says slapping it away with his hand as if he were trying to kill a mosquito. "Ultimate dreams are for lazy people. Ultimate dreams are bullshit."

I lean back in the chair and let out a nervous laugh that echoes throughout the entire business library. There's something charming about an old man who curses.

"I'm eighty-two years old," he says. "There's no time for ultimate dreams. You are either doing it or you're not."

I want to jump in and pepper him with *what-ifs*, like: What if I'm not ready to? What if I'm not sure? What if I don't have enough money to take a break from working full time to build the opportunity no one else in this world can ever give me? But I don't say anything—partially because I know he's right and partially because I know that if I even say the words, "Yeah, but . . ." he'll yell at me to get out. He hasn't done that once in the last fifteen minutes, and I don't want to jeopardize that. I have no choice but to become an early adopter of everything he's saying. It's either that or go back to my tiny apartment and keeping adding to my roommate's tally of Jen's mental breakdowns.

Maybe Ray is right. Maybe I'm not failing enough because I'm too scared of letting go of everything I have, even if what I have feels like a posthurricane kind of mess. I never had plans to start a business called Bridesmaid for Hire. I just had a crazy idea that brought me face to face with my laptop at 9:00 p.m. on a Friday. I remember saying to myself that even if this doesn't work, that's okay, because I have nothing to lose anyway. Maybe I still don't, and maybe that's a truth I needed someone to remind me of every so often. In the end, doing something, even if I'm not ready or sure about it yet, is better than lying on my back and dreaming about it.

Dreaming, I've learned, can be really fun. It gets my body all jittery and my mind working like it's running full speed on a treadmill for the first time in months. But the problem with dreaming is that when I'm done, I've exhausted my mind for the day and have nothing to show for it. I fold my mental notes together and stick them back in a manila folder labeled, "Eventual Plans to Take Over the World." But I forget about them. Or my to-do list makes me forget about them or someone else tells me I'm better off forgetting about them.

"Either do or dream, but don't wait too long to make that decision," he grumbles. "When you're eighty-two, it's a hell of a lot harder to get your ass out of bed in the morning. That's when you're better off dreaming." He laughs like a caffeinated hyena, and all of a sudden, for the first time in our twenty-minute relationship, he shows me something I never thought I would see: he smiles. He smiles right at me, his front incisors almost blinding me with their perfect shine, and in that very moment, I have no choice but to love him.

Maybe the people I admire from a distance for their inspiring and successful lives are inspiring and successful because they've failed so many times behind the scenes—and I have no clue about it. It's not like people post their latest failures on their Twitter account, or speak about them when they're on a *Good Morning America* segment, or add them to their website beside their beloved testimonials.

It's been eight months since I posted an ad on Craigslist that sparked a business I didn't even know was possible. But after I took a chance and posted that ad, I was scared to try anything else. I was scared to make a plan to expand the business, I was even more nervous to hire people, and I had become too attached to let anybody else step in and help me. According to Ray, I was scared of ruining something that would expire if I didn't take action, which was paralyzing me even more.

"Get out of my office, Jen." His lips curl upward in what must be a smile. "And come back when you're ready to fail, fail, fail."

I leave there feeling like somebody pumped all of the oxygen out of my lungs. My legs are shaking and my mind is twisting around Ray's words as I walk the four blocks north and two blocks south to get home.

I can barely explain my Saturday morning to Kerri when I get home, saying only that I met somebody who spoke to me in a way that nobody else had ever spoken to me, and that for some bizarre reason, I had a feeling he was going to be the person who could jolt me out of my slump—and maybe even change my life. I couldn't wait to see him again, but I didn't know when that was going to be.

The next day, as I sit down to make a list of things I'm going to attempt, things that terrify me the most and don't promise me success, I flip open my computer and check my email. At first, I see only deals for 50 percent off on Match.com and 40 percent off a new (and much-needed) blouse from Ann Taylor

Loft. But there's also an email I didn't think I'd see so soon. It's from Ray.

> I've been thinking about the meeting we had yesterday. I think it would be beneficial to have another one. What Saturday in March can you come back? One more thing, Jen. Remember this: regret is what makes you human; failure is what makes you a hero.

I smile so wide that it feels like my jaw might unhinge. This feels better than waiting around for that postdate text from a guy you really enjoy splitting a bottle of half-priced chardonnay with on a first date. It even, I admit, feels better than having your boss call you in to tell you that you're getting an 18 percent raise.

I write back immediately, not wasting any more time:

> Book me for every Saturday in March. I'm ready to learn how to fail like a hero.

chapter fifteen

Oh, You'll Totally Wear It Again

(Twenty Things You Can Really Do with an Old Bridesmaid Dress)

There are some bridesmaid dresses that are plain old eyesores, ones that make you look like a life-sized fruit parfait or strawberry cupcake, even after you pay someone seventy-five dollars to put your hair up in a sleek and modern french twist. Then there are some dresses that, if the fabric is a certain kind of satin, charmeuse, or chiffon, and the sun is hitting you in all the wrong places, you might find your skin literally crawling.

It's true. It happened to me once. I zipped on a black bridesmaid dress cut from georgette fabric for a late May wedding, and my skin immediately broke out in hives. I was posing for a picture with the bride when all of a sudden, I slapped her accidently in the chest. My body suddenly felt that it was being hit with a fire torch, burning and itching wherever the dress rubbed against my skin. My hands were scratching and flailing, and before I knew it, I had cherry-red bumps all up and down my limbs. I looked as bright as a ladybug.

The mother of the bride's cousin handed me two pink pills, and I swallowed them immediately, realizing, only right before, that I was about to take my very first step down the aisle while hopped up on Benadryl: Extra Strength. I tiptoed my way up to the altar, drool slipping off my lips, my head lolling to the side.

I had broken out in hives only one time before that, when I was seven and made cookies with a bottle of expired vegetable oil. But all in all, my body was pretty good at handling foods, insect bites, and even different fabrics. It just didn't have a tolerance for ugly bridesmaid dresses.

When the wedding was over and I was still partially zonked out, my head practically resting on a whipped-cream-stained dessert plate, the bride came over to me and said, "Well, it looks like this is one bridesmaid dress you probably won't wear again." I was too out of it to tell her that even if this dress didn't make my skin sting, I would probably never wear it again.

Brides always trick themselves into believing that the dresses they pick out for their bridesmaids will be something they can toss on again, as casually as a T-shirt or a beach caftan. It helps curb the guilt of asking friends and family to crack into their savings accounts. But I always want to ask these adorably naive brides where they think I'll wear this dress again. My social calendar is filled with solo Netflix and chill nights, not with invitation-only galas and balls at the Waldorf

Astoria. Sure, I could wear it again to another wedding when I'm just a guest, but I'd prefer to spend my off-duty time not looking, acting, or feeling like a bridesmaid. I'd prefer to swap out the duchess satin knee-length lavender number for something Angelina Jolie would wear to the Oscars (or a knock-off version from T. J. Maxx, of course).

The truth, dear brides and bridesmaids, is that you will never wear those dresses again. Even if your heart has good intentions and you're trying to brainwash yourself into thinking a dye job and some tailoring will earn the dress front-of-closet status, we '90s babes know that a hot-pink mesh tank top from Hot Topic is a mesh pink tank top from Hot Topic: we can do what we want to it, but we will never be able to wear it again.

So if your closet is the size of a double-wide sleeping bag and you don't want to use up the precious real estate with body bags filled with polyester, chiffon, and satin, here are some practical alternatives that won't have you stuffing those dresses underneath your bed. (I wonder if monsters look good in blush?)

1. Leave it in your hotel room as a gift for housekeeping since they'll probably have to clean up after your postwedding, hungover, hot-mess self. Maybe they can use it to scrape your fake eyelashes off the countertop. Tulle is particularly effective for this.

2. Try to return it and get your moolah back. Macy's has an exceptional return policy. I once returned a bridesmaid dress I bought there, with three coupons,

and wore for only eight hours at a wedding—though after reading this, they'll probably ban me from returning bridesmaid dresses with the tags ripped off and the bottom looking as if it came in contact with a shredder.

3. Related to point 1, use them as rags around the house. My mom used to do this with old T-shirts that I grew out of (or stained with mustard and was no longer allowed to wear in public). Cut them up into large squares, and use them to dust your dresser or lift freshly spilled wine from your carpet.

4. Sew them into a tablecloth or curtains for your living room. I'm not *that* crafty, but there are YouTube videos about this, as well as grandmas, somewhere, who can help you cut and paste it together. (And no, I'm not talking about on a computer.)

5. Stuff them into the very back of your closet, where the spider webs and cockroach traps live. Have them snuggle beside your high school jeans that fit you like capri pants now. Let them nudge themselves next to your winter boots and pizza-stained snuggie.

6. Give them to the homeless guy who sleeps outside your apartment building. If he stacks them on top of each other, they can form a pretty heavy and well-insulated blanket. You know because after wearing one for eight hours, you got a heat rash on your inner thighs.

7. Never pick them up from the dry cleaners. This may happen without premeditation, and if it does, know

that the dresses will eventually go off to live a better life in some faraway land. The place I used to go to get business suits dry-cleaned (when I briefly wore business suits) told me that clothes left there after ninety days get shipped to a family in Guatemala. I hope the family enjoys the two Ann Taylor Loft clearance rack skirts, neon pink blazer from Forever 21, and three bridesmaid dresses I purposely decided never to go back for.

8. Keep the dresses and stubbornly find a way, a place, and an occasion to wear them again because you can't afford not to: all of your assets are tied up in these one-time party garments.

9. Mail it back to the bride and ask her to walk a mile in the bridesmaid dress she picked out for you to wear.

10. Mail the dress to someone random. Everyone loves getting stuff in the mail! Box up the dress and add a note that says, "One single girl's trash is another single girl's treasure." Google Map a random location, and let FedEx do the rest.

11. Twist it up and stick it in an empty wine bottle. Send it off to sea.

12. Use it as a Christmas tree skirt. Or if you're Jewish, use it as a tarplike tablecloth to place your latkes and applesauce on.

13. Wear it to book club.

14. Regift it, back to the bride, as her thirtieth birthday present.

15. Use it as a gift for a grab bag, secret Santa, or white

elephant exchange. Who knows, maybe someone in the room would prefer to take home yards of chiffon over a candle that smells like cinnamon and Lysol.

16. Wear it to another wedding, but check with that bride first. Make sure the dress is not identical to the one the other bridesmaids are wearing, or even the same style and color. Nobody wants to be the third-wheel bridesmaid, just like nobody wants to be Teresa instead of Barbie. This is a real fear of mine. My doctor claims this is the main source of my sleep apnea.

17. Wear it on a first date. It will be one way for you to show the guy that you're not looking to be his holler-back girl. You are looking for a fully committed, steady relationship that will one day lead the two of you to frolic down an aisle together. Actually, don't wear it on a first date. Maybe save it for a third date when the rest of your crazy crawls out.

18. Wear it to Thanksgiving dinner to dissuade people from asking about your dating life, especially the aunt who loves making "always a bridesmaid!" jokes as you pour gravy over everything.

19. Make it the centerpiece of your Halloween costume. Zombie bridesmaid, anyone?

20 Forget about it. Really, just forget that it exists, like an ex-boyfriend who blocked you on Facebook and told you to never text him at 4:00 a.m. again when you're out dancing with your friends on the

Lower East Side. Forget it as you pack up and leave the hotel. Forget it as you're going through airport security. Forget it in the trunk of the rental car, as it snuggles up beside the spare tire. *Forget it. Just try to forget that it exists.*

chapter sixteen

Those Who Will Remain Nameless

My doorman, Jimmy, calls me Kimmy.

He's been doing that for over three years now. Well, actually, the first year he didn't call me anything; we just exchanged repetitive hellos followed by routine good-byes, simple quick waves as I moved on and he stayed behind. Eventually our relationship got to the next level, and we started having conversations that lasted the length of a burning sparkler and eventually dragged on to the length of a slow-burning cigar.

It was less about what I told him, and more about what he saw that fostered our relationship. He witnessed things that I didn't want to sum up in 140 characters and post on Twitter, or snap with my iPhone and color-correct with a filter or two on Instagram. They were little things, like how I would walk in circles around the apartment building every night at exactly 7:35 p.m., how I waited to close my umbrella until I was halfway into the lobby, or how I would eat only the right side of my pizza crust, the side my fingers didn't touch, and throw away the other half. But also heavy-hitting things, like the time the first guy I ever loved told me, right outside the entrance to my building, that he didn't love me anymore. My doorman watched me cry and pace and pivot, take baby steps back into the lobby, run back outside and toss my cell phone into a thorny rose bush, and retrieve it two days later when he left it for me at the front desk.

Since that moment, Jimmy started regulating my online dating life, offline. If I came home past 10:00 p.m. on any given evening, I had to report my whereabouts, my findings, and my discoveries to him, like a modern-day Christopher Columbus going through customs in Murray Hill. It was as if my Jewish mother had transplanted herself into the body of a forty-five-year-old Irish man dressed in a black and white polyester waistcoat and a magician-like top hat, greeting me with a list of first-date questions, like, "Who was he?" and, "What do his parents do?" and, "Why didn't he hail you a cab after you stuffed your faces with half-priced oysters (which you had to pay for)?"

Jimmy and I even hugged once. When my taxi pulled up to the curb in front of my building after I'd been gone for a two-week vacation in Florida, I fell right into his arms, embraced by his welcome home smile.

And then one day he started calling me Kimmy.

"Good morning, Kimmy," he rattled off to me a year and a half into our nameless, yet very steady, relationship. I kept on walking because my name is not Kimmy and I figured he must have been talking to some other resident while looking directly at me. Maybe his glasses were just a little foggy from the Arctic tundra–like winds of that particular winter. Maybe he thought I was the messy-haired blonde girl with perpetually wrinkled T-shirts who lived in 29B. (Easy mistake to make.) *I'll let this one slide*, I thought to myself, and kept walking toward Third Avenue. It's quite impressive what we convince ourselves of when we can't accept the obvious.

But as I rounded the block, I heard him call out again and again: "Kimmy? Kimmy?" He knew my name was Jen. I had told him that! Well, now that I think about it, I never told him that. I never told him my name.

It's not *that* weird, is it? We spend years in relationships with people and we don't even know their phone numbers. We type their digits in our phones one time and let Siri do the recall whenever we want to give them a ring. Sometimes we even have joint bank accounts with these people! Share a queen-sized bed with their bodies! Bring them home with us for the family's Passover seder! Yet we wouldn't even be able to call them if we lost our phone or if by chance found ourselves in the slammer. So is it really that weird, in this day and age, that I'm in a long-term, strictly platonic, nameless relationship with my doorman?

"Kim?" he said, this time abbreviating the name, as if he had said it many times before, as if my sudden silent treatment was breaking his heart. "What's up with you today?"

I paused in my steps and craned my neck around, my back still facing him, fully realizing that there were no other humans, or even animals, within a 100-foot radius of us. He was talking to me and only me. *I was Kimmy.*

Now, in that moment, I had two very clear and distinct

choices. I could walk up to him and ask who the heck Kim was and why he was calling me that. I could show him my driver's license, or run upstairs and pull out my birth certificate from the linen closet (where one stores all important documents and snacks valued over ten dollars), and show him that my proud parents named me Jennifer Sara Glantz, and if we want to get into the finer details, my mensch of a rabbi blessed me with the Hebrew name Yaffa when I was two. Neither name sounds remotely like "Kim."

Or I could just take on this brand-new identity for the rest of my rent-paying days in this overpriced midtown apartment building and be done with it.

That year, I signed my Christmas card "From Kim" with a blue Sharpie and squiggly hearts. "Happy Holidays to my favorite doorman, Jimmy."

I didn't tell anyone at first about our little name game situation. I hoped, for a while, that maybe I was hearing things. I even tried saying "Kim" so many times out loud, to myself, behind closed doors, that it started to sound just like "Jen." We do the most insane things for the people we care about when we don't want to hurt them.

Kerri had an intervention with me about this one afternoon. We were walking into our building with bags of groceries strapped to our shoulders and our forearms, like Manhattan-dwelling sherpas.

"You know he calls you Kimmy, right?" she asked, disturbed and concerned.

I laughed and waved the comment away with a dismissive flick of my hand. As if I hadn't heard him call me Kimmy 178 times before.

I didn't want to believe it was true. We were rolling into our third year of living there, and Jimmy had become the closest thing I had to a neighborhood best friend, an on-call therapist, a protector of my most intimate and precious secrets. When I started snapping back into reality, realizing that other people could hear him call me Kimmy, I would stop friends and family prematurely in their tracks and body-slam them into the side of my building.

"Now you listen up," I'd say, sticking my index finger into their faces. "I have something very important to tell you."

"What? Are you pregnant? Do you secretly live inside the pizza shop across the street? Are the Feds looking for you because you haven't paid your late library book fines in over a year?"

"Shhh," I'd say, not looking to get busted for another crime. "No, no, it's nothing like that. It's much worse."

I'd instruct them that when they walked into my apartment building and the doorman called me Kimmy, they were to make no sudden moves, flash no awkward smiles, emit no weird giggles, ask him nothing like, "What did you just call her?" My friends would roll their eyes, wrinkle their noses, and look at me like I was nuts. It didn't matter, as long as they didn't blow my cover.

I came close, once. I went to pick up a birthday gift that my mom had sent me when I turned twenty-six, and I asked Jimmy if any packages had come for me. My brain was running hamster-like circles around what could be inside that gorgeous brown birthday box, and I forgot to remember that my mom would have mailed the package to someone named "Jen Glantz." Of course! She had no idea about this name game I was paying over $1,500 a month to play. So when Jimmy saw a package with my address on it, sent to someone named Jen, he shook it in front of my face and said it was a mistake, probably meant for another resident in the building.

"Oh," I said, eyeing the box that inside held all of my theoretical medium-sized treasures from my favorite clothing retailer. "Weird."

I never had the guts to go back and get that package. *My* package. Who knows, the box with the pink, sparkly Forever 21 dress could still be sitting there, waiting to be claimed. Or perhaps someone tossed the box in the trash because it didn't have a rightful owner, and now my flamboyant dresses were buried six feet under in a landfill outside East Brunswick, New Jersey.

The thought of having to walk up to Jimmy at this point in our relationship and tell him that my name is not Kimmy and has never been Kimmy makes me feel icky. It ruins the ebb and the flow of what we have. It makes me think that all of this can be easily solved in one simple way, and one way only: marching down to the Centre Street courthouse and asking the clerk if I can legally change my name to Kimberly—Kimmy for short, and Kim for those who really know me well.

This isn't going to be the last time someone calls me someone else's name. It has now become a regular part of my job.

Rose asks if she can call me Jessica. Her wedding is three months away, and we are smack in the middle of our first phone session together. I have no idea if she pulled the name from a book of the most popular girl names of the '80s, or if the name has significance to her. All I know is that from now on, I'm Jessica.

Here's how it usually works with a client. First, I'll get to know the bride—her pet peeves, her wedding conundrums, and her big-day fears. Then the bride will get to know me and learn about my experience as a bridesmaid for hire. I'll give her some pre-aisle precautions, and we'll discuss what I should say during the champagne toast at the reception, before the cake is cut and the bouquet is tossed. And then, together, we'll get to know "Jessica."

Jessica is the one with the story, the girl who has been places before. The protagonist who enters the wedding from stage left and recites how she knows the bride and how happy she is to be able to stand by her side after all these years. Jessica is the bridesmaid who shows up on the wedding day in my five feet seven inches lanky-armed body.

Sometimes Jessica is Christiania or Meghan with an H. It is always entirely up to the bride. Sometimes I can have as many as three different names and three different stories in one weekend as a bridesmaid for hire.

After a while, it didn't matter what people called me anymore; I was subliminally trained to answer to everything. Whether I was out in a restaurant with terrible acoustics, sitting in the middle row of a movie theater, or taking a quiet walk around the Central Park reservoir on a Sunday afternoon, whenever I heard someone call out a name, any name, a nervous twitch inside me would ignite an immediate answer. Without flinching, I would turn around and wave, say hello, and smile to a complete and total stranger, who was probably just saying hi to her dinner date, chick-flick companion, or a friend she bumped into while also taking a brisk stroll on a casual Sunday afternoon. But just in case she was talking to me, because she recognized me from a rehearsal dinner, the linoleum dance floor, or even perhaps a wedding toast that I gave for a bride I had just met only months ago, I acknowledged her. I transformed, for a couple of seconds, back into that person she might have known for a few minutes, a few hours, or a few days.

"So where did Rose and Jessica meet?" I ask, trying to give birth to our "How do you two know each other?" story—the first, and sometimes only, question people ask at a wedding.

Rose doesn't want anyone, including her five other bridesmaids and her fiancé, to know that she hired me. She made me virtually pinky-promise that before she pressed Send on her signed contract and deposited her payment into my account, this would be our forever secret. She wanted me there as a bridesmaid on her wedding day because she was having panic attacks over how her other bridesmaids were going to ruin what she hoped would be the best day of her life. They were already doing a pretty good job of trying, with their overbearing opinions and their disdain for following directions. She was exerting too much energy keeping tabs on them and making sure they didn't lash out at each other—or her—and ruin everything. She was hiring me as their babysitter, as the peacekeeper, making sure that if they had any diva moments—and she promised me they would—that I would intercept them like a 125-pound linebacker.

I had a track record of falling in love with every person that I met on the job, so I agreed, signed a contract with her, and imagined that this would be pretty easy. I would distract them with candy, jokes, and a night of electric slide–like dance moves.

"It doesn't really matter," she went on, nonchalant and blasé. "Because my bridesmaids already hate you and probably won't speak to you."

"Oh, okay," I responded, caught off-guard, realizing, once again, that with this job, I never know what people are going to say. No matter how many times I work with a bride, I can never predict the situations, the stories, and the plot twists that will fly my way.

"I just want to warn you, Jen/Jessica," she says, giggling over this Frankenstein-like person she had created, "that they might not be the friendliest to you."

I understood why, and I couldn't blame them. They had never heard of me before, and they were probably wondering why they had never seen me at any of Rose's other parties or life milestones, like the birth of her son, Roger, two years ago, or her annual Christmas party where her fiancé would dress up like Santa and she'd be his naughty elf. I didn't shake my booty with them at a nightclub in Atlantic City for the bachelorette party or cry happy tears when Rose opened up a brand-new blender, coffee maker, and set of dish towels at her bridal shower. In their eyes, I was the elusive bridesmaid who showed up whenever she felt like it. I was the girl who always seemed to have better plans, who always put Rose second.

This was nothing new. Most wedding parties felt this way about me—the bridesmaid who pranced into the bridal suite on the morning of the wedding as if she belonged there and would automatically be welcomed. It was customary for me to spend the first thirty minutes surrounded by whispers: "Who is she?" like we were at a first-grade sleepover and I was the new kid in town who hadn't been invited. But this time, I had a feeling things would be different. Rose was hiring me because her bridesmaids were the problem and I was the solution.

On the day of the wedding, I paced back and forth outside Rose's hotel bridal suite for fourteen minutes, figuring out how to make my grand entrance. *Everybody will love Jessica*, I tried to convince myself, wondering what the people watching through the hotel security cameras were thinking about me. *Give her five more minutes*, they were probably saying as they drank their Keurig-brewed coffee and hovered over the tiny black and white fuzzy screen. *Then we'll send security up to have her removed from the premises.*

I repeated the facts over and over to an empty hallway of sleeping hotel guests, singing them like they were the lyrics of a new Justin Bieber song. *Jessica, thirty-two, studied business, likes jazz.* (Jen certainly does not.) *Jessica is in a long-term, long-distance relationship with a guy she met at Rutgers. Rose introduced them, and now they're about to get engaged.* (Jen is certainly not even close to getting engaged.)

All of a sudden, the door of the bridal suite swung open, like a cattle pen, letting out a single bridesmaid who angrily trots up to me. "Can I help you?" she asked pointedly.

"You must be Betsy," I said, matching her face to the gallery of images I had saved in a folder in my brain called "people I want to forget the minute this wedding is over."

She scrunched her face and moved her head in a figure-eight motion. I bit my lip.

"I'm Jessica," I continued, going in for a hello hug, realizing, halfway into the motion that this was not a good idea. I stuck out my hand instead.

She didn't shake anything.

"I'm one of Rose's bridesmaids."

She placed her hands on her hips as if she were about to call the attitude police for backup.

"Okay." I raised my eyebrows at her. "Well, I'm going to go inside now and see Rose."

She continued to block the entrance to the door, leaving me the option of either crawling between her legs or squeezing past her armpit. I chose the latter.

When I saw Rose for the very first time in person, she looked nothing like her photos, which reminded me of every online date I'd ever attempted to go on. I stood there in the middle of the room of unfamiliar women until finally, fifteen slow seconds later, one of them made a rapid move toward me, trampling me to the ground.

"Jessica!" she cried out. I sighed in relief. There she was: my bride, Rose.

Don't say it's nice to meet you; say it's nice to see you, I said over and over in my head before responding.

"Finally!" I said, keeping it neutral and fighting off the anxiety of having five pairs of eyeballs drilling into me at the same time.

"These are Amber, Shelly, and Marque," she said, pointing out who was who among her bridesmaids. As she said their names, they turned away instantly, avoiding all eye and verbal contact. "This is Betsy, but you two already met," she said, flipping me a *beware* kind of a smile. "And this is Janna."

Janna waved hello to me immediately, like a kind human being. Rose told me that none of the bridesmaids liked her either because she was the only one out of the rest of them who wasn't from Newark, New Jersey, so she wasn't able to attend many of the prewedding events either. *Finally, an ally,* I thought to myself.

I plugged in my curling iron and took out bags of candy from my duffle bag, my sweet secret weapon, and made myself at home in a place I wasn't wanted. "Does anyone want a chocolate-covered raisin?"

Nobody moved a muscle. My words hung in the air for a while until they felt awkward and crawled right back into my mouth.

Janna walked over and grabbed a bag.

"Tough crowd," I said to my new loyal gal pal.

"Tell me about it," she said.

That's the funny thing about young friendship; it takes something as simple as a brief moment of shared laughter, isolation, or awkwardness to bond two people together. We're attracted to other people in situations when we desperately don't want to be alone.

Betsy came over to us and interrupted our moment of budding friendship. "Excuse me," she said with a slap of attitude, grabbing a bottle of hair spray that I thought was peacefully communal. "Who do you think you are?"

"Well, I'm Rose's friend from school," I respond. *It looks like my job starts now.* "And I'm a bridesmaid."

I was never a good liar. One time when I was five, I took my mom's wallet out of her purse to use as a prop for an afternoon game of "playing grown-up" (a game I still find myself playing now). When she knocked on my door, interrupting my meeting with high-powered "entre-pen-manures" (as I called them back in the day, and still sometimes do now), and asked if I had seen her wallet, I shook my head back and forth, collapsed into a pile of my own tears, and instantly presented her with the wallet and my sincerest apologies.

But I didn't start this business because I wanted to be a professional liar; I started it to help people. Lying was something I had to do occasionally, though it wasn't on my résumé of skills.

Betsy starts the inquisition off with an easy question: "Where do you know her from?"

"NYU."

"I thought you met in Atlanta?"

"We went to Atlanta," I say, trying not to tremble. "Once."

"Why haven't you shown up at anything in the past five years I've known her?"

"I've been traveling." I grab Janna as a shield of distraction and start combing the ends of her hair. "For work and for love."

"Good excuse," she says, dismissing herself from our Ping-Pong match of questioning to reboot with a caramel macchiato and a cigarette.

Phew, I thought, *I survived.*

Betsy reenters the room, slamming the door shut, squinting her eyes as if she's trying to read the brain waves inside my complicated mind. "There's something weird with you."

"There's a lot weird with me," I say, laughing so hard a half-chewed chocolate-covered raisin almost flies out of my nose.

After being tossed into rooms of standoffish bridesmaids week after week, I've learned that the quickest way to get them on my side, on my A-team, is to help them out with something they need. Whether it's a last-minute pep talk to calm their nerves because they've never walked down an aisle before, or a tampon or a hair tie or blister cream—items I always carry in my bridesmaid survival pouch, strapped underneath my dress, or stuffed into my two-sizes-too-big strapless bra—these small gestures usually earn me a bit of trust. So when Betsy's dress split open, right above her derriere, seconds before she was supposed to lead the bridesmaid entourage down the aisle, you better believe who was there, on her hands and polyester-covered knees, with a sewing kit and a mini-bag of safety pins.

"Don't move," I told her, finally and literally putting her in her place.

The bride was starting to break out in panic-induced hives. The flower girl was getting restless, tossing her bin of flowers upside down and stomping down on a hundred red rose petals. The organist had already started playing Pachelbel's Canon in D, and the guests were turning around in their seats, waiting for someone to walk toward them.

But here was Betsy, with her tangerine-colored underwear shining out of the hole in the back of her dress. I tied a piece of dark blue thread on a sewing needle and got to work. In less than three minutes, the dress was functioning again. *Hello, Project Runway, here I come.*

"It's good for now," I said, taking a deep breath, my heart racing, a nervous bride squatting down next to me to examine my handiwork. "Just don't do any crazy dance moves down the aisle." And together we laughed—until I looked up at Betsy's face, and the bride's, and realized I was the only one here laughing.

Betsy didn't thank me; she eyed the back of her dress in the mirror and brushed off the wrinkles on the front, pretending none of this even happened. She scooped her right arm into the groomsman's left, and they took a step, then another, and then another, down the aisle, away from where I remained hunched over. I shoved the needle and thread back into my bra, where they had been all afternoon in case of an emergency just like this.

Janna tapped me on the shoulder right before I was about to take my first step down the aisle and right after I'd shoved my makeshift sewing kit back into my brassiere. "What are you, some kind of professional bridesmaid or something?"

"Something like that," I said, as if I weren't, and I marched forward into the ceremony, the church door closing behind me like the mouth of a whale.

It's only after dinner is finished and the dessert tables are beginning to sprout up around the room that I heard someone call the name *Jessica*.

It was 10:30 p.m., and there was only half an hour left before I could disappear onto an Amtrak train heading for New York City. I'd sit in the very last car and peel off my fake eyelashes, my blue polyester dress, and this evening as *Jessica*.

I turned around and, two feet away, found my archenemy, Betsy, glowering at me. I wondered what I had done now to get her tangerine-colored panties in a wad.

"Thanks, or whatever. For before," she said, before heading over to the fondue machine.

I nodded, giving her a silent bear hug, my finest and final peace offering. I could smell the invisible incense burning.

When the clock struck 11:00 p.m., I packed up my bags and tiptoed toward the exit door, avoiding any final questions, any unwarranted good-byes.

"Jessica," I heard again. This time it sounded familiar and pleasant. I turned around to find Janna. She pulled out her phone. "Let's be Facebook friends."

"Oh, I don't have an account," I said, because it's true. *Jen* does, *Jessica* doesn't. Janna looks at me like I'm eighty-seven.

This is the part of the job that I dislike the most. Other than a party favor or a photo strip from the photo booth, I can't take anything else home with me from a wedding. Everything must stay there, as is—even the people I meet.

But maybe that's okay. Maybe some people are supposed to enter our lives just long enough for us to share a slice of ourselves and a night on the dance floor before we disappear. That's the strange thing about strangers: you fall in love with a moment in time with them, tattoo that moment onto your memory, and move on, never to see them again.

"You really are weird," Janna said, and we exchanged phone numbers instead. She wrote in her phone, *Jessica the Bridesmaid* and I wrote in mine, *Janna the Bodyguard*. We already had the kind of inside joke that would forever be burned into our memories—or, at least, our iPhones.

She hugged me good-bye, saying she'd like to come to New York City for Christmas. "Maybe we can hang out for a cup of frozen hot chocolate as we watch all the ice skaters spin in circles in Rockefeller Center?"

I nodded my head, my eyes dim with the thought of the friendship we could have under normal circumstances. Could we be friends *this* way? If she came to visit me, my roommate would call me Jen, my doorman would call me Kimmy, and she would call me Jessica. Could we be friends even though she didn't know my real name? Jimmy is one of my closest friends, and he *still* thinks I go by Kimmy. He will never know differently, and if I have anything to do with it, neither will she.

"I hope to see you soon too," I said to her, giving her one last hug and heading out of the giant whale-mouth-like doors, leaving everything as is, including the people, for now.

chapter seventeen

Stand-Up Comedy School Dropout

All I know for sure is that there's a bright light stinging my eyes, and I begin to wonder if this is it—if this is how it's all going to end. The light won't go away when I blink to the left or when I stare to the right. It's as if I just exited a movie theater, my pupils painfully adjusting to daylight.

I've forgotten where I am. I've forgotten what I'm supposed to be doing.

Oh, dear God. Did I die? It's me, again. Jennifer Glantz. Are you still there? I know we haven't chatted since the whole Steve Harvey debacle, and we both know how that turned out. But I need another favor. I need you to turn this light off and let the rulers of the afterlife know that I am not ready to hug them hello yet. There are still slices of pizza in Brooklyn that I want to eat and library fines in Los Angeles that I would like to pay off before I trade in my New York City one-bedroom apartment for a high-rise in the sky. It's just not my time to go, okay?

There's all that talk about how your whole life flashes before your eyes right before you kick the bucket. I think it's happening to me right now. The sharp light is live-streaming a montage of my most sacred memories. I see myself at five, building sandcastles with Styrofoam cups, sitting in the surf full of seaweed. There's me at twelve, tossing a Frisbee across the yard for my dog, Brandy, to fetch, but she decides to run in the opposite direction toward my peanut butter and jelly sandwich instead. Oh, great: me at eighteen, kissing a guy with a metal loop attached to his eyebrow and a tattoo that says, *smile,* in Chinese letters, on his left pec. I see one more. I'm twenty-six, now smooching a guy with a guitar strapped to his back as a homeless man stands next to us burping to the tune of "Mary Had a Little Lamb." Now that I think about it, I wonder what happened to that guy? Not the one I locked lips with—the one with the burps. Those belches were Broadway-worthy. I should have gone back and given him some Tums.

Wait a minute. I feel something. It's my heartbeat. It's knocking loud, louder, so loudly against my chest, my neck, my wrist. I am alive. I know for sure that I am because I tug on my shirt and it's soaking wet. I have never been happier to feel my sweat glands.

I make an X with my arms and furrow my brow until the light is gone, finally. It has moved across the room and is now haunting its next victim, a sign that tells me where I am, that reassures me that I am not walking toward the gates of heaven; I am walking onto the stage at the Broadway Comedy Club.

I notice my feet are now planted in the center of a wooden paneled stage that creaks whenever I shift my balance. I'm moving around a lot, avoiding mouth-to-microphone contact as much as possible. But I realize that the low-key sounds, panicked mantras, and whispers of *oh my god, oh my god, oh my god,* are being announced to the audience thanks to the unforgiving acoustics of this place.

The crowd is already chuckling, probably assuming that the look on my face is part of my act. I'll go with it as long as they keep laughing.

I have to say something. I have to start talking now.

"Dating is expensive and awkward."

I have broken the ice. I have started my tenure as a stand-up comic, and I feel as if I'm going to vomit the two slices of pizza I gobbled before I went onstage.

"The second that bill arrives, us girls, we lose all eye contact. We're shuffling around in our purse, trying to pull our wallet out from a stack of expired Bed Bath and Beyond coupons and hair ties. We look like we're a DJ spinning tracks."

I look out to the packed room of strangers, who are as silent as they would be if someone sealed their lips with Krazy Glue—though, magically, they're managing to guzzle their way pretty easily through the two-drink minimum. There's a brief burst of laughter from a table in the front. I move to the lip of the stage, raise my arm to shield against the bright light once again, and see that Kerri is sitting in the front row. She's bobbing her head up and down, trying to tell me that I'm doing just fine, that I should just keep going, so I do.

"I don't do that. Because I don't have a wallet. So I just say hey, I'll get this one. Because they're supposed to say no, right? Yeah. No: they say yes. And then I'm stuck paying $53 for their steak dinner and my appetizer-sized kale salad with dried cranberries."

I'm only up here on this stage because I'm no good at reading the fine print. I throw away receipts, sign my first and last name on the dotted line, submit payment via my PayPal account prematurely, before I've had a chance to digest what happens if I change my mind.

What happened was late one Friday night, which is when I get most of my dazzling ideas, I ripped my Bank of America monthly statement into ten almost-even strips of paper. On each strip, I wrote down a fear of mine. Fear is what steers us in the wrong direction; it's what wakes us up in the morning like an annoying alarm clock that can be heard three apartments away. I was becoming a twentysomething who was frightened by more things than a middle-aged Jewish mother who sits at home most afternoons and watches Fox News. So I decided to do something about it.

I crumpled up the strips and tossed them into a cereal bowl I had just used to eat my Lucky Charms. Then I turned off my lamps, reached inside, and picked out one, and only one, piece of paper. Whatever fear was written down would be the fear I would conquer this year, the one I would stare down like a cowboy does a bull in an old Western rodeo.

It could have been anything, really. My fears were quite diverse, illogical, and without a distinct pattern. I could have found myself jumping out of a plane with a parachute strapped to my shoulders, eating a chocolate-covered cockroach, or even making myself an appointment with a financial advisor to glance over the damage I'd done to my savings account with my irresponsible habits. But instead, written on the tightly folded piece of paper, was something I feared more than any-thing else. It was something I really didn't want to do. It said: "Go to stand-up comedy school and then perform at a New York City comedy club."

My dad can turn any situation into a punch line. He's made dinner tables, business meetings, and trips to the doctor for a routine checkup his own personal stage to deliver the kind of material that makes people hoot and holler for more. When you're around him, it's best you tuck a napkin over the collar of your shirt, for you never know when he's going to hit you with a joke that will make the lemon-flavored seltzer water flow out of your nose. I got his height, obsession for rock music, and love of a good ice cream cone after dinner, but I wasn't blessed with his natural ability to be funny. Sure, I could memorize jokes pretty well, repeating them over and over in my head just fine. But when it came time to say them out loud, I sounded like a monotone high school biology teacher trying to take attendance.

What scared me the most about doing stand-up comedy was that everyone in the room was paying top dollar to kick back a cold one and giggle on autopilot. It was the comedian's job to flip that switch on. I was pretty sure if I tried to do this at a New York City comedy club, there would be some angry customers demanding a refund for my subpar performance, to say the least.

But a late-night Friday promise is a promise, so I went on-line, Googled "NYC Stand Up Comedy Schools," and within ten minutes, I was a paid-in-full student who was starting class at the end of June. *Oh, the power of the Internet.* I was going to do this. I was going to high-five a fear that made my acid reflux flare up when I imagined doing it.

I was ready for this until one morning, the day before I was supposed to report to comedy school, I decided I didn't want to go anymore. It was more than that, actually. I really couldn't go anymore. My professional bridesmaid Craigslist ad had been discovered that morning, and I was now hiding on the ice-cold bathroom floor at my full-time job, watching my inbox light up on my phone. I was sending calls from reporters straight to voice mail and texting my brother to help me figure out a way to make this nutty accidental situation into a real-life business. In just twenty-four hours, my life had become a blockbuster comedy that I wanted to screen only in the comfort of my own home or on the floor of this bathroom. I was no longer interested in getting up on a stage.

I called them the next morning and begged like a child who was making a case for why she should skip out on school because she couldn't stomach learning about long division for a third day in a row. "You have to let me out of this class. You can keep my fifty-dollar deposit and refund the rest of the tuition; I just need you to take me off the roster."

The woman who answered my panicked phone call was named Martha, and she sighed so loudly it almost started to sound like her natural way of just breathing in and out. You could tell my simple request wasn't unique. Martha was swarmed with calls from last-minute scaredy cats wanting to stay home on their litter box of a couch.

"Fine," she said. "I'll take you off the list."

Phew. That was easy. I was relieved.

"But I'm putting you in the January class. So you have six months to pull yourself together and show up."

"Listen, Martha." It seemed as though she wasn't catching

my drift. "This class sounded wonderful when I signed up two weeks ago. But I've thought it through, and I'm not interested in publicly humiliating myself anymore."

"You have to take this class, Jen," she slammed back, as if she were my dial-a-date therapist.

Poor Martha. She had no idea she was sharing phone waves with the most stubborn human being in the entire world. Once I make up my mind, there's nothing anyone can do or say to change it. If I want to drive left, I drive left. If I want to eat a burrito from Chipotle for lunch, I eat a burrito from Chipotle for lunch. Even if that means my left turn will add an extra forty-five minutes to my commute or the Chipotle next to my apartment is unexpectedly closed for renovations and now I have to take the F train to the M153 bus and then walk seventeen blocks to eat a tofu burrito with extra guacamole, I'm going to do it.

"If you don't show up in January, we won't refund your money. You'll lose the $499."

"I'll see you then," I said, immediately. I knew I would not be able to snooze at night, in my overpriced New York City apartment that I have to work three jobs and eat one-dollar pizza for dinner to afford, knowing that I just tossed $499 up in the air like I just don't care.

"When you're single, everybody you know is trying to set you up with everybody they know. Mid–Pap smear, my gynecologist asked me if I wanted to meet her nice Jewish nephew for dinner. Once my rabbi pulled me aside at a funeral to ask me if there was anybody in the room I'd like to do a mitzvah with. By now, every Jason Cohen or Ian Schwartzberg on the East Side of Manhattan has my number."

A couple of laughs travel across the room. I look toward the back wall at a flashing red digital clock that says I'm up here for another two minutes and forty-two seconds. That's nothing, right?

Wrong. I have suddenly run out of jokes.

I initially forgot about my January back-to-school promise. I really did. I wouldn't be up here if the school didn't have a great accountability system that made my phone ring the night before class was supposed to begin, with a friendly reminder from my pal Martha.

"Is this Jennifer Glantz?"

"It depends. Is this the New York Public Library? If so, the check is in the mail, okay?"

"What?"

"Never mind. Who is this?"

"Martha. From comedy school." I felt like, at this point, she should have said Martha from collections.

"Is it that time of the year already?"

"School starts tomorrow. Do I have to remind you what happens if you don't show up?" Now she was sounding more like Martha from the Brooklyn mafia.

"No. But want to remind me why this class is going to help me at all in life?"

I didn't mean to dish her some attitude, but I was in the middle of running a business, by myself, from the crack between my couch cushions. I didn't have time to think about being funny.

"What do you do for a living?"

"I'm a professional bridesmaid."

Martha laughed so hard I had to move the phone away from my ear.

"That's not one of my jokes. That's the truth. I work weddings as a hired bridesmaid."

"Easy. This class will help you give wedding toasts that don't put people to sleep."

Martha was slowly becoming many things, one of which was a genius. She was right. After a while, all wedding speeches sound exactly the same. Just change the bride and groom's name, an inside joke here and there, and there you have it: a two-minute toast that the guests just want to get through so they can drink from their raised glasses of champagne.

All wedding party speeches start off with poetry about how beautiful and stunning the bride is. The middle is cushioned with a childhood joke; an embarrassing jab to the bride's taste in music, fashion, or her DVD collection; and one aww-inducing story about how she came to the rescue when your world was falling apart. It all ends with a toast to the radiating couple, wishing them a lifetime of happiness, laughter, and of course, love.

But the truth is, it would make more sense, it would be more honest, to wish them a lifetime of limited fights in the middle of the grocery store over which kind of oatmeal to get, adventures that take them more than sixty miles away from their suburban house, and the kind of love that has them waking up in seventy-five years together, whipping the Polident off each other's dentures.

I've started to get creative with my wedding speeches. I've said adios to the usual template and now find ways to make them a little more nontraditional. But that doesn't always work. That doesn't always make for a good speech. The last speech I gave at a wedding, I did it as if it were a game of Mad Libs. There I was, standing up in front of a room full of tuxedo-clad men and Spanx-encased women with a glass of champagne raised at half staff, asking people to shout out a verb, an adjective, and a noun to fill in the missing words of the speech on the spot.

It would have gone down as the most memorable and adorable speech ever given at a wedding if people weren't scratching their heads, trying to remember what an adjective is and what a verb is not. Or if they could hear me over the clinking of forks on plates and the loud chatter of the fraternity boys sitting at table number sixteen. Or, if, just for three minutes, their attention spans could outlast a fruit fly's. Perhaps my own personal guru, Martha, was right. Maybe stand-up comedy school could help bring some natural humor into my wedding toasts and help me entertain 250 glassy-eyed guests who are in the midst of a midparty snooze fest thanks to the open bar.

I'm now two minutes away from writing this experience off as a business expense, something I could reference next week during my meeting with Ray as one of my greatest failures of all time. I just have to figure out a way to improvise, to tell jokes on the spot, since my material stretched for only ninety seconds and I still have ninety more left.

I look down at Kerri, who is rooting for me as if she's cheering on a runner fifty yards away from a marathon finish line. "Go with the bridesmaid stuff," she whispers, and I stand up straight, brush the wrinkles out of my shirt, and go on, talking about a topic I know oh-so-well.

"So, I'm a professional bridesmaid."

The room comes alive with laughter. It is, officially, the most entertaining thing I have said all night.

"Want to know what that really means? It means you have

to lift up the bride's dress so she can pee. Have you ever helped someone pee before? I have. You want to know what happens? All of a sudden, you have to pee too. You find yourself bent over, one hand holding up her dress, one hand covering your crotch, and you're doing a little dance, praying that you don't pee all over the place. But you will."

I can now count the laughs on one hand from the kind souls who are offering me the laughter equivalent of a pat on the back. But five laughs is five laughs. The other sixty people in the room can remain comatose for all I care.

The clock says I have thirty more seconds: thirty more seconds and I'm out of this place. What can I talk about for thirty more seconds? Dating? *Already did that.* Pizza? *There's really nothing funny about pizza.* Food? *Why yes, I'll talk about my slowing metabolism's relationship with food.*

"I can't eat like I used to anymore. I have to eat foods that sound like celebrity baby names. Kale Jolie Pitt. Quinoa Kardashian. Sweet, sweet, Apple Martini, I mean Martin. I'm drinking almond milk. I didn't even know you could milk an almond? Please, somebody, show me the nipples."

The countdown clock is flashing a row of 0s in my face, and the bright light is making its way over from the Broadway Comedy Club Sign and into my eyes once again. My time is up, and I am done.

"I'm Jen Glantz. That's G, l, a, n, t as in tom, z as in zebra." I want everyone in the audience to know who I am and to remember, forever, what I just did. It might not have been the most haha-worthy performance, but for four minutes and thirty seconds, I was doing the Argentine tango with one of my worst fears. "Thank you for coming out tonight."

I backpedaled my way offstage, the bright light enhancing my every move, and wonder if this day will come back to haunt me.

But for now, I'm tugging down on the hem of my sweat-soaked T-shirt, letting my heart squeeze out some final shakes, like the aftershocks of an earthquake. I am alive. I am alive. I am still very much alive.

chapter eighteen

Ghosts of a Bridesmaid's Past

In every group of friends, there's always that one person you can count on, no matter how bone-chillingly cold it is outside, how late at night you're dialing her number for a pick-me-up, or how many candles are starting to fill your birthday cake, to tell you an outrageously good story.

She's the one who seems to always show up a little late to a happy hour, a bridal shower, or a baby's bris with an excuse that sounds as if it belongs in an episode of *Sex and the City*. Some cockamamie story about how she just got pulled over by a cop who had a face like Matt Damon, a body like The Rock, and a voice like George Clooney, which led to some flirty banter and him giving her his phone number on a coffee-stained Dunkin' Donuts napkin instead of a ticket.

I'm talking about the kind of friend who somehow always finds herself as the protagonist in an ill-advised and unimaginable situation that never happens to anybody else you know. She's the one who had to have her parents drive her to an urgent care clinic because she sliced her tongue open during her first kiss. The friend who went on a backpacking trip to a tiny city in Southwest Asia and bumped into her long-term, long-distance, ex-boyfriend whom she hadn't seen in three years. The one who would bite into a hot-pressed tomato mozzarella sandwich during her lunch break and find a piece of pirate's gold inside.

And you know her stories are true because you've been there, in the background, watching it all happen. You've stepped away for one second for one raspberry martini refill, one quick trip to the ladies' room, and come back to discover her doing the limbo with a group of fanny-pack-wearing tourists from Vietnam.

She's the person you find yourself hoping will show up for the quarterly girls-night-out dinner because, when the conversation begins to wind down, after the salad forks have been tossed aside and the first glasses of two-for-one pinot noir have been clinked and drunk, after the stories about refinancing mortgages, choosing the right doula, and bacterial infections from Spanx have been thoroughly discussed, she'll be waiting on deck with a story that starts off with, "You are never going to believe what happened to me."

She's the wild card, the comic relief, the shockingly put-together mess who will have you choking with laughter and brimming with tears within a three-minute span. She's the friend who never seemed to fully grow up, yet her life seems to demand the attention of all the other basic adults at the table who seem to take a weird kind of comfort in their friend's rampant chaos.

I don't know how, but I do know when I became that person for my group of friends. It started in my early twenties when I found myself pulling up a chair to a table full of diamond-ring-wearing, baby-ready gal pals. All of a sudden I didn't fit into the conversations anymore. Every group text message thread, conversation over scrambled eggs and chilled mimosas, and shopping excursion to the J. Crew outlet store went from discussions about rent, promotions at work, and dating to debates about hiring a band versus a DJ for their weddings, buying diapers in bulk, and furniture sales. That kind of stuff became the new normal, and my stories made me feel that I was an alien from Pluto touching down for brunch: "Greetings, Earthlings. Today I am going to tell you about something we have on our planet. It is called Tinder, and it helps us space cadets find someone to rock our intergalactic galaxy."

They couldn't wait to grab my cell phone, tap open a dating app, flip through the carefully chosen photos I uploaded, and read over my bio. It was as if they still wanted me at the round table as a warning of what it feels like to sit on the couch alone on a Friday night, beside a bag of unwrapped, ready-to-eat Hershey Kisses and a stuffed inbox full of unread messages from potential suitors. As if hearing about my online dating stories and offline dating meet-ups made changing dirty diapers feel like a breeze.

They wanted to brush up against a life they were no longer able to live, one that, from far away, seemed more like an impressionist painting than a clear photograph in the gallery of their memories.

"So what about you, Jen?" they ask after everyone at the table has given a routine update on how Baby Boo just said his first words or how Baby-to-Be gave a little high kick and now everyone thinks she'll be born a Rockette.

At this point in the conversation, the engaged ones will be done talking about how many salad spinners they put on their registry, or announcing their formal decision to move their wedding indoors because of the potential forecast of rain six months from now.

The single ones, aka me, will find themselves looking for an excuse to go home early, to leave this adult dinner party before someone has the chance to ask us why we're still single, or if freezing our eggs is part of our (nonexistent) five-year plans. We'll squeeze our eyes shut, trying to send telepathic signals to our roommates, hoping they'll receive them and call from home with some previously agreed-on excuse.

"Oh yeah, Jen! Tell us about the last date you went on."

If I'm too busy getting jiggy with my penne alla vodka and can't clear my throat quickly enough to answer, a follow-up question always finds a way to beat me to the finish line.

"Wait, are you seeing anyone?"

Do daily twenty-minute conversations with my doorman, Jimmy, who calls me Kimmy, count as being in a serious and stable relationship? There's no romantic interest there, but he did offer me a slice of his Domino's pizza once. So I guess you can say I am seeing someone, and I'm very happy.

After over seven years of passing the salt and pepper with these girls, they know that no matter what the happy hour specials are, the day of the week we're breaking bread, or the amount of time that has been X'd off the calendar since our last gathering, I'm good for a story about how I said "I love you" too soon or went out with a guy from Match.com who, three dates in, revealed he had a secret (Kendra) and that Kendra had a nickname (wife).

"You really want to hear one?" I'd double-check in case my tales of defeated love and aborted first dates were getting too stale to be served as the last course before dessert. But they would scoot their chairs closer, plant their elbows on the table, and shove their crumb-filled plates aside, giving me their undivided attention.

"Yes, tell us. Who is it?"

The last time we all powwowed over tapas, they bahahaha'd about the guy who never showed up for our date, the guy who ordered half the menu and then told me he forgot his money at home, and the guy I saw scrolling through Tinder while I was deliberating over what to order as my entrée.

My friends like to say that I attract bizarre situations, as one would attract creepy guys on the subway with their stern eye contact or colds in the winter with their lack of hand sanitizing. I have the type of luck that lands me in the seat across from the kind of guy who snorts when he laughs and picks the pumpernickel seeds out of his teeth when he listens. But I don't think I cling to odd situations purposely, like lint on a little black dress. I just think, maybe, when you constantly do something over and over again (in this case, online dating) and expect something different to happen, you're a bit insane. For me, dating is a déjà vu disaster.

"I went on a date with Lance Bass."

Their mouths gape open.

"Well, I was on a date with someone else, but Lance Bass sat down next to us and we started talking. I offered him some of my roasted hummus and carrot dip."

When I've had enough of the self-deprecating spotlight, I interrupt my own stories halfway through and ask if I can try on all of their engagement rings at once, transforming my bony ring finger into a shiny disco ball. This, to me, is a necessary intermission from recalling my real-life nightmares.

As the years flip over and over like a spinning bingo cage and we entertain each other over catch-up dinners, my role in the group hasn't changed—just the genre of the stories I tell.

In my late twenties, my "you're never going to believe this" anecdotes shift from stories about rock-bottom dates to tales of shuffling down the aisle, often for someone I'd never met before. I now have a book's worth of wedding stories, and I dazzle them with Sports Center–like commentary about how, this week, I had to act as a bodyguard for a bride who fired her maid of honor whom she feared would crash her wedding, and how, last week, I was tasked with finding jumbo tampons for a bride in a tiny town that sold only miniature cardboard ones.

"Tell us the worst bridesmaid story since the last time we saw you," one of them asks.

"You go to, like, a million weddings a year," one of them interrupts, as if she thinks my stories are by now generic, stale, and repetitive. "Aren't they all the same at this point?"

But spending every Saturday at a wedding as a bridesmaid is a lot like spending every Saturday with your baby: it's never the same. One weekend, you go to the playground, another the beach, and another on a road trip to Sesame Street World. One weekend, you have to resuscitate a bride back to life after she has too many prewedding tequila shots, another you have to embark on a top-secret mission to find a missing groom who hasn't been seen in over two hours, and another you find your-self dancing the cha-cha slide while the bride's great uncle Samuel's arm is slung around your neck.

No matter how many pairs of diapers you bring, jars of baby food you pack, and binkies you hand-wash and clip to the edge of your bag, you're never prepared for the out-of-the-blue baby tantrum. Just like, no matter how many packets of Advil, prewedding pep talks, or stain removers you carry with you, you'll never be ready for a wedding disaster.

"Last week, I touched poison ivy," I said, showing off the dried and crusty bumps all over my hands, as if I'm proudly presenting a new tattoo. "The bride wanted to take a picture in a field of flowers outside her hotel room."

Their eyes start to bulge, and I think about what story I should come to the table with next.

"The week before that, I had to give the mother of the bride my bra because she forgot to bring one."

"What did you do about your water balloons?" one of them asks while the others feast their eyes on my B cups.

"I used duct tape," I say, thinking back to how I handed off my double-D-sized strapless bra to someone who could get more practical use out of it than I could. "I just wrapped it around and around and around my chest."

They grab their own chests, imagining the pain of having to rip off the sticky tape when the night came to an end. My body, once smooth and unblemished, has become a living, scar-covered record of professional bridesmaid jobs gone by.

"Okay, but tell us the *worst* thing you ever had to do."

I stick my fork into a slice of chocolate lava cake, lifting a piece the size of my forehead into my mouth.

"Wha abou a goo stowy?" I ask through my mouthful of
ooey gooey heaven.

They purse their lips together and raise their eyebrows
high, as if to say they don't have time for such nonsense. Nobody ever wants to hear about a bridesmaid story gone right,
or a wedding that was as calm as the streets of Manhattan on
a Sunday morning.

"I'm afraid it doesn't make for good dinner conversation."

"Oh, come on, Jen."

"I'm telling you, this story is kind of disgusting."

They lean in closer, like little kids around a campfire at an
outdoor slumber party, waiting for me to tell them ghost stories
about a perpetually single professional bridesmaid.

"I worked a wedding for a couple in Vegas."

Their eyes light up like slot machines, anticipating some
The Hangover–style debauchery.

"But not *Vegas* Vegas. Right outside the Strip, on an open
pasture."

They lean back slightly, confused by this early plot twist in
the story.

"As I went to walk down the aisle, I noticed it was lined
with animal droppings from the wild donkeys that lived there.
So I had two options . . ."

"You could keep walking, or . . . ?"

"I could pick it up."

I thought back to the story my babysitter told me years
ago about the bridesmaid who passed out at the altar and was
tossed aside. How all of the other bridesmaids stood there,
paralyzed, holding their peonies in shock. That story never
sat well with me, and it became my own personal recurring

nightmare. So when I was in a situation where the choice was between doing nothing and letting a bride get poop on her $5,000 Italian silk dress, I reached down and got my hands dirty. Really dirty.

"But the best part was that after the bride walked down the poop-free aisle, the donkeys came back and stood behind them for the rest of the ceremony, waiting to go to the bathroom until after they said 'I do.'"

"That's epic," one of them says. "I knew we could count on you for a good story."

I have a feeling I'll never grow out of being the wild card friend. Even if, one day, we all end up in the same nursing home, I have a feeling I'll have a whole repertoire of brand-new stories. Maybe—well, I hope—they won't be about catastrophic dates or working a wedding as a hired bridesmaid. Perhaps they'll be about how I convinced the nurse to let me order Domino's pizza even though my dentures couldn't handle the cardboard-textured crust. I have a feeling that even if I settle down with a patient husband and we have a minivan full of kids, I'll still be invited to dinner tables across America to tell a story about a wedding or a bad date that will make half the audience cringe and the other half flutter their eyes in utter disbelief.

I think our stories become invisible tattoos that we wear privately until someone, somewhere, shines a light on us and asks us to reveal what we've kept hidden, if only for just a little while.

"Give me another," I say, plunking my cup down on the table and asking the waiter for a refill on my ginger ale. "We have a long night ahead of us, girls."

Chapter Nineteen

Ask a Professional Bridesmaid

(Real Questions from Real Girls)

Dear Jen,

All of my friends are married. The ones who haven't tied the knot yet are engaged and will be married between now and the end of 2017. Sounds like oodles and oodles of fun, right? Well, it would be, maybe, if I had a plus-one. But I don't. I'm the perpetually single one in our group of college pals. Because of that age-old rule that you only get a plus-one if you're in a serious relationship (and a ring is on its way) or you're married, I'm excluded from someone tagging along by my side. You want to know what else I'm excluded from? The table my friends get to sit at with their Hunny Bunny Husbands. I'm an odd number, and tables at weddings are for an even ten. So that means I'm left snagging a seat beside the bride's distant cousin, friend from work who doesn't know anybody else at the wedding, or fourth-grade teacher with the shaggy toupee. My best friend from college is getting married in three months and I'm scared to ask her if I can bring someone. I'm over going to weddings as the single girl. Can I ask her for a plus-one?

Sincerely,

Can I Get a Plus One?

Dear Can I Get a Plus One?

Can I get an amen? *Amen.* I always cringe a little bit when I'm invited to a friend's wedding and the invitation isn't addressed to Ms. Jen Glantz and Guest. By now, I'm also the only single girl at these things too, and while that comes with some perks (catching the bouquet without competition, dibs on which weird uncle to dance with, and not having to worry about having to babysit a drunk date) it also kind of stinks.

You know what I say to those age-old etiquette rules? Go bother someone in your own time period. It's 2016, darling, and we don't just sit around silently when something tickles us ever so slightly in the gut. We open our mouths, er, laptops, and say it in 140 words or less.

So go ahead, say something. If the bride is one of your closest friends and you really will be one of the only single gals there, ask if you can bring someone to the wedding with you so that you're not spending the night rolling your eyes at hand-holding married couples, or slow dancing to a Peter Gabriel song all by your lonesome self.

Ask her, if it's possible, when the wedding gets closer and she has a better sense of how many people are coming, if there's room for you to bring somebody. The bride may be inviting more people than she has space and money for, so the thought of one more person sitting down at table number 15, eating a $250 plate of filet mignon with zinfandel reduction, truffled potatoes, and California vegetables, may make the bridezilla side of her come out to play.

But she kind of owes you a plus-one. Because one glorious day soon, you'll be getting married, and she and her hubby—and, perhaps, by then, three kids—will have an automatic invite to your wedding. Another reason why she should just give you a plus-one now so you can call it even.

Worst case is that she gives you a big fat N-O and you're stuck doing the "Gangnam Style" dance with a bunch of married couples and their diaper-wearing toddlers. That doesn't sound so awful, does it? *Okay, yes it kind of does.*

Dear Jen,

A friend of mine who I'm not very close with anymore asked me if I would be her bridesmaid. I'm torn. Part of me wants to say yes because it could be fun and I'm close with some of the other girls she asked. But the other part of me thinks that I should say no because when (I should say if) I ever get married, I don't think I would make her one of my bridesmaids. I want to have a smaller, low-key wedding, with very few bridesmaids. I just don't want to say yes to her now and feel obligated to make her one of mine in the future. Is that a strong enough reason to say no? Or should I just say yes now and worry about whether I will return the bridesmaid favor later? Help!

> Sincerely,
> Bridesmaid in Waiting

Dear Bridesmaid in Waiting,

Growing up, I went to a Jewish day school, and when I turned thirteen, I found myself at a bar or bat mitzvah every single weekend. In just one school year, I danced the hora and ate a slice of challah bread at over sixty of them. Some Saturdays, I was being herded off to as many as two or three of them in the same night.

But I remember, during that time, people would keep a list of who gave what and who went to which bar and bat mitzvah. That way, after it was your turn with the Torah, you knew how much to give as a gift for all the other parties you attended. Everything was equal. If someone showed up at your bat mitzvah, you went to theirs, no matter what, even if you had strep throat, tickets to a Backstreet Boys concert, or another friend's party that same weekend.

That never sounded right to me, and thankfully, my parents didn't make me operate that way. But a lot of people did. It was safe, and it made sense. It kept you away from any added drama that was already tagged onto a highly emotional event and future emotional baggage that would haunt you if they gave you more money for a gift than you gave to them.

But here's the thing you don't realize when you're thirteen, when you think you have to follow these kinds of rules in order to keep the peace with the people surrounding you during this time in your life. Your bar or bat mitzvah is your special day—no one else's. If you don't want to attend someone's party because they're rude to you and threw a slice of cucumber at your head at lunch last month, and you know they invited you to their bat mitzvah only because their parents made them, then you shouldn't attend.

The same thing applies to us grown-ups. Brides ask friends and family members to stand by their side and be their bridesmaids for different, far-reaching, and sometimes not so obvious personal reasons. Those reasons, however, should never be copied or reciprocated. Because if they are, by the time you get hitched, you might end up with fifteen bridesmaids.

So, if you feel that you should be a bridesmaid for this bride, at this very moment in your life, then say yes. When your big day arrives, you can pick and choose who you want standing by your side, even if it's just one or two very lucky friends.

Dear Jen,

 I recently got engaged, and I'm trying to throw together a list of people I would like to invite to my wedding. So far, my fiancé and I have jotted down quite a long roster of family members, close friends, and people our parents would like to have in the room for our special day. Now we are up to the part where we're deciding if we should invite people from our workplace. My husband works for a larger company (there's close to a thousand employees). He's only going to invite two or three guys he's friends with. I, however, work for a start-up, a company of just fifteen people. I know everyone I work with, and of course, there are some I'm friendlier with than others. But if I invite seven of them, the other eight will feel left out. Am I allowed to pick and choose who I would like to invite? Should I just not invite any of them on account of not wanting anyone to feel left out?

Sincerely,

Invite Only

Dear Invite Only,

 Whenever I go to the grocery store, I make a list of the things I want to buy. But once I get there, I toss so many things that aren't on the list into my basket, which forces me to go back to the front of the store and get a regular-sized cart with wheels. I justify those items too. Like, if I'm buying a loaf of whole wheat bread, then of course, I need to buy peanut butter and jelly, cheese and turkey, and even some I Can't

Believe It's Not Butter. But when I go to the register to check out and the sales clerk is scanning my impulse buys and I'm watching my bill climb to some astronomical number, I think to myself, *Do I really need to take all of these things home and let them expire in the back of my fridge or on the top shelf of my pantry?*

I'm not trying to compare your guests to bottles of pickles and rolls of cookie dough, or any supermarket food for that matter. But it can be tempting to add, add, add people to your wedding guest list because you feel like you need to. Because you feel like, if you don't, you might make someone upset. There's no way around this. We live in a world where we have a whole lot of acquaintances, thanks to Facebook and our pals on Twitter, and very few darling dear close friends. Do yourself a favor, okay? Make a giant list of all the people you would ever think of inviting and put your close friends at the top of that list. Add a giant star next to their names.

What should you do with everyone else on that list? Close your eyes. Imagine your wedding day. Taste the freshly cooked salmon, feel the calluses forming on your feet as you pound the dance floor. Feel yourself kissing your husband after you exchange your passionate and heart-throbbing I dos. See yourself posing for pictures beside the people who raised you and stuck by your side all these years. Keep your eyes closed even longer. Now imagine who's there. Who's beside you? Who are the people you're pulling in tightly, hugging, thanking, and dancing with throughout the night?

Those are the people you should invite.

Dear Jen,

Our wedding was almost one year ago. We finished writing and sending out thank-you notes to our guests just one month after the wedding. While we were handwriting those, we noticed that quite a few people, I would say 18 out of 112 guests, did not send or give us a wedding gift. We started wondering if maybe we lost their check at the wedding or they shipped our gift to the wrong address. Should we say something to those eight people? If so, how do we put it nicely without sounding angry? Without saying, "Hey you! Where's our gift?"

Sincerely,

The Party Is Over

Dear The Party Is Over,

I always get awkward when the conversation turns toward money. Like, on a first date, when the check comes, I cannot just sit there and pretend that I don't see it. I can't just twirl the split ends of my hair or fumble around in my purse and wait for the guy to say, "Oh, don't worry about it. I've got this." I can't even mouth a cohesive set of words that would indicate that I think we should just go dutch and split the whole thing.

So most of the time, I don't say anything. I pull out every single dollar, credit card, and restaurant coupon that I have and throw it on top of the table like a pile of poker chips, as if to say, "I'm all in, dealer!"

Some people aren't this way at all, and I desperately admire them. Some people have no problem coming up to you at an event and saying, "Hey, you owe me $10 for your share of the spinach dip." Or remind you six months after a concert that you need to send them a check for the $50 they spotted you for the ticket.

No matter what kind of person you are, there's some extra gunk spread out on top of this particular situation because we're talking about your wedding here. Not only that, but you threw the party of a lifetime, of your lifetime, for these guests. And that party costs money. Lots and lots and lots of money.

Some couples use the money they receive on their wedding day as a way to pay the vendors for their services. And some couples use it for their honeymoon, a down payment on their first house, or even for a new wardrobe.

Either way, as a couple, you can do what you want with the money. They're your guests' gifts to you.

Which brings me to the gigantic, bright-orange elephant dancing to a Kesha song in the middle of the room. Just because you invited someone to your wedding, paid for them to be there, provided the live music for them to boogie down to, and served them a delicious piece of pork tenderloin, do they have to give you anything?

The answer is no.

It's annoying. It's awkward. It makes you feel like you want to call them up and really stick it to them. Say something quick and blasé like, "Did you enjoy salsa dancing to that Gloria Estefan song? How did you like the mint chocolate chip cheesecake we had for dessert? Oh you liked it? Great. Where the heck is our gift?"

Sure, giving a gift is the right thing to do, and as you've seen, most people will do it. But not everybody does. Not everyone feels as though they should.

Sometimes people can't afford to, forget to, don't want to, don't find the need to, or simply just don't care to.

The rule says people have one year to give you a gift. Chances are, if they haven't sent anything within six months, it's not going to happen— unless you do want to do something about it. So the question is, do you?

Dear Jen,

I don't like to go to weddings anymore. The first few were a blast because my friends and I were fresh out of college and single. We'd toast to our newly married friend and roll our eyes because, let's face it, we felt too young to even know what kind of career we wanted to spend the rest of our lives doing, let alone what kind of retirement fund we should opt in for or who we'd like to marry. But then, as if it happened all of a sudden, my friends started getting engaged left and right. It felt like we all started running the New York Marathon together, except when I slowed down at mile number 5 to grab a cup of water from the sidelines, they sprinted forward without me. Here's the problem: my good friend just got engaged, and when she called to tell me she wants me to be a bridesmaid, I said something like, "If by bridesmaid you mean slow-dance with your cousin all night or flirt with the only other single person there who's probably from Mars, then, no thanks." What I really meant to say was, "Of course." But I don't know how anymore. I don't know if I can stomach it.

Sincerely,

You Know Her . . .

The Single One

Dear You Know Her . . . The Single One,

Halfway through the last wedding I went to, somewhere in between galloping around like a horse to "Gangnam Style" and doing the electric slide, Beyoncé came on the speakers and repeated this: *All my single ladies . . . All my single ladies,* which became the perfect (and most overused) way for the DJ to round up the nonmarried ladies on the dance floor for the traditional bouquet toss.

By now, it's a natural instinct for me. Without even thinking, when I hear that song go on at a wedding, I put down my cheesecake and make my way over to the dance floor.

I'm not a hopeless romantic; I'm just good at following directions.

I'm also good at minimizing embarrassment, and I know, from experience, that it's less embarrassing to tiptoe onto the dance floor and compete with other eligible women for a flower arrangement tied with a ribbon than hide underneath the table and have the bride get on the microphone and shriek, "Where's Jen! OMG we can't start this until someone finds Jen!"

Women take the bouquet toss as seriously as they do a semiannual sale at Bloomingdale's. I was once elbowed so hard in the diaphragm, I couldn't breathe for a couple of minutes afterward. I've been tripped, knocked in the face, bitten, and one time, just one time, bribed to get the heck out of the way.

One time, I caught it and a girl ripped it out of my hands after kicking me in the shin with her fake Louboutin pumps. I knew they were fake because she hit me so hard that the paint from the red bottom came off and left a mark on my leg. I don't think a shoe that costs $1,500 would come apart so easily from kicking the side of a nonmuscular calf.

So I've learned to keep to myself out there. To stand in the back and run in the opposite direction of everyone else when the bouquet goes up in the air (which is typically toward the bar). That way, I'll be far away from the danger zone, and when the girl with the battered tulips rises from the bottom of the pile, we'll all just clap and go back to booty-dancing to the Ying Yang Twins and put our competitive monster selves away.

But one time, when the DJ made the call, it was just one other person and me.

Remember when you used to play the game, Duck, Duck, Goose in kindergarten and the person who wasn't quick enough and got tagged had to sit in the middle of the circle while people screamed "mush, mush, mush"? Well, that's exactly how it felt to be surrounded by 345 married people as I stood beside just one other person, underneath a giant artificial spotlight, in the dead center of a cold dance floor.

I could hear people say things like, "Why are they still single?" and, "Oh my, I feel so bad for them." One elderly lady shouted across the table to her husband, "Boy, do I have a grandson who'd be interested in that!"

The other girl beside me had a serious boyfriend, and when faced with the risk of limping around for the next seven days, she whispered to me and said, "Mind if I get this one?" I nodded my head and moved way, way out of the way.

Being single in a group of married, engaged, or seriously dating people is never a whole lot of fun. It just isn't. It's not fun at dinner or a movie or anytime you're forced to be the one who doesn't have someone to turn to and blow kisses at or call "Babe."

It sucks on a Friday night when you want to go out, but all of your friends are too busy at a husband's work event, or watching *Shark Tank* on the couch, or telling you they no longer have the energy to dance until 4:00 a.m. with a group of sweaty strangers.

But, my sweet dear, let me tell you, it especially sucks at weddings.

The friends who used to say "I do" to Jägerbomb shot after Jägerbomb shot after Jägerbomb shot and laugh endlessly at the idea of spending the rest of their lives on the couch with the same guy, are going to say "I dos" of a different kind.

But, hey, it's not because they look down on you or don't love you or want to make you feel so utterly embarrassed you'd rather hide under the table with bread crumbs and bits of romaine lettuce. I think they're hoping that you'll one day feel the same magical, googly-eyed things they felt when they found love, even if you're not in the mood or ready or interested yet.

Isn't that what we do when we love someone?

We ignore what they want and do exactly what we think is best for them. Even if we're wrong, even if we go a step too far, even if we have no idea what we're doing. Love makes us crazy, my sweet dear. It does.

So zip up that bridesmaid dress, put on the boldest-colored lipstick you have in your makeup bag, drink a cup of green tea (it'll calm you down), and go.

Go to the wedding and dance with your imaginary boyfriend during the slow songs and exchange Facebook info with the souls beside you at table 10 who you'll probably never see again, and when the bride whispers that she has someone dashing for you to meet, smile, shake his hand, and know, just know, that half the people there, the ones taking care of their drunk-by-9:00-p.m. husbands, are envying you just a little bit. Your choices, your freedom, your life.

You still have the magic and the googly-eyed first moments of love coming your way. So when that bouquet is flying in the air, stick your arms out and grab it, as if there's a full floor of people who want it as well.

Just like I know you can.

All my love,
Jen Glantz

chapter twenty

Eggs Sunny-Side Frozen

My favorite place to hide out after "getting lucky" on a date—which means I caught the guy picking his nose with the same hand he was using to eat our shared platter of chips and dip—is the grocery store. There's good lighting there, and it smells nice. Plus, they usually have free samples of some kind of crockpot creation served on saltines and minicups of instant coffee near the pastry aisle. It's as if they know that my postdate, unlucky-in-love self needs a late-night, carb-loaded, caffeine-filled pick-me-up.

I've learned to go to Costco—which has a plethora of samples—right after a nasty breakup, but for a single bad date, my neighborhood grocery store usually does the trick. It's enough to help me get my mind off boogers and satisfy my stomach too.

Mmm, the avocados look ripe today. Maybe I'll pick up a few and make guacamole. Do I even know how to make gua-

camole? Maybe I'll whip up a batch of cookies instead. But not from scratch. I'm no blonde Betty Crocker. I'll get one of those Break 'n Bake cookie rolls. Kale! I need some kale. Maybe I'll make a kale smoothie and then kale chips. Wait a minute, what about kale cookies?

I'm in the middle of my posttraumatic grocery shopping/ therapy session, stuffing a strawberry Pop Tart from a half-opened box into my mouth when I feel my phone buzz in my left hand.

Please don't be Ben the Booger Monster. I shut my eyes tightly and say a prayer near the melons. *Please be somebody, anybody, else.*

It's my mom. I let out a sigh of relief, lean against a display of candy apples, and inhale the pure caramel bliss as I answer my phone.

"Maybe you should freeze your eggs," my mom says the minute I pick up the phone, skipping the small talk.

What an interesting idea, I think, briefly wondering how my mom knows I'm in a grocery store at 9:00 p.m. on a Tuesday before suddenly remembering that moms, like clairvoyants, just seem to know it all.

I wonder if freezing eggs makes them last longer? I'll definitely have a lot left over after the kale cookies, and I am going to be out of town for four days. This mom of mine, she's always thinking about how to save me a penny. What a dime she is!

"Okay, good idea. I guess I should also freeze my bread and my bananas too?" I say. I'm on my third Pop Tart and fourth sample of Folgers espresso, so I'm up for anything.

"No, no," she says impatiently. "I was talking to a guy at the gym today about you and *your* eggs."

This is getting a little odd, I think to myself.

"He's an OB/GYN and mentioned that since you're twenty-seven and not in a serious relationship, you might want to freeze your eggs."

Oh. Those *eggs.* It sinks in almost immediately, like a sudden onset of acid reflux after eating too much tomato sauce, and I understand how wrong I was. Moms aren't like clairvoyants; they're like Time Warner Cable representatives, always saying the wrong thing at the wrong time.

I let out a laugh that's so maniacal that other shoppers near me drop their bags of whole wheat pasta and run away.

"Mom." I take a Lamaze-like deep breath, attempting to remain calm. "Why are you talking about my female reproductive organs and their potential expiration date at the gym?"

"He just asked me about your marital status," she goes on, casually, as if she'd been talking about me to Great Aunt Rita or Rabbi Solomon, not a stranger as he bench-pressed a hundred pounds. "He asked about your dating life, and I told him it could use some work."

That was a nice way of describing it. If my dating track record had a FICO score, it would be in the 500 range. Lenders would view me as high risk, which is also how I viewed most of my dating prospects.

I tend to date guys who are traffic signs. Yield: I have commitment issues. Stop: I'll never be able to love you as much as you love me. Caution: There's a dead-end up ahead, baby. The Mr. Wrong Ways, Slow Downs, Do Not Enters.

Initially it didn't occur to me that this is a problem; after all, I'm just a girl in her late twenties, casually dating and trying to figure out how to tap into her 401(k) to pay off her pesky American Express bills. It wasn't until a support group of my married, almost-married, and want-to-be-married-ASAP friends started analyzing my dating techniques and making me aware of my biological clock that I started to think, *Why do my life plans look like scribbled directions on a used Starbucks napkin?*

"You have a type, you know?" my three-months-pregnant, two-kids-deep friend said to me one evening while we were setting up her tub for bath time. "Unemployed." She stuck up one finger, preparing to tick off a whole list of issues. "Introverted. Doesn't know where he'll be in six months."

I fumbled around with a rubber ducky dressed in a St. Patty's Day outfit, making him zoom across the foamy bathtub water. I wanted to object, deny her ludicrous claims, tell her she was wrong, that you can't group people into buckets based on shared traits when it comes to matters of the heart. But I knew she was right. She was able to summarize my last three flings with three blunt—and true—observations.

I surrendered peacefully, sticking both suds-soaked hands up in the air. "So?"

"Maybe it's time to catch up to the rest of us and break your mold. Date someone different?" She rubbed her hands in a circle around her belly, her own genie in a bottle of sorts. "Date like you have a plan."

I rolled my eyes, mumbling under my breath, "I'll date because I still can."

I tried dating like that before, like I have a five-year game plan in my back pocket and I'm looking for someone, on date 1, to go along with it. Want to know how those dates always end? Poorly. I find myself wondering if I would be absolutely content waking up next to them in sixty-five years, and this is before the appetizers even show up.

"What am I supposed to ask these guys on date 1?" I asked, imagining myself in front of them, sipping my happy-hour-priced wine. "'Where do you see yourself in say ten to fifteen years?' 'Do you want your kids to grow up religious?' 'How do you feel about retiring in Boca Raton?'" All I really want to ask, right off the bat, is where his last adventure was and if he'd like to be a little reckless with me and go skydiving next month in India.

"No," she said, rolling her eyes and wiping the bubbles off her rose-gold wedding band with an *Aladdin*-themed towel. "But you can at least ask them if this is going to be a giant waste of your time."

There'll come a day when you'll notice that your Facebook newsfeed has become a game of "Who's Who?" None of your friends have the same last name as they did when you knew them in kindergarten or high school, let alone five years ago in college, and it doesn't help that their profile pictures are no longer of them taking a duck-faced selfie; those pictures have been replaced by their diapered child wearing a one-sie that says "Potty Like a Rock Star." The days of scrolling through your newsfeed and laughing out loud at photos that your friends posted at 4:00 a.m. from a cash-only bar on the Lower East Side are over. Eyes half open, hands in the air on the dance floor, strobe lights, crushed beer cans—that's all been replaced by videos of their babies burping up applesauce and status updates about how little Gemma Jane took her first poo-poo in the big girl's toilet.

I have no idea how I became the super-single friend. It's

as if I woke up in an alternative universe one day, looked around, and realized everyone else had moved on. I'm the one who gets dating advice spoon-fed to me by married friends who, eight years ago, believed marriage was for boring people. How did all of my friends turn into these family-oriented adults before their twenty-seventh birthday while I was still off living in my third state, working on my fourth job, and dating my fifth Mr. Wrong since graduation? The Venn diagram of our lives is shrinking in the center, and the only way to make sure there's still some overlap is for me to be okay with living my life and to stay involved in theirs—as a friend and as an occasional babysitter (for fifteen dollars an hour, thank you very much.)

I put all the ingredients to make my kale cookies on the check-out counter and tell my mom to put the topic of egg freezing back on the shelf. She virtually pinky-promises me she'll make an effort to stop discussing my dating life—or the time left on my biological clock—with people at the gym.

But I have a feeling it'll come up again—just not the very next morning, at 7:00 a.m., while I'm brushing my teeth and watching *The Today Show*. There it is, a banner flashing across my TV screen: *"Buying peace of mind," more young women save up for egg freezing*.

Matt Lauer is telling me—and every other girl who can't hear the chime of wedding bells in the near future—that it might be smart for me to put my goods in a cooler.

Listen here, Matt: the only thing us single gals want to hear this early on a Wednesday morning is some comforting half-lie, like how coffee is good at preventing wrinkles or how chocolate helps us lose weight.

Welcome to my biological clock dream team, I say out loud to Mr. Lauer. *Make room, mom's friend at the gym and fertile married friends.*

I have two and a half years left before I'll be blowing out thirty candles on top of a Carvel Fudgie the Whale ice cream cake. Even if I go on eighteen Tinder dates a week and make goo-goo eyes at the man of my dreams, I'm not so sure that I'm prepared, right now, for marriage and kids. I want all of that eventually, when I'm ready—not when the world or, unfortunately, my reproductive parts, tell me I *have* to be ready. I have a feeling I'll need to be steered onto that path, slowly, as one is led into a haunted house: with baby steps and maybe a blindfold.

All of a sudden, before I'm even able to properly caffeinate myself, I feel a suffocating amount of pressure to change my dating ways and explore the option of freezing my future babies. Everything around me starts to get blurry.

"Kerri?" I cry out, desperate for backup. Because what are roommates for if not to be there for you when you're about to pass out on the bathroom floor because your life is literally spinning faster than you can catch up with it? But she's still asleep, wisely avoiding eye-opener hour with Matt Lauer.

I'm going to pass out, I start whispering out loud, grabbing onto the edges of the bathroom sink, breathing heavily into a roll of bargain toilet paper I ordered off Amazon for ninety-nine cents per roll. *I'm going to pass out. I'm going to . . .*

When I wake up, I see Matt's eyes shining right into mine from the now-muted TV screen, blinking and winking as if he and I both know what I should do. I pick up my phone and call for help.

"Siri," I say, knowing she'll be there to listen to my latest quarter-life crisis; she always is. "Where does one go to freeze their eggs in New York City?"

I immediately try to cancel that request. I want to start over. I want to be more specific, because I don't have health insurance or the kind of disposable income that makes me privy to luxuries like seeing a Broadway show, shopping at Bergdorf Goodman, or freezing my eggs. "Siri, is there a Groupon deal for egg freezing in New York City?"

Later, after getting nowhere with Siri, I decide to take a stroll over to the fertility clinic and chat with someone in person. I have a lot of questions, like how many eggs they freeze. And where they freeze them. And what happens if the place goes out of business in five years. Do I get my eggs back from them, and if so, do I put them in my freezer next to the pot roast and rugelach? How unromantic would it be if, let's say, five years from now, I have a nice guy over for dinner and he pulls out a Tupperware from the freezer and asks if he should warm it up as a side dish? I would have to say, "No, sweetheart. Those are not pork dumplings; those are eggs. From my ovaries. Extracted through my you-know-what."

I don't plan ahead for anything, so maybe everyone around me is right. Maybe since marriage and kids aren't on my immediate to-do list, I should go ahead and keep a little something stored away for a rainy day—or, say, when I finally decide I'm ready and my body decides that I'm not.

I find myself in an intense staring contest with the glass doors of a midtown Manhattan fertility clinic, pacing back and forth outside, twisting the door open and shut, and shutting and opening it again before I'm finally ready to take a couple of steps and go inside.

"Well, hello there, sweet peach," the receptionist drawls. She has thick, boomerang-shaped eyebrows and hair that almost touches the ceiling. I practically crawl toward her.

"Go ahead and tell me your name, age, and health insurance provider."

Her questions give me something to focus on—and alleviate the urge to run right back outside.

"I'm Jen, I'm twenty-seven, and I don't have health insurance."

"No problem, honey bear," she says, her southern accent making my heart feel like mush, like I'm the most special person who has ever walked through these doors. "We have quite a few payment plan options for you."

Slow down, lady. I snap out of the cradle of her kindness and southern charm and realize I'm probably going to have to stop at Bank of America and apply for a loan on behalf of my neglected love life.

"Fill out this paperwork, baby girl, take a seat, and the doctor will see you in about four minutes."

She hands me a packet of paperwork, and I take a seat in a white velvet chair trimmed with green thread. Everything is happening so fast. I needed a moment to settle in, look at the soothing watercolor paintings on the wall, flip through a parenting magazine, and unwrap a hard candy or two. I figured I would swing by, get a tour of the joint, and come back eventually—not fill out paperwork and make the hard decisions now.

"Actually, I'm not here to do anything today," I say, getting up and handing her back the blank paperwork. I'm terrified they're going to stick me on an operating table the second I sign on the dotted line. I'm not ready for all of this. Not now.

"Don't worry, sugar cube. Today we're only chatting," she says. I wonder if she keeps an Excel spreadsheet of ridiculous yet soothing names to call prospective patients who walk through the door with their knees knocking together in pure and utter fear.

She leads me down a bright hallway into a room with black and white photos of the beach on the wall. I wonder what it would be like to be a hermit crab or an abalone snail; they both stay fertile for life. They're in no rush to find their mate. They are my spirit animals.

The room I'm sitting in is sterile and stark, as if it was painted over with a coat of Wite-Out. There's a circular table in the middle of the room with one box of Kleenex on top. I stuff a few in my purse, because tissues are expensive.

From my previous life experience, I know that when there's a table with nothing else on it but a half-empty box of tissues, that means there's a good chance someone is going to cry. And I know it isn't going to be me.

The doctor walks in and shakes my hand. He has a thin mustache and thick glasses, his shirt buttoned to the top. He starts off our conversation with a question I wish I thought about before I walked into the clinic.

"Why are you here?"

"Matt Lauer told me to come," I answer automatically.

He tilts his head and narrows his eyes. "The guy on TV?" he asks, wondering if maybe Matt and I are related. Perhaps he's my uncle, or I'm his distant cousin.

"Well, I'm twenty-seven," I say, jumping right into the reason for our cryptic exchange on a Wednesday afternoon.

"You're only twenty-seven?" he asks, scanning the paperwork I never filled out. "Then why are you here?"

I look at him, reminding him of my previous answer before going on. "People," I start to say, raising my eyebrows and lowering my voice, as if those people are in this room with us. If he hasn't deemed me crazy already, I'm sure he's marking that box on my chart right now.

"People say that since I'm almost thirty and not on the fast path toward marriage, that I should consider sticking my babies in the freezer." I point down toward my pelvis.

He leans back in his chair, removes his glasses, and nibbles on one of the stems, probably thinking that what he thought would be a quick ten-minute consultation about egg fertility is now going to turn into a thirty-minute therapy session.

"You're only twenty-seven," he says, this time more slowly, in case I missed it the first time. "You have years, years, and years before you should start thinking about doing this. People do it to have as an insurance plan, but I think you're a little too young for this option."

"Well, I'm not in a serious relationship." I clear my throat, holding back that misty feeling I get before tears fall. "I'm not in any kind of relationship, so I don't see myself married with kids or pregnant anytime soon, I guess."

"How do you know?" *If only he knew.* Clearly no one sent him the file on Jen Glantz's botched dating attempts.

"I guess I don't know. I guess I have no idea."

He puts his glasses back on. "There's a lot of talk in the media and online about egg freezing, and how it's better if you do it younger. But I don't think that's true." He clasps his hands together on the table. "It's a slippery slope. Are people going to start doing it when they turn eighteen? Is this going to be the new sweet sixteen gift?"

My eyes bulge at his honesty. Shouldn't he be trying to convince me why I should go home and cash in one of my savings bonds or investment CDs for some pricey procedure?

"There's no right age, Ms. Glantz. There's not even a guarantee that this works." I exhale a load of pressure and inhale the smell of hand sanitizer. "I can tell you that I think you're too young, but if you find yourself in the same position you're in now at, say, thirty-four, then come back and we'll chat."

I look confused, disappointed, like I'm being pulled in two different directions by competing schools of advice that my body doesn't want to subscribe to either way. The world is telling me to freeze my eggs, and the guy with the freezing power is telling me to get back on JDate and live my life.

I get up from the chair and head for the door to leave. He asks me to sit back down. Maybe he's changed his mind; maybe someone just buzzed him with a file on my hopeless rom-com of a love life.

"My daughter is a few years older than you," he says, taking off his doctor jacket and putting on his invisible dad baseball cap. "And the other night, over dinner, I asked her about freezing her eggs."

I let out a nervous laugh. "I bet that dinner didn't end well."

"She still won't talk to me," he says, laughing and shaking his head. "But all I meant by it was, 'You've been married for a few years. Have you thought about having babies?' But I didn't know how to say that directly. Sometimes people don't always know how to say in the right way what they mean."

I don't know why, but in that moment, I start crying, unraveling those stolen tissues from my purse like a magician pulling scarves out of his sleeve.

"So your married friends, your parents, and this Matt Lauer guy, what they're really trying to say is, 'Do you want to have babies eventually?' They care about you and want to make sure you think about that before it's too late. If you don't, you'll really have to spend a lot of money to get other people to help you think about it."

I smile at him, completely reassured. He opens the door and hands me the box of tissues.

"Keep them. And Jen," he says, as if we're longtime pals, as if we often have conversations around circular tables about my reproductive organs. "Enjoy every moment of your plan A, and don't feel so rushed to find your plan B."

To me, there's never been an age limit on finding love or starting a family of my own. It happens whenever it happens, and when it happens for me, whether it's at age thirty-one or forty-five, I'll figure out the details then.

I walk by the receptionist's desk one last time.

"Call us when you're ready, cutie pie." She hands me the doctor's business card, and I clutch it close to my body for a couple of minutes before sticking it in the bottom of my purse to live, for maybe years, beside the expired Bed Bath & Beyond coupons, loose Tic-Tacs, and uncapped pens.

"When I'm ready," I say, exiting the doors and realizing I'm in no rush to figure out when that will be.

chapter twenty-one

DTW to AWOL

It's 3:00 a.m. and I'm at the airport, alone, in Detroit, a city that I've never been to before, looking at the reflection of a person who faintly resembles an exhausted version of myself in the bathroom mirror. I haven't closed my eyes in twenty-three hours. It's been a while since I've stayed up that long, but I've been stuck; I've had no other place to go.

I lean forward, my lips tingling centimeters away from the smooth surface of the glass. The face I see has more lines on it than I remember, my forehead is beginning to look like the staff on a piece of sheet music, and though my acne has packed up its bags and skipped town years ago, it has left its mark on me like an ex-boyfriend. My eyes are drooping into cartoonish teardrops, like a supersad puppy.

My body is trying to tell me something. It's telling me I can't keep going like this. And I'm finally starting to believe it.

Like crazy, I am. I step out of my heels, surveying the damage on my soles, and count the blisters that form a constellation-like pattern on my Achilles tendon.

Beside me is my cell phone, but I have no one to call. Everyone is asleep. Besides, it doesn't work anyway. Last night I dropped it down a staircase, and it bounced off thirteen steps before I was able to catch it. The screen is cracked into a pattern of desolate streams on a map. I have to squint and turn and twist it just to see anything, which I do now—and discover that I have a voice mail from a bride asking me where I am, an email from my boss wanting to talk to me first thing on Monday, and a text from a guy I met at the wedding last night, asking when he'll see me again.

He won't.

"What are you trying to do to yourself?" I ask, my breath fogging up the mirror.

The bathroom attendant hears me, so I look at her and wave, apologizing silently for disturbing her early-morning sink cleaning with my gloomy monologue.

"You are not some kind of superhero," I mumble into a rough paper napkin that could sharpen a knife.

"If you could have any superpower in the world, what would it be?"

You know that a date is taking a sharp turn south when you start asking each other the kind of questions you would hear in an interview with Google. The second he asks where I see myself in five years, I'm going to tap out.

"I don't know," I said, giggling nervously into a plate of tortilla chips. *Is there a superpower that lets me see how this date is going to end? Can I skip ahead to the future and find out if he's going to pick up the check? Walk me home? Lean in when we finally say good-bye and engage in some tonsil hockey?*

"Come on," he prodded. "Pick one."

I took another sip of my margarita, refusing to play along. It tasted like raspberry and Lysol.

"What would you choose?" I asked the waiter, who was delicately removing the guacamole-coated silverware from our table, probably placing a mental bet on how quickly this first-date relationship would come to an end.

"That's easy," he responded, arm full of empty plates, feet shuffling as he went about his business. He stared directly into my eyes, his gaze focused like a laser beam. "I would live multiple lives."

Did he know something about me from my dinner order? Two veggie tacos with beans, two without; two tacos with cheese, two without.

I felt my body flush and my cheeks glow red, as if he'd just exposed me to the world.

"Jen likes that one," my date said, reading into my blush. He was right, and suddenly, I realized, so was the waiter.

Because I was living a double life.

There will come a day, at least once every year, when you will find yourself in the middle of a full-blown emotional break-down, an episode when you lose your cool and your ability to be a functioning, nonhysterical member of society. When you'll be ugly-crying into a bowl of cereal or onto a copy machine you've used a hundred times before that Just. Isn't. Co-operating. When you feel like nothing in your life, not your job or your long-term relationship or your financial investments with Citibank, are going well, though everyone observing you on Instagram or even from a cubicle thirteen feet away thinks that you're fine, that you're perfectly put together, that you're smitten with all of the above. But you know you're not.

I beg you, when that moment happens, try to be in a place where you can hide. Like the back row of a movie theater, or in the dressing room at Target, surrounded by ten items or less. But if it's going to be in public, and most likely it will be, maybe it could at least be somewhere appropriate, like a Rangers game, where the people around you are shouting like cavemen or at the grocery store; people are always losing their minds in the fruit aisle, anxiously squeezing lemons and limes and asking the man behind the produce counter to inspect a bag of plums for them to make sure they're organic.

I couldn't help myself. I was in an airport bathroom, wearing a shredded bridesmaid dress, a hot curling iron in one hand and a loaf of bread in the other, when I had *my* full-blown mental breakdown and identity crisis of 2015.

The loaf of bread wasn't mine. It was from a nice Orthodox woman who found me crying underneath the row of sinks, in a happy-baby yoga pose. She saw me on her way to the third stall from the left, ran out, asked her husband for something that would make the girl on the bathroom floor stop crying, and came back with a fresh-baked challah. L'chaim to her.

I should have tried to make it into the bathroom stall before having this breakdown. People have meltdowns inside stalls all the time, which is the reason they have doors. But it was 7:00 a.m., and a handful of flights were about to board, making it prime time for people to take one last pee. I couldn't outlast them.

I took stock of the numbers. I had been at the airport for four hours for a flight I needed to make three hours ago. I was working as a bridesmaid in two weddings, in two different states, in just one weekend. The moment I was done dancing to "Closing Time" at the first one, I grabbed a party favor, hugged the bride and groom good-bye, and hopped into a taxi to zoom to the airport; I had a 5:00 a.m. flight to Philadelphia to catch, another aisle to walk down, and another set of dance moves to unleash at my second wedding reception in under twenty-four hours. But right before we were about to board, the gate agent got on the loudspeaker and told us there were "some problems" with our plane.

"Deep breaths," I said out loud, as if this were my own personal, calming mantra. *Some problems? Okay, that's okay. They're not* huge *problems. This can be fixed with a hammer and a nail in no time, right?*

Wrong.

"Some problems" lasted over two hours, and by now it was 7:00 a.m., and the gate agent said our flight was officially canceled until further notice. By now, I was supposed to be 583 miles away from here, in the bride's suite, hair in curlers, face airbrushed, dress going through one final pass under the steamer.

The kind lady with the bread in her hand asked me, "What's your name?" trying to get me to snap back into human mode and out of deranged bridesmaid mode.

"It's Jen . . . umm," I thought carefully, wrapping my head around who I was talking to and what the situation was. "Jen Glantz."

The previous night I was Jen Smith, and that day I was Jen Finkelstein. On Monday morning, I would go back to my desk, at my full-time job, as Jen Glantz. I would be as many as three different people in less than forty-eight hours. I was exhausted.

She looked down at the dirty tiled floor. Items from my carry-on bag were scattered everywhere, as if I were making myself at home in a sorority house. An eyelash curler, a strapless bra, a pair of foldable flats. In her hands was an escort card with the name Jen Smith on it from the night before. She rubbed her fingers around the rough edges of the card stock, studying the name and looking back at me, then down once more.

"Who are you?" she asked again, this time observing the wrinkles on my blush-colored bridesmaid dress and the false eyelash glue pilling on my eyelids.

Emotional breakdowns like these don't just show up randomly, like the G train whenever it wants to on a Sunday afternoon, or an ex-boyfriend who decides to ask you out for coffee after five years of radio silence. They brew in our stomachs and erupt at the smallest, most innocuous trigger. It could happen while you're trying to find your black suede wedges while your friend is waiting for you outside, or when you realize you have no idea where Jane Street is in Manhattan and your meeting was supposed to start twenty minutes ago. In my case, it was because my flight was delayed indefinitely. But that's not even why I was on the floor, choking on my own mascara-streaked tears. It was all of the other things: the background characters and the understudies who lived inside me, delivering competing monologues, filling my head with noise. Meanwhile, I, the lead actor, was slumped over in the corner, fanning myself with a Playbill.

"Let me ask you this," the bread lady said, calming me down with a handful of Cheerios she pulled out of her pocket. A magician of breakfast foods. "Why are you in a bridesmaid dress?"

I was breathing slowly, deeply, like I was about to go into labor on the bathroom floor of Terminal 2.

"I'm a bridesmaid for hire," I said cautiously, knowing there was a chance she was going to alert the authorities—or my friends who were already eager to toss me into the loony bin. "I'm late to work, at a wedding, and I can't lose this job because I'm about to lose my other one."

It had been almost a year and a half since I started my business, and my life was a complete mess. Nobody knew any of that because I did a good job of hiding it behind six hundred milligrams of caffeine and carefully written Facebook posts. But there I was, spilling the truth to a lady who was just trying to pee and get home to Crown Heights in Brooklyn. Her eyes fluttered like the wings of a butterfly. But even after all I told her, she didn't try to fly away.

"I work nine hours a day as a copywriter, and then I come home and try to run a business out of my office, which is really just my full-size mattress. I meet brides for dress fittings on my lunch breaks. Sometimes I tell the HR department that I have a doctor's appointment, but really I'm running twenty-five blocks to Fox News to film a segment for a show before

I have to hustle back in time for a 3:00 p.m. conference call with my boss."

Come to think of it, the people I worked with must've thought I had some kind of strange ailment, one that had me leaving work disheveled and returning with my hair combed and curled and my face painted like a clown.

Sometimes guys at work would tell me that their wives saw me on TV that morning, canoodling with Matt Lauer, or in the late-afternoon, high-fiving Steve Harvey, and I would tell them they must be mistaken. That I hadn't left my desk all morning. I was a terrible liar, though I was becoming an expert escape artist.

"I'm not a businesswoman," I said to the bread lady. "I majored in poetry."

She nodded her head, trying to relate. "You know what's happening? You're living two people's lives with one person's heart."

My date leaned forward, excited to whip out an SAT word from his past. "There's a name for that."

The waiter put his tray of dirty plates down on an empty table beside us. "Oh yeah?"

"Yeah. It's called bilocation."

"Sounds like something the doctor prescribes for constipation." I laughed so hard, snorting directly into a dish of mild salsa.

"Bilocation," the waiter repeated out loud, hoping if he said it enough times, it would somehow become real.

"My superpower would be to find a way to be okay with living just one life at a time," I said.

"Sounds boring," my date said, clinking his empty glass of Patrón against the fistful of dirty forks in the waiter's hand.

The bread lady wiped away my tears with a tissue, and then something happened. Something made me realize why falling apart on the floor of an airport bathroom in the arms of a complete stranger, who was in danger of missing her own flight, is never a good idea: she started crying too.

Airports are the worst place to have a mental breakdown. Everybody around you is already on the verge of having one themselves because security confiscated their extra-large jar of organic peanut butter, or they realized that their gate, F17, is in a different terminal than all the other F gates are and now they have to navigate their way back to the AirTrain in thirty minutes.

So when it happens to you—and it will happen to you—don't do it in an airport, because if you do, it will create a domino effect. I was ninety minutes into my breakdown, and now a crowd of women had gathered beside me and the bread lady, oohing and ahhing over us on the bathroom floor.

"We're going to get you on a flight to Philadelphia," one of them said between her own strangled sobs.

"Yeah!" they all exclaimed in unison as if we were at a feminist gathering in the 1960s.

I left the bathroom with the cord of my curling iron wrapped around my shoulder and my carry-on bag unzipped, wedding invitations and Band-Aids streaming behind me. I walked up to the gate agent's desk with an army of equally unstable women behind me. *How's that for oversized baggage, JetBlue?*

"My name is Jen Glantz," I said to Rhonda, the lady behind the counter, her hair fastened together with a sheet of bobby pins and her lipstick melting onto her two front teeth. She looked at me like whatever I was about to say, she'd heard many times before. "I'm just wondering if, um . . ."

She tapped her pen against the linoleum desk, rolling her eyes before I even finished my sentence.

"Listen, I need to get to Philadelphia in the next two hours," I went on. By now, my Sisterhood of Traveling Emotional Breakdowns had hugged me good-bye, wished me luck, and dispersed to their own gates.

"Yeah?" she said, pointing to a line of people behind me fanning themselves with expired plane tickets. "So does everybody else. Next!"

I turned around to the man walking forward to take my spot at Rhonda's desk and held up my index finger, silently asking him to give us a few more minutes alone. He took three steps back because when someone asks you to do something, and she is in a beaten-up bridesmaid dress, with makeup stains all over her face, her hair a bee's nest of tangled curls, you have to do it.

I leaned forward. "I'm about to get fired from my real job, and if I don't make it to this wedding," I said, pointing at my dress like Vanna White, "I'm going to be fired from this job too. So could you please do me a favor and book me on another flight so that I can stop scaring these passengers with my unstable emotions and embarrassing airport attire???"

She picked up her walkie-talkie and I took a few steps back, all the way back. I couldn't end up in airport security looking like this. I couldn't have the TSA calling up my parents and making them hop on a last-minute flight from Florida to Detroit to pick me up from the airport holding facility. Imagine what the car ride home would be? It would be 1,214 miles of *Jennifer, we told you so. We told you that you were doing too much of that and too much of this. You should have focused all your energy on one thing: dating what's-his-name instead.*

I leaned down against a metal beam in the middle of the terminal and rested my head in my clammy hands. I had no place else to go.

A girl with a tricep full of colorful tattoos sat down next to me, plugged in her cell phone, and snapped pictures of the crowded airport.

"Hey," she said, handing me a wet wipe from the inside of her backpack. "You look like you could really use this."

"What makes you think that?" I said, laughing as I grabbed the wipe from her hand and began rubbing off all of the gunk off my face.

We weren't going anywhere, any of us. They were sending more people in lime green vests with tool belts strapped around their waists onto our plane to fix it. Even if we left three hours from now, I would miss the whole thing. I wouldn't be there for the bride to walk down the aisle. I wouldn't even be there for a slice of almond vanilla wedding cake.

"I saw your performance over there," she said. "I wanted to give you a standing ovation. Or a Xanax."

I looked at her with eyes that said hug me, and she did.

"You know," she went on, handing me a candy gummy worm. "You're not the only twentysomething girl in the history of girls who's trying to do two things at once."

I blew my nose into a sock from my still-open carry-on bag.

"What I'm trying to say is, you're not alone. Consider yourself a modern-day Cinderella."

"I bet Cinderella didn't have this many blisters," I said, showing her the pads of my feet.

I wondered what would happen to me if I left one of these on-sale Guess shoes from the clearance rack of DSW on the floor of the airport. Would my Prince Charming find it and locate me inside my tiny apartment in Midtown East? Probably not. Airport security would confiscate the shoe and swab the insides to see if there were any chemicals on it before sticking it into one of their industrial-sized trash cans.

The girl sitting beside me was wrong. I was nothing like a modern-day Cinderella. I was more like a modern-day Tasmanian devil.

And then the knights in shining armor showed up. If you consider brightly colored construction vests to be armor.

I watched as the airplane repairmen exited the plane, and my heart soared with hope. Rhonda got on the loudspeaker and cleared her throat to get the attention of the crowd of aggravated passengers. "Good news," she said, flatly. "You can all get on the plane now."

I hugged my new friend once more and thanked her for the candy, the wet wipe, and the early-morning quarter-life-crisis perspective.

The plane would take off in a couple of minutes, and I would make it in time for the ceremony, right before the second bridesmaid took her first step down the aisle. I would do the cha-cha slide on the dance floor beside the other guests I'd just met that night, and I'd give a toast to a lifetime of love and adventure to a bride and groom I'd also just met that night. Finally, I would make it home and crawl out of another polyester dress and toss on my cut-up Van Halen T-shirt. On Monday, I would walk up to my boss with a fresh cup of coffee in hand and listen as he said this was hard for him but he had to let me go. The company was downsizing and I was on the list of people getting laid off.

I would be okay because I'd already met my quota for emotional breakdowns that month, right? Wrong. But I would find a way to walk out of there and say good-bye, going back, once again, to a life where I could be just one person, with one job, perhaps even with a new goal of finding just one person to love.

The previous sixteen months were an adventure, an experiment that mixed up all the pieces of my life and bound them together with dental floss. I entered people's lives at the last minute, I sat in front of TV cameras in front of national audiences, I went to work every day, and I came home at night to another job. I was slowly becoming so many things to so many people that I was losing every part of myself.

I couldn't handle it all, okay? But who were the right people to admit that to if not the strangers at DTW airport before 9:00 a.m.?

"You're not a superhero," the bread lady said, boarding a plane at the gate next to mine. "You are *just* Jen Glantz."

I sat down in 9B, in between two men in business suits. *I'm just Jen Glantz.* I puffed up the layers of my tattered bridesmaid dress and slipped my feet into a fresh pair of socks, realizing, for the first time in 456 days, that I was okay with that.

chapter twenty-two

Good-Bye, Cold Feet

I am no good at good-byes. It's my tragic character flaw and my own personal kryptonite. It's also what makes me a prime candidate for the show *Hoarders*. I stuff my dresser drawers, kitchen cabinets, and empty suitcases with things that no longer serve a purpose in my life. Things like a clown costume I wore for Halloween in 2010, twenty bottles of Shout stain remover that I won years ago through an online opt-in contest, and about twelve rolls of wrapping paper, though I can't remember the last time I bought somebody something that needed to be covered in shiny paper with a print of little elephants swimming in a pool. (That roll was only fifteen cents at CVS—I had to grab it.)

I'm even worse at saying good-bye to people, even when it's casual, mutual, or forced by an expired parking meter. The second I feel the phone call leaning toward pregnant pauses or the coffee date beginning to stall out over empty mugs, I try to keep things going as long as I can. I rattle on as if I'm on auto-pilot and watch as the other person fiddles with the crumbs of a long-gone croissant or stifles a yawn. But the very second I feel an, "All right, well . . ." or an "Okay, I'm taking off . . ." about to come out of their mouth, I wrestle on my coat, smile wide, and bolt toward the exit door. Or if I'm at home, blab-bing on the couch, I keep things easy: I just hang up.

By now, my good friends know to tread lightly around me. Even their reaching for the handle of their purse and giving me a blasé, "This was great . . ." is enough to make me dine and dash. But for those lucky victims who meet me or call me for the first time, they always send a follow-up text that asks, "Did I say the wrong thing?" or "Did you just lose service?" I always reply with the truth: I am not good at lingering good-byes.

I've been known to leave jobs in the most jaw-dropping and infamous way possible, whether or not the leaving is on my terms or theirs. I left my first job in New York City by telling my boss, who, I was fully convinced was the brother of Cruella de Vil, that I loved him with every ounce of my beating heart before handing him my resignation letter and sneaking down the fire escape. At my second job, when rumors of layoffs were floating through the air, my boss called me into his office, shut the door, and told me he had some bad news for me. That's when I got my tush off the bright yellow chair, went straight to my desk, shoved the stapler and the family-sized jar of peanuts into my purse, and saw myself out of that place before he had the chance to tap into his inner Donald Trump and announce that I was fired.

But saying good-bye on dates is its own cup of tea—the

aggressive, overly brewed, undrinkable kind, in my opinion. Whether he's someone I'm Thanksgiving thankful that I'll never see again, or someone I'm finger-crossing will text me the second I get home, my response at the end of the night is always the same: as soon as he starts talking about how much fun he had, or how those were quite possibly two of the oddest hours of his life, I pull back and run in the opposite direction, sending an air hug his way as I race down the stairs toward the rat-infested subway station. If a guy wants to give me a smooch or a warm bear hug, it needs to be done at the spur of the moment, at the most nonsensical time—say, right as I'm buttering my third dinner roll of the night or getting all hot and heavy over my stance on global warming. If he waits for the end of the date, it's always too late. I'll be all the way on the other side of Manhattan island by the time he figures out what the heck just happened.

Saying good-bye means that something is over. Even if that something is temporary, like the end of an afternoon shopping trip to Target with your best college girlfriends, or something permanent, like an unexpected phone call in which your boyfriend of three years tells you he just doesn't love you anymore, saying good-bye leads to heartbreak. And I am not a masochist. I don't enjoy the pain of wondering when and if I'll see a person, a place, or a thing ever again. So I avoid the final hug, the see-you-soon closing statements, and turn the finality of a period into an ellipsis. If someone says good-bye and nobody hears it, does the good-bye really count? I am on team No Way, José with that one.

My therapist, also known as a couple of deep-diving Google searches and a scroll through WebMD, has told me that I hold

on to things longer than I should, which is a nice way of saying that I have something called separation anxiety. Dogs have
this, which is why they whimper when you leave them behind
and go about your day. I don't whimper; I just don't let the
person leave. That is why I've never successfully been able to
break up with someone before. I've tried and failed miserably,
approaching the conversation with an outlined script of how
to tell him it's time for us to part ways. Instead, I jabber on
about how I think we should spend even more time together
and suggest that maybe Taco Tuesday can become a real, con-
sistent thing with us.

I guess it's because I'm scared that I'm wrong. They might
not be the best match for me, they might be above average
in the lazy department, and they might revel in pushing my
buttons when I'm already coming to the table with my hair on
fire, but what if they change? Or maybe I can be the one to
change? What if it's too soon to know? What if they're the *one,
my one, my one and only,* and I'm about to prematurely kick
them to the curb with a be-all and end-all good-bye?

The last time I found myself in dire need of pulling the
plug on a three-month stint with a guy I could no longer
stomach sitting beside, even in a dark movie theater while
stuffing my face with popcorn and a large cup of Diet Coke,
the guy beat me to it. *Thank God.* But it wasn't that simple;
he didn't just leave me a voice mail detailing how this *thing*
between us was coming to an end, or send me a Facebook
message that said he would have to defriend me on social
media and in real life. He texted me, saying he didn't think
he could do *this* anymore, and asked if we could meet that
night to talk. Normally I wouldn't go, knowing that the in-

person conversation would end with me being Ms. Fix It, a tool belt full of promises buckled around my waist, or him slapping me in the face with verbal good-byes. But right as I went to swipe left and permanently delete the history of our text messages, a new message appeared on my phone from one of my brides. She asked if we could talk because she couldn't do this anymore.

"Listen, I just wanted to set boundaries with you." I called her on the way to meet my guy for our own dreaded good-bye. "I just wanted to put a stop to 4:00 a.m. texts about which style of garter you should buy. We can work this out!"

"No, no, Jen," she jumped in. "This isn't about you. This is about Matt and me. I just don't know anymore. I don't know if he's the one I want to marry."

This wouldn't be too alarming if, say, this conversation were happening any time but two days before her wedding. Tricia had hired me almost eleven months ago, and we'd spoken once a week since then. This was the first time she was telling me about her second thoughts, her ice-cold feet, her plans to perhaps call this whole wedding off. "What if there's somebody better out there for me? What if my real soul mate is sitting at a coffee shop, wearing a plaid long-sleeve shirt and unwrinkled khakis, coding a website, waiting for me to sit down next to him with my double-shot espresso and ask him for the Wi-Fi password?"

Little did she know she was talking to a loveless disaster. The kind of girl who breaks everything she touches, even poor guys' hearts. I was starting to believe I wouldn't know who the love of my life was even if his arms were wrapped around me and he was whispering the intimate details of our future together. How was I supposed to help her when half of the time I confused the feeling of falling in love with acid reflux?

But it was easy. It's always easier when someone else plays the role of fickle princess and you get to be her talking animal sidekick.

"I think," I began, trying to be a notch more credible than Google and a notch less credible than a licensed therapist, "there's no such thing as just *one* soul mate. There are a lot of people who could be really great for us, who could make our world shake. But if you have someone in your life you thoroughly enjoy and can put up with most of the time, maybe that's worth the risk of taking yourself off the market."

That, alone, was the scariest thing I'd learned about love, after finding it and losing it, and finding it again. Just because we've fallen in love, doesn't mean we have to stick with that person if that love turns into a mere and morbid uggghh. We don't get just one shot at love; I truly believe we get many. The trick is to recognize when we're really happy with someone and when it's time to move on.

"Have you found your person, Jen?"

In that moment, as I was crossing over to Third Avenue, it hit me. I had been talking to Tricia for almost a year now, and I knew everything about her: the kind of polyester sweaters she likes to wear from Express and the type of birth control she's on that regulates her cycles and her mood swings. But she didn't know much about me. To her, I was just this voice pumping advice over the phone. A buttoned-up professional who seemed to have it all figured out. But really, I was just good at helping other people make decisions, say their good-byes, decide when to hire a DJ and fire a caterer. Behind the phone, whenever I looked in the mirror, I was just a complete and utter disaster.

Isn't that just the way it is? We give Dear Abby–worthy advice to our friends, but for ourselves, we ignore the warning signs; we lay face-down on our beds and kick our legs up and down as we decide what to do and what not to do, when to stick around and when to pack up our bags and head west.

"Quite the opposite." I decided to tell Tricia the truth. "I'm on my way to get broken up with by a guy I was too scared to break up with myself."

"We're very different," she said.

"I hang on too long," I added, finishing her sentence.

"And maybe I run away too fast."

I remember a lady I used to work with once told me that the first time she got married, she walked down the aisle muttering under her breath, "Man, this is going to suck if I have to do this again." She had known weeks earlier that marrying this guy was not a good idea.

"How did you know?" I asked her, curiously.

"Because I never missed him when I left."

That was another thing about good-byes: either they were suffocating, like sitting inside of a helium balloon, or they were nothing at all. If you ever wanted to know how you really felt about someone or something, say good-bye to it.

"Matt makes me happy," she said, though both of us were old and mistake-riddled enough to know that happiness is never enough. "But what if I can find someone who makes me happier?"

"I can't help you decide whether you should marry Matt," I

told her, because that was the truth. Even if she told me everything about their relationship, I would still not know enough.
She was the only one who knew whether she was just having cold feet or listening to the rumblings of her gut. "But I
do think, right now, you should jump into your car and drive
somewhere far away, just for a little bit. See how you feel. Do
you want to go back home, or do you want to keep driving until
you reach the Arctic Circle?"

Outside, the air still carried a dense chill. It wasn't quite
summer yet, though everyone was breaking out the flip-flops
and jean shorts, hoping that it was. Mike was waiting for me,
tapping his toes against the battered sidewalk and leaning
against the scaffolding just outside the bar. I had just hung
up with Tricia, unsure if her car would be parked back in her
driveway tonight or on a boat to Santorini, but now it was time
to figure out my own love life.

"Hey, there," he said, leaning in for a hug. I let him have
one.

"Listen, I know what you're about to say." For the first time
in the history of my good-byes, I didn't run away. I curled my
toes, looked into his eyes, and stood there, like a child awaiting
punishment.

"I just don't know what happened, Jen. But I don't feel like
you're into this anymore."

Almost as bad as my breakup skills were my pretending
skills. It was written all over my face for weeks that I was holding on to something I wished would let me go.

"I'm really sorry," I said, grabbing his arm and keeping my
mouth shut. I wasn't going to try to make things better between us. I wasn't going to promise Monday Movie Nights

or Smoothie Saturdays. I was going to end this like a mature, wanna-be grown-up I was hoping I'd be for real someday.

Sometimes people make decisions for us. They break our hearts before we have the chance to break theirs. Sometimes that's what we need them to do.

As we started walking away from our ninety-day romance, I turned around and shouted his name.

"Hey, Mike," I called out. "Good-bye."

"Good-bye, Jen." He waved, and just like that, it was over and done.

Maybe good-byes can be quick and painless, like pulling off a Band-Aid or wiggling out a loose baby tooth, if you do it the right way. But maybe, if you do it and it hurts like heck, then you know that you need to retrace your steps back into that person's arms as soon as you possibly can.

I didn't run back to Mike because I knew that I didn't want that. But I did stick around, on that street corner, right outside the bar, and cry. I was single again. Alone. Back to square one.

"What do you think is wrong with her?" a lady with a southern accent asked her husband in a shrill whisper.

There were taxis zooming by us, a guy announcing the next showing of a comedy club performance down the street, a group of fifty school kids passing by, slapping each other on the back and laughing like hyenas. Yet through it all, I could still hear them perfectly.

"I don't know. Why don't you ask her?"

I took a break from the waterworks and turned around to face them. She was what I imagined she'd look like: fanny pack, hair-sprayed bouffant. They seemed like the kind of people who gave really deep, intense hugs and kept rolls of Mentos in their pockets.

If you ever want to feel better about your problems, tell them to a stranger. That's probably why Tricia turned to *me* forty-eight hours before she was supposed to zip herself into a lace wedding dress and a life of forever with Matt.

I told them about my breakup, about my first-ever good-bye.

They patted me on the back, and she pulled out a Hershey Kiss that was beginning to melt from the heat of her fanny pack. They tried to tell me everything would be just fine and dandy.

"Well hooey! There are other fish in the sea."

And maybe where they're from, there is a proper sea, and there are plenty of fish inside of it. But here in New York City, we have concrete, steel, glass, buses filled with tourists, and buildings that tower high above our heads. It would have made more sense for them to say something like, *There will be other rats on the subway.*

But I understood what they meant. And I even hugged them good-bye.

chapter twenty-three

Thirty Wedding Songs I Never Want to Dance To Again

1. "The Macarena." You think this song retired with scrunchies and overalls? You're wrong. It still comes out to haunt us during hour 3 of the wedding reception. And like zombies in our Saturday best, we bust out the moves that have been permanently engraved in our memories.
2. "Piano Man." I once saw a groomsman strip down to his underpants during this song. The image of his beer gut shows up like a hologram on the dance floor whenever this song comes on.
3. "Wonderful Tonight." I would look wonderful too if I wasn't wearing a tapioca-colored bridesmaid dress that makes me look like a Cabbage Patch Doll.

4. "Sweet Caroline." This song instantly sends me back to Friday nights drinking $1 shots and $2 Natty Lites at the local college bar. Let's leave it there.

5. "The Electric Slide." You can actually do these dance moves to any other song and they match the beat perfectly. This is a seasoned wedding vet and a midwestern grandma's time to shine on the dance floor.

6. "New York, New York." The song during which everyone locks arms and high-kicks, like they're auditioning to become a Rockette.

7. "Happy." I would be happy if I was dancing to this song with a plus-one.

8. "I Wanna Dance with Somebody." This is what I say to myself in the mirror after I get a wedding invitation that is addressed only to my lonesome self.

9. "I Got a Feeling." I enjoy this song only because they say "mazel tov" and sometimes people think they are saying "monotone."

10. "Love Shack." Once you dissect the lyrics to this song, you realize the four-year-old version of yourself singing it must have been terribly entertaining for the adults in the room.

11. "Don't Stop Believing." When everyone busts out their electric air guitar and sings like they're an '80s rock-and-roll superstar.

12. "Celebration." I feel like I'm back at a bar mitzvah.

13. "Brick House." It has been a lifelong goal of mine to have someone describe me saying, "She's a brick . . . house."

14. "Baby Got Back." Nobody wants to know that your anaconda doesn't want some unless you got buns, Hun.

15. "Living on a Prayer." This is when I leave my dignity and my voice on the dance floor.

16. "We Are Family." I never get the hint and depart from the dance floor when this beat drops, which always leaves me in the background of family photos, boogying alone.

17. "Single Ladies." I'll leave it at that.

18. "Cha Cha Slide." I appreciate that the exact moves are called out and easier to understand than IKEA instructions, but I'd prefer to dance to a song that doesn't remind me of the hokey pokey.

19. "Shout." The part in the song when everyone shimmies down to touch the dance floor with their hands is usually the part of the song when I realize I'm too old and don't have the leg strength to get back up.

20. "Gangnam Style." I was never very good at galloping.

21. "Cupid Shuffle." When everyone is moving to the right, I always find myself moving to the left.

22. "Come On Eileen." Yes, come on. Put down your sixth cocktail. It's time to go home.

23. "Girls Just Want to Have Fun." I once danced with an eighty-six-year-old grandma to this song who was twerking during the *they just wanna, they just wanna* part.

24. "Wobble." I look like I'm grinding coffee beans when I dance to this song.

25. "Whip/Nae Nae." Sometimes I confuse these dance moves with "Gangnam Style."

26. "Bohemian Rhapsody." I wish we could just jump to the second half of the song, when the beat picks up and everyone can jump around like they're tap dancing in a Broadway show.

27. "The Twist." A true throwback for the adults in the room—not the wannabe adults who think a throwback is a picture they post on Instagram from a year or two ago.

28. "Cotton Eye Joe." My goal for this song is not to elbow, knee, or stab someone with my toes.

29. "Time of My Life." By the time this song plays, I'm trolling tables, looking to stick my fork into any and all uneaten slices of cake.

30. "Last Dance." By this song, I hope I'm already halfway home.

chapter twenty-four

Love Always Perseveres

"Love is patient."

I take a deep breath of cool air through my nose, letting it burn all the way down through my lungs. When I exhale, my eyes fly toward the watchful guests, my attention bouncing like a quarter in a washing machine. I see the grandma, who is wiping away tears of joy with the edge of a lace handkerchief. I see a family of four, dressed in their October best. I zoom in on the dad, who's bobbing his head in silent approval of what this day means for his family for the rest of his life.

All of a sudden, I feel an elbow digging into the meat on my ribs. It's the pastor.

"Keep reading," she whispers through a frozen smile, her lips barely moving.

I continue: "Love is kind . . ."

The groom is gripping the hands of his bride like a metal

binder clip on the rolled-down end of a bag of potato chips. His eyes meet hers before falling to the grass, his smile taking over.

When you're bursting with happiness, your facial muscles take turns showing it. Your eyes go first, pushing your lids wide open, then your mouth follows suit; even your ears perk up. The bride's eyes are everywhere. On her groom, the crowd, me, and then, ultimately, on the uncut, dewy grass.

I know she sees all 150 guests squirming in their ties, or adjusting their hemlines and leaning forward in their white resin folding chairs, cotton cardigans draped over their collarbones.

I know they look at her thinking she must be the happiest person in the room. How could she not be? She found her Mr. Forever, something that requires constant vigilance, like finding an outlet in an airport or a size small at a sample sale. She has something that I have found, lost, found, and lost again, like car keys or an unpaid American Express bill that got stuck in the sections of Sunday's paper.

Keep it separate, Jen. Put it in a place you'll remember, people always say, as if I'm begging to forget it, as if somehow, in some way, I want to lose it. This bride has found love, and even better, she's found a way to hold onto it.

The guests are jet-lagged. They smell like hotel shampoo and conditioner, and their tummies are full of watered-down coffee and continental breakfast. I can tell the men spritzed on extra cologne when they got out of their rental cars and the women applied an extra coat of Roma tomato red lipstick before taking a seat. They're all here for this early-afternoon celebration because it means something to them.

The bride looks at me once more, like a puppy that's scared her owner is going to leave her home all afternoon.

"Jen. You can go on," she says, as if there's a chance I might not.

I nod. "It does not boast. It is not proud."

"Okay, okay, let me try this again," I said to Monica. It's a week before her wedding, and this is the seventeenth phone call we've had. We've never met face to face; she's in Georgia, and I'm in New York, but we've become close enough that we finish each other's sentences and laugh at jokes from weeks past.

I wanted, once more, to run through all of the facts that I had memorized about her because in just seven days, I'd be sitting in seat 9b on my flight to Georgia and exiting the airplane as Jen Smith, her friend since we were fourteen.

I'd made note cards, each one handwritten in pencil with some fact about Monica. I took them with me everywhere, snuggled at the bottom of my purse for whenever the F train got too moody or a first date was running late, or while I was massaging a homemade apple cider vinegar and Greek yogurt mask onto my face. (Thanks, *Cosmo*.)

"Thirty-one as of August, born in Sacramento, vegan who occasionally flirts with a piece of salmon, met me at Newton High School."

"Hewton High School," she cuts in, with a chuckle. It's fun getting to know someone else, but it's even more fun listening to them getting to know you.

"Hewton High," I say three times over before going on. "You have a sister in Germany, a brother in Kentucky, and your mom lives five miles away, behind the Stop and Shop, on the south side of town. Your son's name is Dallas, he's thirteen going on twenty-six, and he lives with you and Rick, who you met about five years ago when you were traveling for your job as a data analyst. You're known as a hot blonde nerd at the office."

She laughed again, and I started to as well. Laughter, like yawning, is contagious, but only once you've made a connection with another person; otherwise, your mouth doesn't even move.

"Anything else I should know?" I asked, patting myself on the back for remembering the facts without glancing at any of the note cards that were now displaced across my full-size mattress.

"Actually," she said with a pregnant pause, as if she were searching her own mental database for the precise information to retrieve. "There's one more thing."

"Sure, what is it?" I asked, pulling out a blank note card and uncapping a ballpoint pen with my teeth.

"The guy I'm marrying . . ."

"Rick," I interrupt, name-dropping him casually, as if we've known each other forever.

"Well, he's gay," she said, rushing through the bomb she'd just dropped. "And I'm marrying him for a different kind of love."

Love does not dishonor others, it is not self-seeking, it is not easily angered.

I threw the pen and note card on my bed and started pacing around the twenty square inches of spare floor space in my bedroom.

I waited in silence, trying to conjure up something to say,

waiting for a *just kidding* to follow, like a joke that shows up unexpectedly at the wrong party, when it belongs next door, with the Natty Lite beer and the strobe lights. But I knew Monica—or, at least, I thought I knew her—and she didn't joke like that. Everything she said was with purpose, with heart, with intention. I could wait there, counting my steps for hours, but I knew that a *just kidding* was not going to come.

"Jen?" she said, wondering if I was still on the line.

"Hi, yes." I responded. "I'm still here. It's just, I, umm . . ." I didn't know what to say.

"That's okay," she cut in.

"I guess I'm wondering why you're marrying him, then?" I asked as I searched for the right response that would make Monica feel comfortable and allow me to make sense of the situation.

"What are you? Some kind of journalist?" she joked. That was her way of humoring the situation, her way of letting me know that she felt comfortable telling me all of this but also not comfortable at the same time. Like when we tell someone something serious and then laugh after, as if to say, *I'm okay, but also may need you to walk on tippy-toes with your questions and judgment for the next five minutes so nobody gets hurt.*

"Well, what do you mean by a 'different kind of love'?" Thinking, wrongly, in the moment, that there is only one kind, just like a person foolishly thinks there is only one way to order steak.

She went on to tell me how they started dating, how she liked him, as one would like anyone with an edge of charm and a heart full of kindness and compliments. She told me about the way her stomach would fill with butterflies when her phone lit up with his name, or how she would have trouble not smiling when he said her name out loud, at the dinner table.

Things didn't get as intimate as she would have liked, so a year into their relationship, she asked him why not.

"That's when he told me," she said, calmly, the memory filtered by still fresh. "He loved me, but in a different kind of way."

Rick, she went on, was attracted to guys. He wanted, one day, to be able to be in love with a guy, but was terrified what his conservative family would think. He told her that he wasn't ready to live his life as a gay man. Monica was attracted to the way Rick made her feel, how he helped raise her son, how he made her up-in-the-air life seem stable for once. She wanted to make him feel comfortable and hoped one day, in the future, he would go off and live the life he was meant to. She wanted to be there for him in a way he couldn't trust anyone else in the world to be there.

Monica spoke for sixteen minutes straight, without pausing for anything more than a deep breath. I paced back and forth in silence, repeating the story she was telling me in my head, trying to grasp every single bit about it.

Rick was gay. Monica was straight. Rick was scared to be gay. Monica wanted stability in her life. Rick wanted stability in his life. Monica wanted to help Rick by being there for him, so he could one day live his life as an openly gay man.

I wanted to interrupt. I wanted to ask her, "Why marry him?" Skip the paperwork, the $50,000 event, the pain you're going to cause the people around you when they one day learn this was all a sham. I understood that she wanted to be there for him and he wanted to be there for her, but I didn't understand why they had to fool others in the process. Why they had to disguise the lives they wanted behind a diamond ring.

"So why marry him, right?" she went on. I exhaled, relieved that she had asked the question I so desperately wanted to know the answer to.

"Yes, why? Why do that when you know it has an expiration date? When you know that one day, you'll both go your separate ways?"

"Because I love him, and he loves me," she said, without a moment of hesitation, as if she had been waiting for someone to ask her this but no one ever had. "Love between two people is never the same; when you add everything up, it always yields a different number."

I sighed, overwhelmed with emotion for someone who had become a part of my life, and I, a giant part of hers, despite the fact that we'd never met before.

"Jen," she cried out, desperate for a virtual hug of approval. "Haven't you been in love before?"

"I have," I said, wondering who the journalist was now. "Twice."

"So tell me this, was the first time the same as the second time?"

Love keeps no records of wrongs.

The second time I was in love, I told the guy after twenty-one days of knowing him. We were eating a burrito and he told me that I had a chunk of guacamole on my eyebrow. I told him, "I love you."

But he didn't say it back. Spoiler alert: they don't always do. Love isn't fair; it works the same way a carnival game or a slot machine does. Just because you give it your all and hit the pad as hard as you can with a hammer, you might walk away without that stuffed animal the size of your torso. It takes more than effort to land the ultimate prize: someone who loves you back.

He told me that he didn't know. *How do you not know?* I wondered. *Either you're in love or you aren't. Either you want to eat pizza or you don't.*

He told me he would know by January, so I waited around for four months, because love for a person doesn't expire like milk or a parking meter. If you love a person, you have that feeling forever, like a birthmark, until you optionally, painfully, have it removed.

Eventually he told me he didn't love me back, and I finally understood what one-sided love feels like: making out with a plastered wall, or sending undeliverable pieces of mail, over and over and over again. Eventually you have no choice but to take that love elsewhere, whether to the frozen desserts section of Trader Joe's on a lonely Friday night or Tinder.

I sat on the edge of my mattress pad, thinking about that guy, that burrito, those three words I blurted out so quickly. That unadulterated feeling. I thought about Monica and Rick and how those three words meant something entirely different to them. To me, I wanted the phrase to mean allegiance, and I wanted it to be endless. To her, it meant safety. It meant growing together before, one day, they would, rightfully, grow apart.

I listened to Monica and watched the skyscrapers darken against the Manhattan skyline as they fell asleep outside my window. I often thought during the daytime, from twenty-six floors up, that it looked as if everyone was doing the same thing. But at night, who knew; you can't see into the windows of those buildings once night falls.

I thought about the person who helped approve the shapes of these buildings. Who gave his thumbs up, the ultimate okay, to have it look so messy, so uneven, so all over the place that if you tried to draw them, your hand would get exhausted from the ups and the downs, the curves and the nonsensical dips. I couldn't help but cringe at how the skyline looked at that moment: a mouthful of crooked teeth that needed a year and a half of braces to straighten out, to make everything line up. But love, and every single thing I've ever tried to get my hands on, seemed to make much more sense when it was a little bit imperfect, broken in, flawed around the edges. And I did love this skyline, after all.

Love does not delight in evil.

"I just need you to be there for me," she said. "Ever since I hired you, you have been there for me more than anyone else in my life, and now this, this thing I just told you . . . nobody else can ever know. Nobody else will ever understand."

The pastor steps on my toes, wanting to make sure that I'm still awake, that I'm still committed to reading these words out loud. I let the air out of my nose, unexpectedly, like a deflating balloon.

"Love rejoices with the truth," I say.

I'm thinking about the moment right before the ceremony as I fluffed the waterfall of lace cascading from Monica's dress. Her flower girl stood eagerly by her side, waiting to take her very first step down the aisle.

"Do you want to know a secret?" I asked the flower girl.

"Mmhm," she replied, lollipop in one hand and a basket of hydrated flower petals in the other.

"Find a person you love, but not because they're good at smushing their lips against yours or because their hair is a perfect shade of cinnamon."

She giggled at the thought of lips smushing together. I laughed too.

"Love always protects," I tell her, no longer holding back the words.

"Where do I find that?" she asked, thinking beyond the rainbow-colored wooden doors of her kindergarten classroom and the swing sets on the sandy playground.

"You'll probably find it in the place that makes the least sense," I said, hoping that she'd remember those words when she was my age.

"Love always trusts," I say now.

I fell in love for the first time when I was twenty-two with a guy who said I was too young to fall in love. There's no age limit on love, like there is on an R-rated movie, but was there a time limit? Because after seven months, the *I love yous* turned into *How are yous?* which turned into *I'll call you back laters*, which turned into silence. Until one day, when May was pushing April out of the spotlight, he called me and told me he didn't love me at all anymore.

That was when I threw my phone into a rose bush in front of Jimmy, my doorman, and told myself that I would never love again. Once was enough. I would retire, move to a sunny condo in Florida, and feast on early bird specials at local kosher restaurants.

But love, like a night of drinking that leaves you with a nasty hangover, or a stomach filled with unsettling food that makes you spend a couple of hours hunched over the toilet, has a way of quickly fleeing, making you forget the pain and *never again* promises that come with it.

The pastor leans toward me to grab the microphone out of my shaky hands, and I signal with bulging eyes that I'm ready to finish up this poem, which has taken me three minutes to read when it should have taken me only one.

"Love always hopes."

If love had a texture, I think to myself, it would be like rice pudding, filled with chunks that make it hard to swallow. Love is the reason for my acid reflux. Long-distance love is the reason I don't have a 401(k). One-sided love is the reason I can't help but try to fall in love again. This was my experience with love, and it was my kind of *different*.

Monica is the sixteenth bride I've worked with this year, and I realize now that each one I've worked with got married for a *different* kind of love. Some brides married the first person they kissed; some married for the third time to the fourth person they loved. There were times I watched brides get married to grooms who didn't seem to love them at all.

I look at the crowd once more, particularly at the long-

married couples who've probably heard this passage from Cor-
inthians a million times, maybe even at their own weddings.
I eye Rick and then Monica, tossing them a hint of a smile
before glancing at the pastor, who's giving me shade for my
long, drawn-out performance.

Finally, I look down at the wrinkled piece of paper in my
hand, covered in smudged ink and immortal words.

"Love always perseveres," I say. And I mean it, like never
before.

Acknowledgments

One More Thing Before You Go

This book wouldn't exist if not for all the people who told me it never would. My ninth-grade teacher, a boss I had when I worked for a magazine, the first book agent I hugged hello, and the handful of publishers over the years, who all said the same thing: you're not going to make it as a writer. I can't thank you enough for telling me that I wasn't good enough. That alone kept my fingers dancing on the keyboard and my mind racing with ways to make this happen, when it almost didn't. And it did, because I'm not very good at listening to other people, and I'm even worse at giving up.

This book also wouldn't be alive if not for the people who fought to get it into your hands. My agent at Writers House, Stacy, and my agent at CAA, Olivia—thank you for being my champions.

To my editor at Simon & Schuster (Atria), Jhanteigh, you

saw the raw, unedited version of this book, so in some weird way, you saw the raw, unedited version of me. I must tell you this: thank you for picking up the phone when the book proposal landed in your lap to say that you wanted me to write a book that wasn't just about wedding horror stories, but instead about what I learned from all of the bold and beautiful experiences that I've lived through. Thank you, thank you, thank you for giving me the chance to write my freaking heart out.

The stories inside wouldn't exist if not for their main characters: the friends who put up with me, the brides who made me a bridesmaid, and the guys who were brave enough to take me on a date. Thank you for letting me tap-dance inside of your world.

To Ray, who told me, simply, that I needed to write out of order. But not out of order like a broken-down bathroom stall, but out of order in the sense that it was most important to write what I felt like writing at that very moment. His words jolted me to write this entire book in two months. I didn't have much of a choice: what Ray says goes.

To Jess and Sarah, thank you for supporting and loving me no matter what situation I find myself in. You are truly *professional* best friends.

To my roommate Kerri, thank you for calling me a professional bridesmaid and for never calling me crazy—even though you have every piece of evidence in the world to do so. You have sat beside me, on our very comfortable couch, through many ups and downs over the past six years. You are the closest thing I have to a soul mate.

To Adam, a thousand thank-yous for showing me how to squeeze the positive out of every day and every challenge. And for your love; every single ounce of it.

And to my doorman, who asked me, every day for three years, when my next book would come out—this one is for you. Love, Kimmy.

But I pinky-promise you that you wouldn't be reading any of this right now if not for my family, who love me enough to reassure me, constantly, that I can do anything I set my mind to.

To my brother, who turned Bridesmaid for Hire into something real; my dad, who is the loyal president of my unofficial "fan club"; and to my mom, who is the voice inside my head, always reminding me to never, ever give up, that I'll never know unless I try, and that it only takes one person to say yes. You have always believed in me, long before I was ready to believe in myself. I love you to the moon and back.

One last thing: This one is for *you*. Thank you for supporting me and buying this book. You are making the dream I've had since I was six years old come true. Please accept one million virtual hugs, and, when we meet in person, a slice of pizza, on me—one-dollar pizza, of course; I still have hefty library fines I need to pay off.

All my love,
Jen Glantz

About the Author

Jen Glantz is the world's first professional bridesmaid and founder of Bridesmaid for Hire. She's the heartbeat behind the website *The Things I Learned From* and the author of the Amazon-bestselling ebook *All My Friends Are Engaged*. She can be found in New York City wearing old bridesmaid dresses to the grocery store, or on first dates, and double-fisting slices of one-dollar pizza.